PHILOSOPHICAL CLASSICS

General Editor: P. GRAY LUCAS

THE
LEIBNIZ-CLARKE
CORRESPONDENCE

THE
LEIBNIZ-CLARKE
CORRESPONDENCE

TOGETHER WITH EXTRACTS FROM
NEWTON'S *PRINCIPIA* AND *OPTICKS*,
EDITED WITH INTRODUCTION AND
NOTES BY

H. G. ALEXANDER

MANCHESTER UNIVERSITY PRESS
BARNES & NOBLE, NEW YORK

© Manchester University Press

Published by
Manchester University Press
Oxford Road, Manchester M13 9PL
1956

Reprinted in a paper edition 1976

ISBN: 0 0669 4

Published in the U.S.A. by
Harper & Row Publishers Inc.
Barnes & Noble Import Division

Produced by offset lithography by
Unwin Brothers Limited
The Gresham Press, Old Woking, Surrey, England
A member of the Staples Printing Group

TABLE OF CONTENTS

CONTENTS

PREFACE

The exchange of papers between Leibniz and Clarke is the most frequently cited of all eighteenth-century philosophical controversies. For their contemporaries it was the final confrontation of 'the mathematical philosophy', represented by Newton and his champion Clarke, and 'the metaphysical philosophy'. To many modern observers it appears to mark one of the final stages in that temporary emancipation of the natural sciences from philosophy and theology, which made possible the progress of science in the two succeeding centuries.

This is the first complete edition in English since 1738. The text follows exactly that of the first edition of 1717 prepared by Clarke himself, except that the spelling has been modernized, italics and capital letters have been removed, and the arrangement of the marginal references and footnotes simplified. The original punctuation has been retained. Clarke's translation of Leibniz's papers is extremely accurate, and editorial comment has been necessary only at a very few points.

Since the Correspondence is chiefly concerned with the wider implications of Newton's physics, we have added an appendix containing those passages in the *Principia* and *Opticks* which are mentioned in the Correspondence, and also the sections in which Newton expresses his general views on philosophy and scientific method.

I must thank Professor S. E. Toulmin of Leeds University for advice on a large number of topics ; Mr. E. Wild and Mr. M. B. Glauert of Manchester University for their help with the sections of the Introduction on relativity and Newtonian dynamics ; Professor G. Martin of Mainz for the information contained in the note on p. xlv ; and the general editor of the series for his assistance throughout.

H. G. A.

August, 1955.

ABBREVIATIONS

References to the Correspondence are given by paragraph numbers, e.g. L.I.1 for the first paragraph of Leibniz's first paper, C.IV.15 for the fifteenth paragraph of Clarke's fourth reply. Clarke numbered the paragraphs in his replies to correspond to those in the previous paper of Leibniz, e.g. C.III.5 answers L.III.5.

G.— *Die philosophischen Schriften von G.W. Leibniz*, ed. C. J. Gerhardt.

G.M.—*Leibnizens mathematische Schriften*, ed. C. J. Gerhardt.

INTRODUCTION

I

THE ORIGIN OF THE CORRESPONDENCE

The collection of papers which is now known as the Leibniz-Clarke Correspondence consists of five papers by Leibniz and five replies by Samuel Clarke. They were written in the years 1715 and 1716, and originally published in 1717 in an edition prepared by Clarke. Leibniz had been engaged in a controversy with the Newtonians for several years and in 1715 wrote a letter to Caroline, Princess of Wales, strongly criticizing the philosophical and theological implications of Newton's work. The first paper in the Correspondence is part of this letter. Clarke, a friend and disciple of Newton, attempted to answer these charges in a paper given to Caroline and sent by her to Leibniz.

The Newton-Leibniz Controversy, 1705–1716

The Correspondence was the last phase of a general controversy between Leibniz and the Newtonians which had started in 1705. The original point at issue was whether Leibniz or Newton had been the first to invent the calculus. With each accusing the other of plagiarism the dispute was protracted and acrimonious. Newton at first remained in the background and allowed his case to be argued by his friend Keill, a skilful and outspoken controversialist; Leibniz was more restrained, believing for many years that Keill's articles must have been written without Newton's approval.

Gradually the dispute spread to other issues, of which

the most prominent was Leibniz's attack on the Newtonian theory of gravity. He first made this criticism in print in the *Theodicy*, published in 1710 (*Discours de la Conformité de la Foi avec la Raison*, §19), where he accuses Newton of reintroducing the outmoded idea of action at a distance. He repeated the charge in a correspondence with the Dutch physician Hartsoeker, published in the *Journal de Trévoux* of 1712 and reprinted in the *Journal des Savants*. In this letter Leibniz refers to gravity as 'an occult quality' and says that it would be a perpetual miracle if planets were to move in circular orbits without some medium impelling them. Newton himself addressed a reply to the editor justifying his use of the concept of gravity, but his letter was never published.[1]

Leibniz's criticisms were also answered in Cotes's preface to the second edition of the *Principia* (1713), in a passage so forthright as to make Leibniz describe the preface as *pleine d'aigreur*. Even more strongly worded were two articles by Keill in the *Philosophical Transactions* of 1714, translated and reprinted in the *Journal Littéraire*. Keill here dismisses Leibniz's claim to have developed the calculus independently, and goes on to reject Leibniz's theory of gravity and pour scorn on his whole philosophical method.

During this controversy the only exchange of letters between Leibniz and Newton was in the winter of 1715–16 after the Correspondence with Clarke had begun. The intermediary was the Abbé Conti, a Venetian then visiting London, to whom Leibniz wrote defending himself from the accusations of plagiarism in the calculus and criticizing Newton on various grounds. In addition to his usual remarks on gravity, Leibniz in this letter touches on several points discussed in the Correspondence and concludes by accusing Newton of departing from the experimental method in physics.

Conti showed this letter to Newton, who wrote an indig-

[1] Brewster, *Memoirs of Sir Isaac Newton*, II, 283.

nant reply addressed to Conti but clearly intended for Leibniz. As far as is known, this correspondence ended with Leibniz's answer to this letter of Newton's.

The sections of these letters which deal with philosophical issues are reprinted in Appendix B (pp. 184–188); the remaining parts concern the calculus and are omitted.

Samuel Clarke (1675–1729)

Leibniz's letter to Caroline extended the dispute between him and the Newtonians to theological and philosophical issues. Undoubtedly the Englishman best qualified to deal with such questions was Clarke, who had a considerable knowledge of theology, philosophy and science.

Clarke's scientific work consists of two translations into Latin. The first (1697) was of Rohault's *Physics*, which was the standard Cartesian text-book on the subject; the other (1706) of Newton's *Opticks*. In his edition of Rohault Clarke added copious footnotes expounding parts of Newton's physics so that, in places, the footnotes refute the text. This composite work became very popular, was reprinted several times, and even translated into English. It was still used as a text-book in Cambridge as late as 1730.

In philosophy and natural theology, Clarke's reputation rested on the two sets of Boyle lectures which he delivered in 1704 and 1705. The first set is devoted to proving the existence of God by a method ' as near mathematical as the nature of such a discourse would allow '. In the second Clarke tries to show that moral laws are as certain as the propositions of mathematics.

Like Newton, Clarke's theological beliefs were strongly tinged with Arianism. His book *The Scripture Doctrine of the Trinity* was so violently criticized by orthodox churchmen that he was removed from his position as one of Queen Anne's chaplains. Voltaire—who had a very high regard for Clarke—tells a story (*Oeuvres*, 1785, LV, p. 96) of how Gibson, Bishop of Lincoln, prevented Clarke's elevation to the See of Canterbury by telling Princess Caroline that Clarke was the most learned and honest man in her dominions, but had one defect—he was not a Christian.

Caroline, Leibniz, and Clarke

The letter from Leibniz to Caroline, which begins the Correspondence, was one of a series of letters exchanged by Caroline and Leibniz in the years between her arrival in England and his death. These concern both personal matters—such as Leibniz's arrears of pay—and philosophical and theological questions. The parts of these letters which bear on the Correspondence are given in Appendix B.

Caroline's friendship with Leibniz had begun in her youth when she had stayed at the Court of Berlin with Frederick I and his wife Sophia Charlotte, who was herself a close friend and disciple of Leibniz. It was renewed in 1705 on Caroline's marriage to the Electoral Prince of Hanover, later George II of England, as Leibniz was librarian and political secretary to the Elector. Her acquaintance with Clarke appears to have been the result of her efforts to find someone to translate the *Theodicy* into English. Although Clarke refused to undertake this, he became a frequent visitor at court and eventually almost took Leibniz's place as the Princess's philosophical mentor.

The letters of Caroline to Leibniz show that she took a close interest in the debate between him and Clarke. At first she was strongly in sympathy with Leibniz, but later became converted to Clarke's views on some of the topics under discussion. Her letters also provide evidence that Clarke asked Newton's advice before writing his replies, and that Leibniz considered the exchange of papers sufficiently important to be published.

II

THE ARGUMENT OF THE CORRESPONDENCE

Summary of the Argument

The Correspondence as published in 1717 starts with the part of Leibniz's letter to Caroline in which he asserts that Newton's works have contributed to a decline of natural religion in England. He refers to two passages in Newton's writings. The first is where Newton speaks of space as the 'sensorium of God', a phrase which Leibniz interprets as meaning that space is God's sense-organ. The other is the passage which implies that God occasionally intervenes in the universe; Leibniz comments that such a theory assimilates God to a watchmaker who has from time to time to wind up and even to mend the watch he has made.

In later papers Leibniz makes other criticisms. One of these is the charge that gravity is a scholastic occult quality, and that it would be a miracle for planets to move round the sun without some medium to impel them. Another is that the notion of a vacuum is only a ' pleasing imagination ' which can be disproved on *a priori* grounds.

The major part of the Correspondence starts from a discussion of the principle of sufficient reason, namely that there must be a sufficient reason why everything is as it is and not otherwise. Leibniz in his third paper accuses the Newtonians of not understanding this principle. For it entails the principle of the identity of indiscernibles; and this can be used to refute the Newtonian theory of space and time according to which points of space and instants of time are real, distinct, but indiscernible entities. Leibniz develops, in opposition to this, his own theory of space as the order of coexistent phenomena, and time as the order of successive phenomena. That is, space and time are for Leibniz not real substances but relations, and consequently ' ideal things '.

All these points are taken up by Clarke. He tries to

explain what Newton meant by saying that space 'is, as it were, the sensorium of God' and shows that this does not imply that God needs any sense-organ. Clarke admits that on Newton's theory God has to intervene in the universe, but denies that this derogates from God's perfection since such interventions are part of his plan. This gives rise to a discussion of the notion of the miraculous, in which Clarke repudiates the accusation that gravity is, for the Newtonians, a perpetual miracle, and retorts that Leibniz's pre-established harmony which precludes any interaction between soul and body, would be far more miraculous.

When in his fourth paper he comes to discuss the existence of the vacuum and the nature of space and time, Clarke cites empirical evidence in support of the Newtonian position. He interprets Guerike's experiments with the air pump and Torricelli's work with mercury barometers as conclusive proof of the existence of vacua. As further evidence he refers to other experiments which show that different liquids have different specific gravities and provide different degrees of resistance to moving bodies. These results, he suggests, indicate that some substances contain more matter per unit volume than others, and that therefore there must be, in at least some substances, empty space between the ultimate particles of matter.

In his treatment of space and time Clarke refers to the arguments used by Newton in the *Principia* and the experiments quoted there. Clarke argues that these show that one must distinguish absolute from relative motion, and therefore absolute space and time from relative space and time. He goes on to say that, in themselves, space and time are neither substances nor relations, but attributes. He clearly implies that they are attributes of God but refuses to say so explicitly when pressed by Leibniz.

The following are detailed comments on some of the more important topics.

Natural Religion [L.I.1] [1]

The correspondence develops out of Leibniz's accusation that Newtonian views are contributing to a decline of natural religion in England. This was a charge that must have particularly incensed Newton and Clarke. In the *Principia* and *Opticks* Newton had expressed his conviction that his discoveries in physics provided new evidence for the existence and providence of God; in their Boyle lectures, both Clarke and Bentley had drawn arguments for God's existence from Newtonian physics; and Newton had written to Bentley about these lectures, ' When I wrote my treatise about our system, I had an eye upon such principles as might work with considering men for the belief of a Deity, and nothing can rejoice me more than to find it useful for that purpose ' (first letter to Bentley, 10th December 1692).

Space as the Sensorium of God [L.I.3, L.II.3–4, L.III.10–12, L.IV.24f., L.V.78f.]

The first point in Leibniz's attack on Newton's theology is that Newton regards the universe as independent of God since God is represented as needing an organ, namely space, in order to perceive created things. This is a reference to the two passages in which Newton speaks of space as the sensorium of God. In *Opticks*, Query 28 (Appendix A, p. 174), he writes : ' . . . does it not appear from phenomena that there is a Being incorporeal, living, intelligent, omnipresent, who in infinite space, as it were in his sensory, sees the things themselves intimately, and throughly perceives them, and comprehends them wholly by their immediate presence to himself : of which things the images only carried through the organs of sense into our little sensoriums, are there seen and beheld by that which

---

[1] Since Clarke numbered the paragraphs of his replies to match those of Leibniz's papers, only the references to Leibniz's papers are given here and at the head of the following sections.

in us perceives and thinks '. The other passage occurs in Query 31 (Appendix A, p. 181) where he speaks of God ' who being in all places, is able by his will to move the bodies within his boundless uniform sensorium '.

From these passages it is clear that this odd expression, which Leibniz criticizes, is the result of Newton's acceptance of the representative theory of perception in its most extreme form. Our human sensoria are the internal cinemas to which images are conveyed by the various sensory nerves. But if God is to perceive what happens in the world, he must do so in a less indirect way. Newton therefore suggests that all space is, as it were, God's sensorium.

The point of Newton's remark is brought out in a passage in Addison (*Spectator*, No. 565, July 1714). ' Others have considered infinite space as the Receptacle, or rather the Habitation of the Almighty : but the noblest and most exalted Way of considering this infinite Space, is that of Sir Isaac Newton, who calls it the *Sensorium* of the Godhead. Brutes and Men have their *Sensoriola*, or little *Sensoriums*, by which they apprehend the Presence, and perceive the Actions, of a few Objects that lie contiguous to them. Their Knowledge and Observation turn within a very narrow Circle. But as God Almighty cannot but perceive and know everything in which he resides, infinite Space gives Room to infinite Knowledge, and is, as it were, an Organ to Omniscience.'

God's Intervention in the Universe [L.I.4, L.II.6f., L.III.13f., L.IV.38f., L.V.99f.]

The other specific criticism levelled by Leibniz in his first paper is that Newton has a very imperfect conception of God, since he represents Him as being too inefficient to make a perfect machine. This refers to the passages where Newton suggests that God intervenes in the universe. Clarke answers this by arguing that because God is both creator and sustainer of the universe, it would not derogate from his perfection if he were to intervene in it from time to time.

This particular issue belongs to the theological problem of providence. Newton's reasons for postulating such interventions were, however, scientific rather than theological : some divine action was apparently necessary if the universe were to maintain its present form.

It seems from remarks in the *Opticks* that, for Newton, God acts in the world in two, or possibly three, different ways. He has to prevent the fixed stars from falling on each other (*Opticks*, Query 28, and the third letter to Bentley). His second task is that of adjusting the Solar System from time to time. In Query 31 (Appendix A, p. 180) Newton refers to the irregularities which arise in the motion of the planets because of the disturbing influence of the other planets, and he suggests that these irregularities will increase 'till the system wants a reformation '.[1]

Leibniz and Clarke both interpret Newton as assigning a third task to God, that of maintaining constant the amount of motion in the universe. This is apparently necessary since ' by reason of the tenacity of fluids . . . and the weakness of elasticity in solids, motion is much more apt to be lost than got, and is always upon the decay ' (Query 31, Appendix A, p. 176). It was shown in the nineteenth century that in cases like the collision of inelastic bodies this loss of motion—if one interprets motion as energy—is only apparent. For, although the bodies lose some kinetic energy, this energy appears as heat ; that is, the mean kinetic energy of the molecules is increased. Some of Newton's contemporaries, including Leibniz (cf. L.V.99), had made similar suggestions, but there was little, if any, empirical evidence for such a theory at the time.

---

[1] It was only after Newton's death that it was shown that the effects on any one planet of the others would cancel out over a long period. The fact that, according to Newton, the planetary orbits were unstable, was one of the reasons why continental scientists were slow to accept his theory.

It is therefore assumed in the Correspondence that, according to Newton, God has to intervene supernaturally to conserve the amount of motion in the universe. But it is not certain that this was Newton's view. In the *Opticks*, Query 31 (Appendix A, p. 178), he writes : ' There is a necessity of conserving and recruiting it (*sc.* motion) by active principles such as are the cause of gravity . . . and the cause of fermentation.[1] . . . For we meet with very little motion in the world, besides what is owing to these active principles.' This suggests that for Newton active principles are not special divine interventions, but the action of natural causes. There is, however, an important difference between the Latin edition of 1706 which Leibniz read, and the second English edition of 1717, quoted here. For in the 1706 edition, the last phrase of the passage quoted is ' owing either to these active principles or to the dictates of a will ' (*vel ex his principiis actuosis vel ex imperio voluntatis oritur*). The omission of the last phrase may, like other changes in the same query, have been made with Leibniz's criticisms in mind.

Gravity [L.III.17, L.IV.45, L.V.118–123]

At the end of his third paper, Leibniz introduces the familiar charge that it would be a perpetual miracle if bodies were to move freely in the aether about a fixed centre. This is the same criticism that he makes in all his later writings : gravity in Newtonian physics is either an occult quality or a perpetual miracle.

This rejection of the concept of gravity is an immediate consequence of his general denial of action at a distance. The motion of the planets was explained by Leibniz in terms of vortices of aether, following Descartes.

From his correspondence with Huygens (G.M.II, 142 ff.), it is clear that Leibniz never worked out this

---

[1] Newton's two active principles, gravity and fermentation, regarded as sources of energy, would now be called potential energy and energy released by chemical change.

theory in detail. The only actual argument he gives in support of it is the fact that it explains why all the planets move round the sun in the same direction—a fact which Newton interpreted as proof of God's design. When Huygens, like Newton in the *Principia*, objects that the theory of vortices is incompatible with the elliptical orbits of the planets and with the infinitely varied paths of the comets, Leibniz answers that these difficulties can be overcome, but never explains exactly how it is to be done.

Newton and his followers always rejected Leibniz's criticisms of gravitational theory with some indignation. For Newton's official theory of gravity had been clearly stated : gravity was a force whose reality was proved beyond doubt by phenomena ; as a real force it must have a cause ; but there were insufficient data to enable him to put forward publicly any hypotheses as to its cause. This is the view which Newton stresses in the General Scholium in the second edition of the *Principia* (Appendix A, p. 170) when he writes *hypotheses non fingo*. In the letter to Bentley also (1693), ' You sometimes speak of gravity as essential and inherent to matter. Pray do not ascribe that notion to me, for the cause of gravity is what I do not pretend to know and therefore would take more time to consider of it '. And in the preface to the 1717 edition of the *Opticks*, ' And to show that I do not take gravity as an essential property of matter I have added one question concerning its cause, choosing to propose it by way of a question because I am not yet satisfied about it for want of experiments '.

But though this was the official Newtonian view, there was some justification for Leibniz's criticisms. Roger Cotes, in his preface to the second edition of the *Principia*, in several places speaks as if gravity were an essential property of matter—in spite of Clarke having warned him against giving such an erroneous impression of Newton's views.[1] Newton and Clarke also had written passages

[1] See Edleston, *Correspondence of Sir Isaac Newton*, p. 158.

which suggested something very like the continual divine action which Leibniz ridiculed. In his third letter to Bentley, Newton says : ' It is inconceivable that inanimate brute matter should, without the mediation of something else which is not material, operate upon and affect other matter without mutual contact ' ; and Clarke in his Boyle Lectures (*Works*, II, p. 601) speaks of gravity as due to something ' superior to matter *continually* exerting on it a certain force or power ', the world therefore ' depending every moment on some superior being, for the preservation of its frame '.

The Vacuum [L.II.2, L.III.9, L.IV.7, 21–23, PS., L.V.33–35]

Leibniz uses two arguments against the existence of vacua in nature. He argues first (L.II.2, etc.) that the more matter there is in the universe, the more perfect it will be ; and therefore God will have filled the whole universe with matter. His second argument (L.IV, PS.) is that if there were vacua, there would be no sufficient reason for determining the exact proportion of matter to empty space.

These, however, were not the considerations which had first led Leibniz to deny the existence of the vacuum. In his youth he had accepted the Cartesian theory according to which extension and matter were equivalent terms and *vacuum*, therefore, a self-contradictory expression. Leibniz abandoned this view on his discovery in dynamics of inertia (mass). For, if matter was only extension, it would be equally easy to move large and small bodies. (See e.g. *Specimen Dynamicum*, G.M.VI, 234–246.) He writes, for example : ' I make the very notion of *materia prima* or of mass consist in this passive force of resistance (involving impenetrability and something more) which is always the same in bodies and proportional to their size ' (G.IV.5). Leibniz later returned to the opinion that there was no vacuum. This first rejection of the Cartesian theory explains why he always held the non-existence of a vacuum to be a contingent rather than a necessary truth—that is, its truth depended on the principle of sufficient reason, not just on the principle of contradiction.

In the Correspondence (L.IV, PS.) he tells how he abandoned the 'pleasing imagination of a vacuum and atoms'. The phrase gives the clue to his real reasons for denying the vacuum. For Leibniz, the vacuum and atoms went together, so that the choice was between this picture of the universe—the picture that Newton accepted—and what was essentially the Cartesian view of an infinite plenum with infinitely divisible bodies moving in vortices of aether. Once Leibniz rejected atoms, he also had to reject the vacuum.

For denying atoms he had several reasons. It involved a breach of continuity to suppose that at a certain stage in division one came to ultimate units; philosophically, atomism led to materialism since the atoms would inevitably be regarded as fully real; the existence of atoms would contradict the principle of the identity of indiscernibles; and in dynamics they would contradict the principle of the conservation of moving force (kinetic energy) since atoms are hard and inelastic, while for motive force to be conserved all particles would have to be perfectly elastic (cf. G.VII.285 note).

Having once abandoned his former belief in a vacuum and atoms, Leibniz never seriously considered the empirical evidence which was adduced by Guerike, Torricelli, and the Newtonians. In the Correspondence (L.V.34–35) he mentions some of the experiments but claims that they do not prove the existence of a vacuum for there will still be, in the apparent vacuum, beams of light, magnetic effluvia and other matter 'void of heaviness'. To Clarke's argument that the different resistances of mercury and water show that mercury is more dense, Leibniz replies that it is not so much the quantity of matter as its 'difficulty of giving place' (viscosity) that causes resistance.

Leibniz is, in fact, right in arguing that viscosity is a more important factor than density in the resistance of liquids to moving bodies. His attempt to deal with the first objection by postulating matter ' void of heaviness ' is less satisfactory. Both Leibniz and the Newtonians agreed that matter was to be defined by its inertial properties, and so matter without inertia, as seems to be implied here, is self-contradictory.

The Principle of Sufficient Reason [L.II.1, L.III.7–8, L.IV.1–2, 13–20, L.V.1–20, 66–73, 76–77]

One of the topics discussed at length by Leibniz and Clarke is the interpretation to be placed on the principle of sufficient reason. Leibniz claims at the beginning of his second paper that from this one principle (together with the principle of contradiction) one can deduce the whole of metaphysics and natural theology. In reply Clarke admits the importance of the principle but suggests that sometimes the reason may be the mere will of God as when He created any body in one part of space rather than another. From this there ensues a dispute about the principle of sufficient reason as applied to God's actions, a discussion of the principle of the identity of indiscernibles, and the whole argument about the nature of space and time.

Closer examination of Leibniz's work shows, however, that at least three distinct principles are indiscriminately referred to as the principle of sufficient reason. There is first what would now be called the causal principle, viz. that nothing happens without a cause. Clarke always interprets the principle in this sense and thus argues that sometimes the sufficient and only reason for an event may be the will of God.

This, however, contradicts the second form of the principle, that God must always have a motive for acting. With human actions, the sufficient reason may be either a motive or, in the case of motiveless actions, e.g. stepping left foot first across a threshold, a cause such as a sub-

conscious perception or passion : for God, the sufficient
reason must always be a motive.

The third principle is a stronger form of the second :
God must always act for the best. Leibniz uses this in
arguing that there cannot be a vacuum since the more
matter there is in the universe, the more perfect it is.

The Principle of the Identity of Indiscernibles [L.III.2–6, L.IV.3–6, L.V.21–26]

Although Leibniz usually speaks of the two principles
of contradiction and sufficient reason as adequate for
metaphysics, he occasionally (e.g. L.IV.5) seems to regard
the principle of the identity of indiscernibles as equally
important. There are two forms of the principle.

The first is virtually an application of the modern verifica-
tion principle—that if there is no method of distinguishing
between what are alleged to be two distinct states of affairs
then there is in fact only one state. Leibniz uses this
principle to show that no meaning can be attached to
Clarke's contention that the whole universe might be moved
in space. Although he applies the principle in the form
' God could have no reason for moving the whole universe ',
this reference to God is unnecessary. God's choice is here
impossible, not because He has to have certain motives for
choosing, but because there are not two genuine alternatives
between which choice is possible.

The other and more usual sense of the principle is that
there cannot exist two indistinguishable things. In the
Correspondence (L.IV.3 etc.), Leibniz deduces this from
the principle of sufficient reason by arguing that God could
have no motive for arranging two identical pieces of matter
in one position rather than the reverse. This argument
is, however, fallacious. For consider the example of a
chess problem. If a chess player sets out to arrange the
pieces on his board in accordance with the diagram of a
problem, he will be confronted with choices. For if on
the diagram there are white pawns shown on KR4 and

QB2, he will, when he takes the first pawn piece out of the box, have to decide on which of those two squares on his board to place it. If he was Leibniz's God—who always acts rationally—or Buridan's ass, he would never succeed in setting out the problem at all.

The position of the man who invents the problem is quite different. For when in his mind, he decides to put pawns on KR4 and QB2, no choice is involved ; the pawns, as it were, only come into existence *in situ*. Now clearly God, when he created the world, was in the position of the man who invented the problem, not the man who set it out on the board. God would have been confronted with a choice only if he already had the constituent parts of the universe piled together in a box, or if he first devised the plan and then had to create it one part at a time.

This fallacious line of argument was not, however, Leibniz's only reason for holding the principle. Almost certainly he regarded it as a necessary consequence of his whole theory of monads, according to which each monad mirrored the universe from its own point of view. From this it would seem to follow that every monad is different. But this argument is also invalid. One weakness is that Leibniz is relying on a spatial analogy although he holds that spatial relations are unreal. The other is that even if the analogy is accepted, there is no reason why the universe should not be symmetrical. If one had a two-dimensional universe shaped like this,

1	2	3
·	·	·
4	5	6
·	·	·
7	8	9
·	·	·

then monads 1, 3, 7, 9 could be identical, and monads 2, 4, 6, 8, even if they did each mirror the universe from their own viewpoints.

Space and Time [L.III.2–6, L.IV.8ff., L.V.27–32, 36–65, 79–80, 104–106]

The theory of space and time put forward here by Leibniz is the same as had been expressed in all his later writings : space is the order of coexistent phenomena ; time is the order of successive phenomena ; and both are ideal. Leibniz contrasts this view of space and time as dependent on things with the Newtonian theory of space and time as real independent entities. This is the theory implied by Clarke when he speaks (C.II.1.) of God choosing to create any body in one part of space rather than another.

The ideality of space and time follows, for Leibniz, from the fact that they are neither individual substances nor aggregates of individual substances ; for only these are fully real. This line of thought is most clearly expressed in his fifth paper (L.V.47) where he compares spatial and temporal relations with the ratio between two lengths. Such a ratio between two lines can be considered in three ways : as a ratio of the greater to the lesser, in which case logicians would regard it as an accident inhering in the former ; or as a ratio of the lesser to the greater ; or ' as something abstracted from both '. In this third way the relation is in neither subject but ' being neither a substance, nor an accident, it must be a mere ideal thing, the consideration of which is nevertheless useful '. That is to say, propositions which concern space and time, like statements about ratios, cannot be expressed in subject-predicate form ; therefore space and time cannot be fully real. Nevertheless they must not be taken as unreal and groundless since ' their truth is grounded in God ' (*New Essays*, II.13.17).

A relational theory of space and time appears to imply that no meaning can be attached to such phrases as *absolute position* or *absolute motion*. It would seem to be impossible to say that A is moving and B and C stationary rather than that B and C are moving and A stationary. Leibniz draws this conclusion explicitly in one of his letters to Huygens (June 1694, G.M.II.184).

> For if there are 1000 bodies, I still hold that phenomena cannot give us any infallible way of determining which are moving and in what degree; and that each separately could be considered as being at rest . . . Mr. Newton recognizes the equivalence of hypotheses in the case of rectilinear motion, but with regard to circular motion he believes that the effort which revolving bodies make to recede from the axis of rotation enables one to know their absolute motion. But I have reasons for believing that nothing breaks this general law of equivalence. [Leibniz does not state what these reasons are.]

But there are other passages which contradict this. In some of these it is suggested that moving force (kinetic energy) is real, and therefore when a body possesses moving force it has an absolute and real motion. In his letter to Huygens just quoted he writes: ' As for the difference between absolute and relative motion, I believe that if motion, or rather the moving force of bodies is something real, as it seems one must admit, it is necessary that it has a *subjectum*.' The same view is expressed more clearly in the *Discourse on Metaphysics*, § 18, and *Phoronamus (Arch. f. Gesch. d. Phil.* I.577).

In the Correspondence also, Leibniz admits (L.V.53) that ' there is a difference between an absolute true motion of a body and a mere relative change of its situation with respect to another body. For when the immediate cause of the change is in the body, that body is truly in motion.' Clarke naturally enough claims that this admission is quite incompatible with the theory that space is only the order of coexistent bodies. But Leibniz does not say here whether it is ever possible in practice to determine in which of several bodies the cause of their change of relative position lies and so to discover which is truly in motion. He may therefore have held that the distinction between absolute and relative motion is metaphysical, not physical : that is, the absolute motion of a body can never be experimentally determined ; and so the concept of absolute motion is of no use in physics. Such an interpretation is supported by his statement in the *Discourse on Metaphysics*, that moving force is a metaphysical concept. There is, however, no doubt that this admission of the distinction between absolute and relative motion is inconsistent with his general theory of space.

Clarke raises three main objections against Leibniz's relational theory. One of these (C.III.2, etc.) is that the theory is self-contradictory since it implies that if the whole universe were displaced, it would still be in the same position—which is impossible. Leibniz points out that this objection evades the whole point at issue.

Clarke's second argument (C.IV.13, etc.) is that experiments show that it is necessary to distinguish absolute from relative motion ; but absolute motion implies absolute space and time. Most of his examples are drawn from the Scholium to Definition 8 in the *Principia*, the section in which Newton elaborates his theory of space and time. The Scholium is discussed below, pp. xxxiv–xl.

The third argument which Clarke uses against Leibniz (C.III.4), is that space and time cannot be merely relations, since they are quantities. Leibniz attempts to meet the objection (L.V.54) by saying that numerical ratios are relations but yet ' have their quantity ' ; but it is difficult to see how the analogy holds. In fact, the objection shows that any relational theory of space and time is radically incomplete unless supplemented by an analysis of the process of measurement. Leibniz never provides such an analysis.

This deficiency in his theory is also evident in the Correspondence when he discusses the finiteness of the universe and the existence of the vacuum. Leibniz holds that the universe is spatially infinite, though finite in time, and that there are no vacua ; but he explicitly states that these are contingent truths. Although God could have willed otherwise, he has not done so because an infinite, fully-filled universe is the best possible.

But, Clarke asks, how could the universe possibly be finite if space is relational? What meaning can be attached either to the finiteness of the universe or the existence of vacua unless space is regarded as independent of material things?

In an essay on the Correspondence,[1] Broad attempts to meet this objection. He suggests that, on the relational theory, the statement that the universe is finite can be interpreted thus: if the distance PQ is taken as standard, then there is a finite number N such that for any points x, y the distance xy is less than N times the distance PQ. The statement that there are no vacua in nature might be interpreted by developing the definition of an empty linear segment as a pair of particles PQ such that there was no particle between them—a definition that seems to presuppose the infinite divisibility of matter.

Such an interpretation, however, goes far beyond any suggestion made by Leibniz, who never realized this weakness of his theory. In fact, like his opponents, Leibniz in his less reflective moments seems to have thought of space as some infinite aethereal substance containing and, at the same time, permeating the material world.

Clarke, however, does not confine himself to defending Newton's theory and attacking Leibniz's. He also puts forward a theory of his own—that space and time are neither substances nor relations, but attributes. This theory also appears in Clarke's Boyle Lectures (*Works*, II, 527–530), but there is no evidence that it was held by anyone else on the Newtonian side.

As Leibniz points out, such a view is untenable. It implies either that space and time are properties of a God who pervades the whole universe; or else that they are properties which belong to one thing after another—'subjects will leave off their accidents, like clothes; that other subjects may put them on'. A passage in Des Maiseaux's preface to his 1720 edition of the Corres-

[1] C. D. Broad, *Ethics and the History of Philosophy*, pp. 168–191.

pondence shows that even Clarke realized some of the difficulties of the theory.

Since the terms *quality* or *property* have normally a sense different from that in which they must be taken here, M. Clarke has asked me to warn his readers that " when he speaks of infinite space or immensity and infinite duration or eternity, and gives them, through an inevitable imperfection of language, the name of qualities or properties of a substance which is immense or eternal, he does not claim to take the term *quality* or *property* in the same sense as they are taken by those who discuss logic or metaphysics when they apply them to matter ; but that by this name he means only that space and duration are modes of existence of the Substance which is really necessary, and substantially omnipresent and eternal. This existence is neither a substance nor a quality nor a property ; but is the existence of a Substance with all its attributes, all its qualities, and all its properties ; and place and duration are modes of this existence of such a kind that one cannot reject them without rejecting the existence itself. When we speak of things which do not fall under the senses it is difficult to speak without using figurative expressions ".

Measurement of Force (C.V.93–95)

In Clarke's fifth paper there occurs a long footnote in which he discusses the proper way of computing the impulsive force of a moving body. Clarke is here taking up an issue which had been disputed for the previous thirty years and which was to continue under dispute for the next thirty. On the one side Leibniz and his followers maintained that the ' force ' of moving bodies should be measured by the product of mass and velocity squared (mv^2) ; on the other, the Cartesians and the Newtonians contended that it should be measured by the simple product of mass and velocity (mv). (This, of course, is not the same as the Newtonian concept of force as mass multiplied by acceleration.)

Both sides were, to some extent, right ; for, as Newtonian dynamics was developed, it became clear that both concepts were important. The product mv is called *momentum* and the product $\frac{1}{2}mv^2$, *kinetic energy*. What had appeared to some of the contestants as a dispute about facts, was seen to be a dispute as to which concepts should be taken as basic in mechanics—and both were found to be indispensable.

The concept of momentum is, for example, useful in considering the collision of inelastic bodies ; since in such collisions, momentum is conserved, but not kinetic energy. On the other hand, in experiments where work is done against such forces as gravity, considerations of energy are more important. Leibniz, therefore, draws his examples from cases such as raising weights while his critics consider experiments with colliding bodies.

Leibniz's opponents also cite from statics examples in which we would now apply the principal of virtual work (or virtual velocities). Leibniz, however, points out that these examples are quite irrelevant.

What has contributed most to confound force with quantity of motion is the abuse of the theory of statics. For we find in statics that two bodies are in equilibrium when in virtue of their position their velocities are inversely as their weights, or when they have the same quantity of motion. . . . [*sc.* This is an example of] the case of *dead force* or the infinitely small motion which I usually call solicitation which takes place when a heavy body tries to start moving and has not yet acquired any impetuosity ; and this happens precisely when bodies are in equilibrium and trying to descend are mutually hindered [G.M.VI.2,18].

In the footnote in the Correspondence, Clarke accuses Leibniz of being led into error by considering only the distance traversed by a falling body and not the time of its descent. The point of this comment can be seen by considering a body moving under the action of a constant force (P), where force is used in the Newtonian sense of mass (m) multiplied by acceleration (f). Let the velocity at the beginning of the interval be v, at the end v', the distance covered s, and the time taken t.

Then by Newton's second law of motion

$$P = mf$$

Since P is constant, and therefore f,

$$Pt = mft = m(v' - v) \quad . \qquad . \qquad . \qquad (1)$$
$$= \text{change of momentum}$$

Now since the acceleration is constant, the mean velocity during this motion $= \frac{1}{2}\,(v' + v)$

$$\therefore \frac{s}{t} = \frac{1}{2}(v' + v) \quad . \qquad . \qquad . \qquad (2)$$

Multiplying corresponding sides of (1) and (2),

$$Ps = \frac{1}{2}m(v'^2 - v^2)$$
$$= \text{change of kinetic energy}$$

In dynamics the product Pt is called *impulse*, Ps *work*.

Clarke is therefore right when he suggests that if one considers only the displacement of a body acted on by a force, the concept of kinetic energy will be taken as fundamental, and if one considers only the time during which the force acts, the concept of momentum. The fact that in dynamics the concept of momentum was developed first is due, as Mach points out, to a historical accident. In his experiments with falling bodies Galileo at first tried to find the relation between the final velocity of the body and the distance through which it had fallen. He failed to do so, but succeeded instead in discovering the relation between the final velocity and the time of descent. If he had succeeded with his earlier experiments, the concepts of work and kinetic energy would have been developed first and would have seemed to many more fundamental than those of impulse and momentum.

The dispute about moving force came effectively to an end after the publication in 1743 of D'Alembert's *Traité de Dynamique*. D'Alembert points out that *force* is a word with no clear meaning and that the consideration of different problems will lead to different concepts of force. He also comments :

Rather than understanding by the word force some sort of being which resides in the body, one should use it only as an abridged way of expressing a fact—in the same way as, when one says that one body has twice the velocity of another instead of saying that in equal times it traverses a distance twice as great, one does not mean by the word velocity something inherent in the body.

D'Alembert must be referring to Leibniz, who not only regarded force as something actually possessed by the body, but even thought of it as more real than space, time, or motion. 'It must first of all be recognized that force is something wholly real even in created substances ; but space, time, and motion have something of the nature of mental entities' (G.M.VI.247). Newton is sometimes criticized for having lapsed unintentionally into metaphysics in his scholium on space and time. Leibniz in discussing force consciously digressed into metaphysics. 'The distinction between force and quantity of motion is important *inter alia* for judging that we must have recourse to metaphysical considerations separate from extension in order to explain the phenomena of bodies' (*Discourse on Metaphysics*, § 18).

III

THE PROBLEM OF SPACE AND TIME

At least three different questions can be distinguished in what is sometimes called the problem of space and time. There is the question of the ontological status of space and time or more simply, ' What are space and time ? ' There is the scientific problem as to which concepts of space and time are most useful in physics. The third is the epistemological, or perhaps psychological, question of how we come to acquire our knowledge of space and time.

To some extent these three questions intermingle ; and to some extent they merge into further problems such as the relation of God to space and time. Nevertheless it is not seriously misleading to say that Leibniz and Clarke were primarily concerned with the first question, Newton with the second, and that the third was first discussed seriously by Kant. It is true that the Correspondence touches on the second problem as, for instance, when Clarke argues that space cannot be relational because it is treated quantitatively in physics. But, in general, the scientific arguments adduced by Clarke are only re-statements of Newton's position as expressed in the *Principia*.

In the eighteenth century both the first two questions were widely discussed. Wolff and other disciples of Leibniz in Germany, and writers on natural theology in England continued to dispute about the exact nature of space and time and their relation to the Deity. Maclaurin, Euler and other mathematicians and physicists wrote about the Newtonian notions of absolute space and time. Only Kant took up all three problems and discussed them together.

By the end of the century these disputes had died away. The metaphysical and theological problem no longer interested philosophers to the same extent and the scientific problem appeared to have been settled. Newtonian mechanics had succeeded in explaining the tides, the paths of the comets, and the irregularities in the movement of the moon ; and therefore its theoretical foundation had to be secure. Even the invention of non-Euclidean geometries, while giving rise to some discussion of the relation of geometry to physical space, caused few qualms among scientists : if Newtonian mechanics used Euclidean geometry, space must be Euclidean. Only with Mach and Einstein was it shown that the examination of the basic concepts of Newtonian dynamics could still be fruitful.

The three sections which follow deal with certain parts of the history of the space-time controversy. The first contains an analysis of the treatment of space and time in the *Principia*. The second discusses the work of various writers on the space-time problems in the period from the death of Leibniz to Kant. The last summarizes and discusses the criticisms of Newton's theory made by Mach and Einstein.

NEWTON'S THEORY OF SPACE AND TIME IN THE *PRINCIPIA*

Newton's distinction between absolute and relative space and time occurs in the scholium to Definition 8 of the *Principia* (Appendix A, pp. 152–160). He comments that ' the vulgar conceive the quantities, time, space, place and motion under no other notions but from the relation they bear to sensible objects '. But it is ' convenient to distinguish them into absolute and relative, true and apparent, mathematical and common '. In the rest of the scholium he explains this distinction and indicates certain cases in which absolute motions can, in practice, be distinguished from relative motions.

Some commentators argue that Newton is uncritically reproducing metaphysical—or theological—presuppositions, in spite of his avowed resolution to admit nothing but principles drawn from phenomena. Weyl writes : ' Newton's conviction of absolute space was an empirically unsupported and theologically impregnated belief.' [1] Burtt [2] and Whitrow [3] suggest that Newton was influenced by the semi-mystical theories of Henry More.

Such explanations are totally unnecessary. The belief that it makes sense to talk about the real as opposed to the relative motion of a body, is not confined to the followers of Henry More ; both Galileo and the Inquisition thought it meaningful to ask whether the earth really moved.

Nor was the belief that absolute motion is different from relative motion just a commonly held assumption taken

---

[1] *Mind and Nature*, p. 59.
[2] *The Metaphysical Foundations of Modern Science*, pp. 257 f.
[3] *British Journal for the Philosophy of Science*, IV, 37.

over uncritically to form part of the foundations of the Newtonian system. On the contrary, the purely physical considerations which Newton adduces were sufficient to lead anyone at that time to accept the assumption. Even Leibniz admitted the distinction although he thought that it could be reconciled with his own relational theory of space.

Newton's reasons for distinguishing between absolute and relative space and time are most easily understood in the case of time. In the scholium to Definition 8, Newton comments that experiments with pendulums and observation of the eclipses of Jupiter's satellites [1] show that the natural solar day is unsatisfactory as a standard of time. We should now normally express this by saying that the solar day varies in length at different seasons of the year as the earth traverses different parts of its elliptical orbit. But it would be more accurate to say that there is a discrepancy between time as measured by pendulum clocks and time as measured by successive southings of the sun ; that there is also a discrepancy between time measured by the periods of revolution of Jupiter's moons and time measured by the sun ; but that there is no discrepancy between time as measured by Jupiter's moons and time as measured by pendulums.

To-day, largely as a result of Poincaré's work, almost all scientists would regard the adoption of a standard of time as a matter of convention or choice rather than of truth or falsehood. In practice we adopt whichever standard enables us to use the simplest physics. From this point of view the seventeenth-century scientist had two alternatives : he could either maintain the solar day as the standard of time and say that the position of the earth in its orbit affected both the beat of pendulums and the

---

[1] Roemer's observations of Jupiter and her moons, and his consequent deduction of the velocity of light, were made in 1676. Newton was therefore able to make allowances in his calculations for the velocity of light.

motion of Jupiter's satellites ; or he could take another standard and say that the solar day varied in length. The second scheme is clearly the simpler and scientists therefore adopted it taking as the standard of time the sidereal day, i.e. the period of revolution of the earth on its own axis relative to the fixed stars.[1]

One can however easily understand how they regarded this substitution as standard of the sidereal day for the solar, not as the result of a choice between two alternatives but as the discovery of a more accurate way of measuring time—and to say that one has discovered a more accurate measure of time seems to imply that one has achieved a closer approximation to an absolute real time.

Very similar arguments apply to space. Where Newton went beyond his predecessors was in making explicit the reasons why one wants to say that the earth has both a velocity of translation and a velocity of revolution about its own axis.

Observation suggests that the more isolated a body is from the influence of other bodies, the more nearly is its velocity constant ; Newton makes this an axiom of his system. But velocity is always velocity relative to some frame of reference. The problem then arises of finding a frame of reference to which this axiom is applicable ; that is a frame of reference with respect to which bodies move according to the laws of Newtonian dynamics. But by postulating enough special forces, almost any frame of reference can be made to satisfy this requirement. One must therefore try to discover a frame of reference for which the minimum number of types of force have to be postulated in order to explain the motion of bodies. Such a frame is usually called an inertial frame.

It is, however, the case that if bodies move according to

[1] This account is oversimplified. (1) For convenience, the *unit* adopted is not the sidereal day but the mean solar day. (2) The standard clocks are only checked against astronomical observations over a long period, i.e. the actual sidereal day is not regarded as absolutely constant.

Newtonian laws with respect to one frame, they will also move according to Newtonian laws with respect to any frame which has a uniform velocity of translation relative to the first. There are therefore an infinite number of inertial frames. Thus on Newtonian theory all one can do is to discover the set of inertial frames; one then says that these frames have zero absolute acceleration and zero absolute rotation.[1] One cannot distinguish any one frame among that set and say that that frame has no absolute velocity.

This means that one can discover absolute accelerations and absolute rotations but not absolute velocities. For if a body is accelerating or rotating with respect to one inertial frame, it will have the same acceleration or rotation with respect to all inertial frames; this will be its absolute acceleration or rotation. But if it has a uniform linear velocity with respect to one inertial frame it will have a different uniform velocity with respect to every other frame.

Newton suggests in the scholium that there are two ways of distinguishing absolute accelerations and rotations from relative. The first is if one can observe the action of forces; for real forces produce real and not merely relative accelerations. Later it was seen that this method was theoretically impossible. For although the concept of force seems to be independent of any other, in Newtonian dynamics force is defined in terms of acceleration (Def. 4 and the First and Second Laws of Motion). That is to say, the fundamental way in which one can discover that a force is acting is by observing the acceleration it produces.[2]

The second way in which one can discover an absolute motion is by observing rotations. In the former case the argument was that real accelerations must result from real

[1] This is now regarded as part of the definition of *absolute acceleration* and *absolute rotation*.

[2] For a full discussion of Newton's Laws of Motion see G. Buchdahl, *British Journal for the Philosophy of Science*, II, 217–235.

causes—real forces ; in the case of rotation, there appear to be real effects from which one can deduce the reality of the cause. This is because any body which moves in a circle has an acceleration at any moment directed towards the centre. A body will therefore only move in a circular orbit under the influence of a centripetal force. If one then moves one's frame of reference to the body in its orbit —or, what is equivalent, to a point on the surface of a rotating body—there will appear to be a force acting not towards the centre but away from it. This is the so-called centrifugal force, a force which to the stationary observer is only the natural tendency of bodies to continue moving in a straight line.

There are several phenomena which show the existence of centrifugal force. In the case of Newton's bucket of water, it causes water molecules to go towards the edge of the bucket and so make the surface concave. Equally obvious are the effects normally attributed to the rotation of the earth on its axis. At the equator centrifugal force is greater than anywhere else on the earth's surface and therefore g, the acceleration of freely falling bodies, is at a minimum. This fact was first observed in 1672 when it was found that pendulums beat more slowly at the equator than in higher latitudes. Another phenomenon attributed to the effect of centrifugal force, is the oblate figure of the earth (i.e. the equatorial diameter greater than the polar). This is analogous to the shape of the rotating water in the bucket in that the particles are attempting to recede from the axis of rotation.[1]

Perhaps the most impressive experiment of all is Foucault's pendulum, first demonstrated in 1851. This is,

---

[1] Historically this was a deduction made by Newton (*Prin.*, Bk III, Prop. 19) and only confirmed by geodetic measurements after his death. It was, however, indirectly confirmed by the fact that the precession of the equinoxes can be explained by Newtonian theory on the assumption that the earth is spheroidal in shape (*Prin.*, Bk III, Prop. 39), the calculated amount of precession agreeing with observation.

essentially, the demonstration that if a pendulum were suspended at the pole, it would swing in a plane which rotated uniformly with respect to the earth—or, as it is usually interpreted, that it would swing in a plane which remained fixed as the earth rotated.[1]

All these phenomena suggest that the earth possesses an absolute rotation. There are two reasons for rejecting the alternative that the earth is at absolute rest and the diurnal revolution of the stars ' real '. Firstly ' if it [sc. this revolution] was real an immense centrifugal force [acting on the stars] would arise, which could not but discover itself; because they move in free spaces, and the solid orbs have been exploded upon the most evident grounds ' (Maclaurin, *Newton's Philosophical Discoveries*, p. 107). The other reason is that if the earth were at rest, the centrifugal force which acts on terrestrial objects would be a real force whose cause was the fixed stars. Such a theory would mean attributing major physical effects to the influence of the most distant of all bodies (cf. p. xliii below). For these reasons only a frame of reference with respect to which the earth is rotating and the fixed stars are at rest is an inertial frame.

One would like to believe that this is all Newton meant when he introduced the concepts of absolute space and time. Such an interpretation is supported by his equating the distinction between absolute and relative space and time, with the distinction between ' mathematical and common ' space and time. This recalls the distinction made in his preface to the first edition of the *Principia* (p. 143 below), between geometry and mechanics. There geometry is said to be concerned with ideal straight lines and circles even though ' artificers do not work with perfect accuracy '. Similarly one might interpret the scholium as

---

[1] A similar phenomenon is the Coriolis force, which, like centrifugal force, is an apparent force manifested when a body is rotating. Its effects are experimentally observable, e.g. in the deflection of the trade winds.

saying that space and time are ideal entities which it is helpful to consider in theory, although they may not exist in reality.

Unfortunately it is easy to cite other passages in which Newton treats absolute space and time as real even though perhaps unknowable. The phrases ' absolute time flows equably ' and ' absolute space remains always similar and immovable ' ; Hypothesis I of Book III ' that the centre of the system of the world is immovable ' ; Proposition XI ' that the common centre of gravity of the earth, the sun and all the planets is immovable ' : all these show that Newton thought he was doing more than just identifying the set of frames of reference with respect to which the laws of dynamics would take the simplest form.

But although the theory of space and time as real entities can be called metaphysical, Newton was not led to it by asking the metaphysical question, ' What are space and time in themselves ? ' Newton himself never discusses this question or related questions as to their reality. There are only three passages in his main works which bear on such metaphysical issues. Two are the remarks in the *Opticks* in which space is spoken of as the sensorium of God ; the other is the short passage in the General Scholium in the *Principia* about God and space and time—and Newton was seventy-one when he wrote this. All three passages are primarily about God and are intended by Newton not to establish any theory as to the nature of space and time, but to prevent any interpretation of his work as derogating from the perfection of the Deity.

THE SPACE-TIME CONTROVERSY FROM LEIBNIZ TO KANT

Thümmig and Wolff

A paper by L. P. Thümmig, a pupil and disciple of Wolff, which answers Clarke's fifth reply, is appended in the German edition of the Correspondence, first published in 1720. It contains little of interest and at one point—where he admits that a universe in motion would differ from one at rest, but says that God would have no sufficient reason for causing it to move—Thümmig has clearly misunderstood Leibniz. This edition of the Correspondence also contains a foreword by Wolff.

Berkeley

Berkeley's *De Motu* (1721) contains a discussion of the Newtonian concepts of absolute space and time, which is in some respects more important than that of either Leibniz or Clarke. The subject was one on which Berkeley had written in *The Principles of Human Knowledge* (1710). There he had criticized the use physicists made of the terms 'force' and 'gravitation' in explaining the motion of bodies, and rejected the idea of absolute space on the grounds that the distinction between absolute and relative motion was invalid. But, like Leibniz, he apparently contradicts himself. For although he denies that absolute motion can be distinguished from relative, he admits that when two bodies change their position with respect to each other 'it may be that only one is moved, namely that on which the force causing the change of distance is impressed'. In the *De Motu* this contradiction does not occur, since he points out (Paras. 11 and 15) that forces are only known by their effects, that is, by the motion they cause.

In the *De Motu* Berkeley refers to the writings of both Newton and Leibniz. He does not, however, cite the Correspondence.

English Critics of Clarke

A series of more lengthy writings in English on the subject of space appeared in the years 1731–5.[1] Although these

[1] John Clarke : *A Defence of Dr. Clarke's demonstration of the being and attributes of God. A Second Defence . . . A Third Defence . . .*
Joseph Clarke : *Dr. Clarke's Notions of Space examined. A further examination of Dr. Clarke's Notions of Space.*
Edmund Law : *Notes to translation of Archbishop King's Origin of*

mention the Correspondence, they are mainly concerned with a passage in Clarke's Boyle lectures where he writes, ' When we are endeavouring to suppose that there is no Being in the Universe that exists necessarily, we always find in our minds some ideas, as of infinity and eternity, which to remove, that is to suppose no Being, no Substance in the Universe, to which those attributes or modes of existence are necessarily inherent, is a contradiction in the very terms.' Against Clarke were Joseph Clarke, Isaac Watts, Edmund Law ; in his defence, John Clarke and John Jackson. The interest of these works is now merely antiquarian.

Voltaire

Voltaire's *Éléments de la Philosophie de Newton* (first complete edition 1741) is a popular exposition of Newton's physics. It is of some historical importance since it contributed very considerably to the spread of Newtonian doctrines on the Continent. The first section deals with Newton's metaphysics. In this Voltaire discusses such topics as natural theology, liberty and necessity, and space and time. He frequently cites the Correspondence and, in each case, sides with Clarke against Leibniz. Few, if any, new arguments are adduced.

Maclaurin

Another semi-popular exposition of Newtonian physics, which contributes in passing to the controversy on space and time, is Maclaurin's *An Account of Sir Isaac Newton's Philosophical Discoveries*, published posthumously in 1750.

Evil. An Enquiry into the Ideas of Space, Time, Immensity, and Eternity, etc.

Isaac Watts : *Philosophical Essays on Various Subjects.* Essay 1. *A fair enquiry and debate concerning space, whether it be something or nothing, God or a creature.*

John Jackson : *The Existence and Unity of God proved from his Nature and Attributes. A Defence of a book entitled the Existence and Unity of God.*

Maclaurin discusses several of the issues raised in the Correspondence to which he frequently refers. He defends Newton from the accusation that his theory of the universe is incompatible with the omnipotence and omniscience of God. He discusses at length the various experiments and observations (e.g. the oblate figure of the earth) which seem to demonstrate that the earth possesses a real rotation, and repeats Newton's conclusion that one must distinguish absolute from relative space and time. Maclaurin also strongly criticizes Leibniz for adopting the wrong estimate of ' moving force ' and, more generally, for constructing an elaborate philosophical system instead of using the true scientific method, analysis followed by synthesis.

Euler

Euler published in 1748 an interesting paper *Reflexions sur l'espace et le temps*, Memoires de l'Academie des sciences de Berlin (*Oeuvres* III, 2, p. 376). This short essay contrasts the opinions of the ' mathematicians ' (i.e. the Newtonians) with those of the ' metaphysicians ' (Leibniz and Wolff), and sides with the former. Euler's main argument is that the principles of mechanics—e.g. that a body continues in its state of rest or uniform motion unless acted on by external forces—have been shown by experience to be true, and that such principles imply the reality of absolute space and time. ' If they say it is with respect to the fixed stars that it is necessary to explain the principle of inertia it would be very difficult to refute them seeing that the fixed stars . . . are so far from us. But it will be a very strange principle in metaphysics and contrary to other of its dogmas to say that the fixed stars direct bodies in their inertia.' He goes on to point to another weakness in Leibniz's account—that he gives us no way of measuring space and time. ' I very much doubt whether the Meta-physicians will dare to say that the equality of spaces ought to be judged by the equality of the number of monads which fill them ', and ' if time is the order of successive events . . . two times ought to be equal during which the same number of successive happenings occur. But if one considers a body which goes through equal spaces in equal times by what changes or what body must one judge the equality of these times?'

Euler then considers the question of how we acquire the ideas of space and time. He admits that we do not get them by sensation, but points out that it cannot therefore be assumed that they are ideal things. Although we get them by reflection the way we do so is very different from the way in which we form ideas of genera and species. This remark recalls Kant's discussion of the problem.

Euler also discusses space and time in his *Theoria Motus Corporum solidorum* (1765). Here he admits that by experiments we can only discover relative motion; but he asserts that the laws of mechanics presuppose that bodies are, without relation to other bodies, either at rest or in motion, i.e. absolutely at rest or in absolute motion.

Boscovitch

In 1755 a remarkable paper [1] on space and time was published by the scientist Boscovitch, an Italian Jesuit of Serbo-Croat extraction. The paper is divided into two parts. The first, ' on space and time ', purports to give an account of the ' real ' nature of space and time. The position of objects in space and time is taken to consist in the relations they have to points of space or to instants of time which are treated as real entities. This is essentially the same as the Newtonian theory.

The second part of the paper, ' Space and time as we know them ', takes a completely different approach. Boscovitch asserts that we can never know absolute location either in time or space. He adds, ' Moreover, it might be the case that the whole universe within our sight should

[1] Contained in an appendix to *Philosophiae Recentioris* by Benedict Stay, and republished as a supplement to his own *Philosophiae Naturalis Theoria* 1763.

daily contract or expand while the scale of forces contracted or expanded in the same ratio ; if such a thing did happen, there would be no change of ideas in our mind, and we should have no feeling that such a change was taking place.'

Unlike all earlier writers, Boscovitch's discussion of space and time includes an analysis of the process of measurement. He takes the case of length and points out that whenever we measure an object against a standard rod we employ two general axioms of measurement : things which are both equal to the same multiple or submultiple of another are equal ; and things that coincide are equal. We also presuppose that the standard rod is constant in length. But, he asks, are we right in assuming that a wooden or iron ten-foot rod is the same length after it has been moved ? According to Boscovitch's own theory of physics it cannot be the same length, since the forces which connect the points of matter will have been altered. Even on ordinary physical theory there may be compression or dilation of the rod as it is moved.

The obvious problem is how these two theories of space and time are related. How can we proceed from experiments involving space and time ' as we know them ' to theoretical physics which uses the concepts of space and time ' as they really are ' ? Boscovitch never faces this difficulty. In fact one of the shortcomings of his theoretical physics is that it has practically no experimental foundation.

Kant

There is no doubt that Kant knew of the existence of the Correspondence and was acquainted with the general nature of the controversy between Leibniz and the Newtonians.[1] It was his dissatisfaction with both views

[1] On a sheet of paper presumed by the editor of the Academy edition to be notes for a lecture on space and time, Kant twice briefly mentions Clarke and Leibniz together, on the reality of space and again of time, along with Hobbes, Descartes, Wolff, and others, and also mentions

that led him to his critical theory of space and time[1]—and to his whole critical philosophy, since his theory of knowledge is an extension to knowledge in general of his solution to the problem of knowledge in mathematics.

Kant discusses the nature of space in his first published writing, *Thoughts on the true estimation of living forces* (1746–9). This work is a belated contribution to the controversy about the measurement of force. In it Kant tries to show that the measure mv is correct in mathematics (i.e. formalized theoretical dynamics) and the measure mv^2 correct in nature—a suggestion of little value. Near the beginning of the work (§ 9) Kant outlines a possible relation between space and force. ' It is easily proved that there would be no space and no extension if substances had no force to act outside themselves. For without a force of this kind, there is no connexion, without this connexion no order, and without this order no space.' He goes on to suggest that the fact that bodies interact with a force varying inversely as the square of the distance between them, explains why space has three dimensions.

Kant's general theory of space at this time was a development of Leibniz's. Space is the relation of coexistents. But whereas Leibniz leaves the relation undefined, Kant explains it in terms of forces.

The *Nova Dilucidatio* (1755) and the *New System of Motion and Rest* (1758) also show that Kant in his early years accepted the Leibnizian account of space and time. In the *Nova Dilucidatio* (*Works*, Acad. ed., I, 414) Kant remarks, ' Since place, situation, space, are relations of substances . . .' In the *New System* he writes : ' I should never use them [*sc.* the terms motion and rest] in an absolute sense

Newton's view of space as God's sensorium. The sheet of paper is dated by the editor to the period 1775–7. There is also a somewhat earlier note on the sensorium. (*Works*, Academy edition, XVII, 699, Refl. 4756, and XVII, 432, Refl. 4145.)

[1] For a full discussion of the relation between Kant's theory of space, time, and matter, and the theories expressed in the Correspondence, see G. Martin : *Kant's Metaphysics and Theory of Science.*

but only relatively. I ought never to say that a body is at rest without adding in respect of what things it is at rest, and never to say that it is in motion without naming the objects in respect of which it changes its relation. Even if I thought I could imagine a mathematical space empty of everything as a receptacle for bodies, that would not help me. For how could I distinguish the parts of it and the different places, if they were not occupied with something corporeal ' (II, 17).

A few years later, Kant entirely abandoned Leibniz's theory of space and time and adopted the Newtonian account. Two factors in particular influenced him. The first was a reading of Euler's *Reflexions sur l'espace et le temps*, the second his discovery of the puzzle of incongruent counterparts.

In the *Attempt to introduce the concept of negative magnitudes into philosophy* (1763) Kant, after mentioning Euler, complains about metaphysicians who try to discover the nature of space and motion abstractly without paying attention to the data given in mechanics. *The First ground of the distinction of regions in space* (1766) makes Kant's change of view explicit. Here he quotes Euler as having shown that it is impossible to assign any meaning to the laws of mechanics if one assumes that the concept of space is obtained by abstraction from the relations of things. Kant goes on to argue positively for the reality of absolute space. Consider the difference between two incongruent counterparts such as a left hand and a right hand. The difference cannot lie in the internal relations between the parts of each object ; for the relation between, for example, the thumb and fingers of the left hand is exactly the same as the relation between the corresponding parts of the right hand. It cannot lie in the relations between the hands and external objects, because if a hand were the only thing in the universe, it would still have to be either a right hand or a left. The distinction must therefore lie in their relation to absolute space even though thi relation 'is such that it cannot itself be immediately perceived'.

Kant did not hold the Newtonian theory of absolute space and time for long. To regard space and time as real entities was to raise all sorts of unanswerable problems about the relation of God to space or about the infinity of the universe—problems which appear in the *Critique of Pure Reason* as the Antinomies. Moreover the puzzle of incongruent counterparts did not necessarily imply the existence of absolute space ; it could equally well be resolved if space was the form of human intuition.

The theory of space and time as forms of sensible intuition is first put forward by Kant in the *Inaugural Dissertation* of 1770. Kant rejects the Newtonian view as ' pertaining to the world of fable ' and as ' placing a stumbling block in the way of certain rational concepts . . . such as questions concerning a spiritual world '. The Leibnizian theory is equally unacceptable since it would make geometry an empirical science and thus deprive it of its necessary universality. But if space and time are the forms of human sensibility, all phenomenal objects—and only phenomenal objects—will be in the one space and time, since they are all objects of the same kind of sensible intuition. Thus God, spirits, and other noumena will be entirely independent of space and time ; and one geometry will necessarily be valid for all sensible objects.

In the *Dissertation*, Kant considers for the first time how we get our knowledge of space and time—the problem which for him was the fundamental one. He takes up two points which Euler had made. The first is that we do not acquire the ideas of space and time by sensation but by reflection ; the second that they are not abstract ideas like ideas of genera and species. Kant develops both lines of thought. He points out that our knowledge of space and time cannot come from sensation since they are pre-supposed in all our sense-experience. He concludes that, since the ideas of space and time are neither sensible intuitions nor general concepts, space and time themselves can neither be substances, attributes, nor relations ; the only alternative is that they are pure intuitions which are forms of all human sensibility. This is the same theory of space and time as that expressed in the *Critique of Pure Reason.*

MACH AND EINSTEIN

It was difficult for any physicist in the nineteenth century to criticize the concepts of Newtonian dynamics. On the assumption that the planets possessed an absolute rotation on their own axes and moved in elliptical orbits round the sun, the astronomers had been able to reduce the whole solar system to order. If one admitted that the planets possessed real, absolute rotations, then, it seemed, one also had to admit that it was meaningful to speak of absolute time and absolute space.

Electro-magnetic theory helped to make scientists more ready to accept this idea of an absolute space which ' remained always similar and immovable '. Just as sound is normally propagated by waves in the air, so electro-magnetic radiation was taken to consist of waves in an aether, their velocity of propagation relative to this aether being constant. The aether was thought of as being— except for minor local variations—both uniform and at rest. It was, therefore, easy to run the two ideas of absolute space and an aether together and to regard dynamics and electro-magnetic theory as, in this respect, supporting each other.

The first important critic of the orthodox theory of absolute space and time was Mach, who in his *Die Mechanik,* 1883 (translated into English as *The Science of Mechanics*), attacks the assumption that absolute rotation is observable. All that can be observed is rotation relative to the fixed stars. ' Can we fix Newton's bucket of water, rotate the fixed stars and *then* prove the absence of centrifugal force ? The experiment is impossible, the idea is meaningless, for the two cases are not, in sense-perception, distinguishable from each other. I accordingly regard these two cases as *the same case* and Newton's distinction as an illusion.' And of the law of inertia (Newton's first law of motion) he writes : ' When we say that a body preserves unchanged its direction and velocity in *space*, our assertion is nothing more than an abbreviated reference *to the entire* universe.'

Mach's criticisms were based solely on epistemological considerations, and they therefore had very little immediate influence among scientists. When Einstein published his Special Theory of Relativity in 1905, the surprising failure of experiments devised to discover the motion of the earth relative to the aether (e.g. the Michelson-Morley experiment) was well known. His theory, though revolutionary, was therefore much more readily acceptable.

The Special (or restricted) Theory of Relativity extends the relativity of velocity and position from dynamics to electro-magnetism. Newtonian dynamics recognizes that it is impossible to discover a system's absolute velocity (as opposed to acceleration or rotation) ; for any frame of reference moving with a uniform linear velocity relative to an inertial frame is itself an inertial frame (cf. above, p. xxxvii). On the other hand, nineteenth-century electro-magnetic theory suggests that velocity relative to the aether can be discovered. What Einstein does in his Special Theory is to make two postulates : that the laws of nature, both electro-magnetic and dynamical, are the same for all frames of reference in uniform relative motion ; and that light *in vacuo* is propagated with a constant velocity which is independent of the states of motion both of the emitting body and of the observer. The theory consists in the working out of the consequences of these two postulates.

The Special Theory has two implications which bear on the controversy about space and time. It shows not only ' uniform velocity relative to absolute space ' to be unobservable, but also ' uniform velocity relative to the aether '. It also shows that the distinction in physics between space and time depends on the observer. For, if to an observer at rest with respect to one system of reference two events appear to occur at the same time in different places, then to an observer at rest relative to another system of reference moving uniformly relative to the first system, they will appear as separated both in space and time—although the effect will only be observable if the relative velocity is comparable with the velocity of light. It was this aspect of the theory that led Minkowski to make his famous remark, ' Henceforth space by itself and time by itself, are doomed to fade away into mere shadows and only a kind of union of the two will preserve an independent reality ' (*The Principle of Relativity*, Einstein and others, p. 75).

Einstein's General Theory of Relativity (1916) is an extension of the principle of relativity from systems of reference in uniform relative motion to all systems of reference in any kind of motion. Two considerations in particular influenced Einstein here (*The Principle of Relativity*, pp. 112 f.). The first was the epistemological difficulties, pointed out by Mach, in the concepts of absolute space and time. Einstein says that to explain the oblate figure of the earth as due to the rotation of the earth relative to absolute space is to introduce a ' factitious ' and ' unobservable cause ' and like Mach holds that the distant masses of the stars and their motion relative to the earth must be regarded as the real cause.

The other consideration was the equality of gravitational and inertial mass, which in Newtonian physics is a basic, unexplained empirical fact. Newton himself never provides a clear definition of inertial mass. In Definition 1 of the *Principia* he defines mass as density multiplied by volume. This is unsatisfactory, because if density is taken in the modern sense of mass divided by volume it is trivial, and if in the seventeenth-century sense of specific gravity it assumes the proportionality of gravitational mass (weight) and inertial mass. It is clear however that Newton had in mind a different concept of mass, the purpose of this definition being to express the empirical fact that there exist substances such that bodies composed of them have (inertial) masses which are proportional to their volume.

If one wanted to produce a formal definition of mass in Newtonian physics one would have to proceed in some such way as the following : take some force, reproducible at will, such as that provided by a compressed spring ; take some body as the unit of mass ; measure the velocity acquired by this body when the force acts on it during a short interval of time ; then if under the action of the same force during the same interval, another body is given $1/n$ times the velocity, it will by definition have a mass of n. This is inertial mass, the concept which is fundamental in Newtonian physics.

Then take a balance, and taking the same body as unit, construct a body which when placed in the other pan balances the first ; then put these two bodies in the same pan and construct a third body which balances them ; this will, by definition, have a gravitational mass (weight) of 2. It will then be found by experiment that a body of n inertial mass has a gravitational mass of n and vice versa. (Newton actually established this fact by experiments with pendulums.)

Einstein, however, pointed out that if one considers two frames of reference K and K', where K' has a uniform acceleration relative to K (this could equally well be described as K having an acceleration relative to K'), a body moving in K with a constant velocity as a result of its own inertia will have in K' a constant acceleration independent of the material composition and physical state of the body. Now in Newtonian physics gravitational accelerations have this property of being independent of the nature of the body. Thus what appears in one system as a body moving in a uniform gravitational field can be regarded in another system as a body moving uniformly under its own inertia. These two descriptions, Einstein claims, are physically equivalent. For this point of view to be possible it is essential, not just accidental, that gravitational and inertial mass should be proportional. This is the position taken up by Einstein in his General Theory of Relativity.

By generalizing the argument, Einstein was able to formulate a law of gravitation for the statement of which all frames of reference are equivalent. This new gravitational theory enabled him to explain the movement of the perihelion of Mercury's orbit,[1] an anomaly which had puzzled astronomical physicists for some time—and also to predict the phenomenon of the bending of light in a gravitational field as later observed during total solar eclipses. The General Theory, it is therefore claimed, has been to some extent empirically confirmed.

One point, however, should be noted about the General Theory in its present form. As we have seen, Einstein had two theoretical aims in forming his theory. He wished to show that the equality of gravitational and inertial mass could be regarded as a consequence of the wider principle of the equivalence of different frames of reference. He also wished to explain why frames of reference with zero rotation relative to the fixed stars were inertial frames ; for this—or the equivalent statement that the fixed stars have, on the whole, no angular velocity relative to absolute space—was, in Newtonian physics, an unexplained empirical fact. The General Theory satisfies the first aim but not the second. For, according to the theory, a test particle would possess inertial properties even in an otherwise empty universe. If inertia was due to the gravitational effect of the whole universe, as suggested by Mach and Einstein, this would not be so.[2]

[1] The ellipse in which Mercury moves, gradually rotates at a speed which cannot be explained solely on the basis of the disturbing influences of the other planets.

[2] cf. D. W. Sciama, *Monthly Notices of the Royal Astronomical Society*, vol. 113, No. 1, 1953.

It is difficult to estimate the importance of the General Theory of Relativity in the dispute about space and time which started with Newton. Sometimes it is suggested that Einstein has shown the phrases ' absolute rotation ' and ' absolute acceleration ' to be meaningless. But this is mistaken. For there is still, according to any relativity theory, a difference between inertial and other frames of reference. Thus if ' absolute rotation ' is interpreted as rotation relative to an inertial frame, it still is as meaningful a phrase as in Newtonian dynamics.[1]

The aspect of the General Theory which is philosophically intriguing is that those properties which were previously thought of as physical are there regarded as, in some sense, geometrical. It is almost impossible to estimate the general implications of this part of the theory because of the difficulty of interpreting any theory couched in a complex mathematical form. But in expositions of the theory phrases like the following are common.

' The corner stone of Einstein's theory of gravitation is that space-time is not uniform and that its varying intrinsic character accounts for the varying acceleration of a particle as it moves through the gravitational field.'—NUNN.

' The existence of gravitational energy becomes a physical property of space.'—KOPFF.

' We have reduced the theory of fields of force to a theory of the geometry of the world.'—EDDINGTON.

' The gravitational field influences and even determines the metrical laws of the space-time continuum.'—EINSTEIN.

' The ten functions representing the gravitational field at the same time define the metrical properties of the space measured.'—EINSTEIN.

---

[1] General relativity shows that at any point the gravitational field may be ' made to disappear ' by a suitable choice of a frame of reference, just as in Newtonian physics centrifugal force can be eliminated by a shift of frame. But whereas in the latter case, a set of frames can be found which will eliminate centrifugal forces everywhere, no frame can be found which will eliminate gravitational forces everywhere.

Such remarks suggest—as do, to some extent, mathematical expositions—that in the General Theory of Relativity, space-time is given some sort of reality. For part, if not all, of what is meant by calling a thing real is that one can ascribe properties to it. It is possible that the theory could be given an alternative exposition which would avoid this implication. It might be interpreted in terms of the behaviour of every sort of measuring rod and clock in a gravitational field; or in terms of one geometry being more convenient in certain circumstances than another. But, as explained at present, the General Theory does seem to imply the reality of space-time and the meaningfulness of speaking about its properties. (It was largely dissatisfaction with this aspect that led E. A. Milne to develop his Kinematical Theory of Relativity.)

We are therefore left with a somewhat paradoxical conclusion. To some writers it has seemed that when in the Correspondence Leibniz criticizes the concepts of absolute space and time, he is anticipating Einstein. On the other hand, Leibniz's fundamental postulate is that space and time are unreal. No one therefore would have rejected more strongly than he a theory which ascribes properties to space-time. If, therefore, one insists on awarding points to Leibniz and Clarke, in the light of modern physics, it is perhaps best to call it a drawn contest.

PREVIOUS EDITIONS OF THE CORRESPONDENCE

1. *A Collection of Papers which passed between the late learned Mr. Leibnitz and Dr. Clarke in the years 1715 and 1716 relating to the Principles of Natural Philosophy and Religion*, London 1717 (English and French on facing pages, Leibniz's papers translated by Clarke and Clarke's replies translated by de la Roche).

2. *Merckwürdige Schriften welche . . . zwischen dem Herrn Baron von Leibniz und dem Herrn D. Clarke über besondere Materien der natürlichen Religion in Französ. und Englischer Sprache gewechselt und . . . in teutscher Sprache herausgegeben worden von Heinrich Köhler,*

Frankfurt and Leipzig (Jena) 1720 (German ; with a foreword by Wolff and an answer to Clarke's fifth reply by L. P. Thümmig).

3. *Receuil de diverses Pièces sur la Philosophie, la Religion Naturelle, l'Histoire, les Mathematiques, etc., par Mrs. Leibnitz, Clarke, Newton, & autres Autheurs célèbres*, vol. I, Amsterdam 1720 (edited by Des Maiseaux, French).

4. *The Works of Samuel Clarke, D.D.*, vol. IV, London 1738 (English and French).

5. (2nd edition of Köhler, 1720) *Des Freyherrn von Leibniz Kleinere Philosophische Schriften . . . ehedem von dem Jenaischen Philosophen Herrn Heinrich Köhler Teutsch übersetzt nun auf das neue übersehen von M. Caspar Jacob Huth der teutschen Gesellschaft in Jena Senior*, Jena 1740.

6. (2nd edition of Des Maiseaux, 1720) Amsterdam 1740.

7. *Viri illustris G. G. Leibnitii Epistolarum Pentas una cum totidem responsionibus D. Samuelis Clarkii . . . latinitate donavit et adjectis notis uberius illustravit Nicolaus Engelhard*, Groningen 1740 (Latin ; with Thümmig's answer and extensive notes by the translator).

8. (3rd edition of Des Maiseaux, 1720) Lausanne 1759.

9. L. Dutens : *G. G. Leibnitii Opera Omnia*, vol. II, Geneva 1768 (French).

10. (2nd edition of Dutens, 1768) Geneva and Berlin 1789.

11. J. E. Erdmann : *G. G. Leibnitii Opera Philosophica*, vol. II, Berlin 1840 (French).

12. A. Jacques : *Oeuvres de Leibniz*, Paris 1842 (French ; re-issued 1844, 1847).

13. P. Janet : *Oeuvres philosophiques de Leibniz*, Paris 1866 (French).

14. O. Klopp : *Die Werke von Leibniz*, Hanover 1864–84, vol. XI (French ; includes most of the general correspondence between Leibniz and the Princess of Wales, which accompanied the exchange of papers).

15. C. J. Gerhardt : *Die philosophischen Schriften von G. W. Leibniz*, vol. VII, Berlin 1890 (Leibniz in French, Clarke in English, with a few additional documents).

16. A. Buchenau and E. Cassirer : *G. W. Leibniz, Hauptschriften zur Grundlegung der Philosophie*, transl. by A. Buchenau and edited by E. Cassirer, Leipzig 1903 (German ; includes extensive notes giving answers that Leibniz might have made to Clarke's fifth reply).

17. (2nd edition of Buchenau and Cassirer, 1903) Leipzig 1924.

THE CORRESPONDENCE

On the opposite page is printed the relevant part of the original title page. The edition of 1717 also included as an addition separately paginated *Letters to Dr. Clarke concerning Liberty and Necessity* ; *From a Gentleman of the University of Cambridge* [actually R. Bulkeley] : *With the Doctor's Answers to them,* and *Remarks upon a Book* [by A. Collins], *Entituled, A Philosophical Enquiry concerning Human Liberty.*

A
COLLECTION OF PAPERS

which passed between the late Learned

Mr. LEIBNITZ

AND

Dr. CLARKE

in the years 1715 and 1716

relating to the

PRINCIPLES

OF

NATURAL PHILOSOPHY AND RELIGION

With an Appendix

★

by SAMUEL CLARKE, D.D.
Rector of St. James's, Westminster

★

LONDON :   Printed for   JAMES KNAPTON
at The Crown in St. Paul's Churchyard
MDCCXVII

TO
HER ROYAL HIGHNESS
THE PRINCESS OF WALES

Madam,

As the following papers were at first written by your command, and had afterwards the honour of being severally transmitted through Your Royal Highnesses hands : so the principal encouragement upon which they now presume to appear in public, is the permission they have of coming forth under the protection of so illustrious a name.

The late learned Mr. Leibnitz well understood, how great an honour and reputation it would be to him, to have his arguments approved by a person of Your Royal Highnesses character. But the same steady impartiality and unalterable love of truth, the same constant readiness to hear and to submit to reason, always so conspicuous, always shining forth so brightly in Your Royal Highnesses conduct ; which justly made him desirous to exert in these papers his utmost skill in defending his opinions ; was at the same time an equal encouragement to such as thought him in an error, to endeavour to prove that his opinions could not be defended.

The occasion of his giving your Royal Highness the trouble of his first letter, he declares to be his having entertained some suspicions, that the foundations of natural religion were in danger of being hurt by Sir Isaac Newton's philosophy. It appeared to me, on the contrary, a most certain and evident truth, that from the earliest antiquity to this day, the foundations of natural religion had never been so deeply and so firmly laid, as in the mathematical and experimental philosophy of that great

5

man. And Your Royal Highnesses singular exactness in searching after truth, and earnest concern for every thing that is of real consequence to religion, could not permit those suspicions, which had been suggested by a gentleman of such eminent note in the learned world as Mr. Leibnitz was, to remain unanswered.

Christianity presupposes the truth of natural religion. Whatsoever subverts natural religion, does consequently much more subvert Christianity : and whatsoever tends to confirm natural religion, is proportionately of service to the true interest of the Christian. Natural philosophy therefore, so far as it affects religion, by determining questions concerning liberty and fate, concerning the extent of the powers of matter and motion, and the proofs from phenomena of God's continual government of the world ; is of very great importance. 'Tis of singular use, rightly to understand, and carefully to distinguish from hypotheses or mere suppositions, the true and certain consequences of experimental and mathematical philosophy ; which do, with wonderful strength and advantage, to all such as are capable of apprehending them, confirm, establish, and vindicate against all objections, those great and fundamental truths of natural religion, which the wisdom of providence has at the same time universally implanted, in some degree, in the minds of persons even of the meanest capacities, not qualified to examine demonstrative proofs.

'Tis with the highest pleasure and satisfaction, that the following papers upon so important a subject, are laid before a Princess, who, to an inimitable sweetness of temper, candour and affability towards all, has joined not only an impartial love of truth, and a desire of promoting learning in general, but has herself also attained to a degree of knowledge very particular and uncommon, even in matters of the nicest and most abstract speculation : and whose sacred and always unshaken regard to the interest of sincere and uncorrupt religion, made her the delight of all good Protestants abroad, and by a just fame filled the hearts of all true Britons at home, with an expectation beforehand, which, great as it was, is fully answered by what they now see and are blessed with.

By the Protestant Succession in the illustrious house of Hanover having taken place, this nation has now, with the blessing of God, a certain prospect, (if our own vices and follies prevent not,) of seeing government actually administered, according to the design and end for which it was instituted by providence, with no other view than that of the public good, the general welfare and happiness of mankind. We have a prospect of seeing the true liberty of a brave and loyal people, firmly secured, established, and regulated, by laws equally advantageous both to the crown and subject : of seeing learning and knowledge encouraged and promoted, in opposition to all kinds of ignorance and blindness : and, (which is the glory of all,) of seeing the true Christian temper and spirit of religion effectually prevail, both against atheism and infidelity on the one hand, which take off from men all obligations of doing what is right ; and against superstition and bigotry on the other hand, which lay upon men the strongest obligations to do the greatest wrongs.

What views and expectations less than these, can a nation reasonably entertain ; when it beholds a King firmly settled upon the throne of a wisely limited monarchy, whose will, when without limitation, showed always a greater love of justice, than of power ; and never took pleasure in acting any otherwise, than according to the most perfect laws of reason and equity ? When it sees a succession of the same blessings continued, in a Prince, whose noble openness of mind, and generous warmth of zeal for the preservation of the Protestant religion, and the laws and liberties of these kingdoms, make him every day more and more beloved, as he is more known ? And when these glorious hopes open still further into an unbounded prospect in a numerous royal offspring ? Through whom, that the just and equitable temper of the grandfather ;

the noble zeal and spirit of the father ; the affability, goodness, and judicious exactness of the mother ; may, with glory to themselves, and with the happiest influences both upon these and foreign countries, descend to all succeeding generations ; to the establishment of universal peace, of truth and right amongst men ; and to the entire rooting out that greatest enemy of Christian religion, the spirit of Popery both among Romanists and Protestants : and that Your Royal Highness may your self long live, to continue a blessing to these nations, to see truth and virtue flourish in your own days, and to be a great instrument, under the direction of providence, in laying a foundation for the highest happiness of the public in times to come ; is the prayer of,

> Madam,
> > Your Royal Highnesses
> > most humble and
> > > most obedient servant,
> > > Sam. Clarke.

ADVERTISEMENT TO THE READER [1]

The reader will be pleased to observe

1. That the following letters are all printed exactly as they were written; without adding, diminishing, or altering a word. The marginal notes only, and the Appendix, being added.

2. That the translation is made with great exactness, to prevent any misrepresentation of Mr. Leibnitz's sense.

3. That the numbers of sections in each of Dr. Clarke's papers, refer respectively to the numbers or sentences of each of Mr. Leibnitz's papers immediately foregoing.

[1] Clarke inserted in the original edition a large number of marginal references. In this edition we have omitted those which refer to subsequent paragraphs of the Correspondence, to previous paragraphs of the same paper, and to Clarke's Appendix of passages from Leibniz ; but we have added before each section of the Appendix a list of the paragraphs in the text where Clarke had inserted a reference to that section. The many marginal references to Leibniz's Fifth Paper in Clarke's Fifth Reply have been incorporated into the text. His remaining references (i.e. those to previous papers) are printed as footnotes.

Clarke's footnotes have here been assigned letters ; numbered footnotes are the editor's. Square brackets in footnotes indicate editorial insertions.

MR. LEIBNITZ'S FIRST PAPER

being

An Extract of a Letter [1] Written in

November, 1715

---

1. Natural religion itself, seems to decay (in England) very much.   Many will have human souls to be material : others make God himself a corporeal being.

2. Mr. Locke, and his followers, are uncertain at least, whether the soul be not material, and naturally perishable. [2]

3. Sir Isaac Newton says, that space is an organ, which God makes use of to perceive things by.   But if God stands in need of any organ to perceive things by, it will follow, that they do not depend altogether upon him, nor were produced by him.

4. Sir Isaac Newton, and his followers, have also a very odd opinion concerning the work of God.   According to their doctrine, God Almighty [a] wants to wind up his watch from time to time : otherwise it would cease to move.   He had not, it seems, sufficient foresight to make it a perpetual motion.   Nay, the machine of God's making, is so imperfect, according to these gentlemen ; that he is obliged to clean it now and then by an extraordinary concourse, and even to mend it, as a clockmaker mends

---

[a] The place Mr. Leibnitz here seems to allude to is as follows [Clarke then quotes the passage in Query 31 of Newton's *Opticks*. ' For while comets move in very eccentric orbs . . . wants a reformation ', given in Appendix A, p. 180].

---

[1] To Caroline, Princess of Wales.   See Appendix B, p. 189.
[2] Locke, *Essay IV.3.6* and *First Letter to Stillingfleet.*

11

his work ; who must consequently be so much the more unskilful a workman, as he is oftener obliged to mend his work and to set it right. According to my opinion, the same force and vigour remains always in the world, and only passes from one part of matter to another, agreeably to the laws of nature, and the beautiful pre-established order. And I hold, that when God works miracles, he does not do it in order to supply the wants of nature, but those of grace. Whoever thinks otherwise, must needs have a very mean notion of the wisdom and power of God.

DR. CLARKE'S FIRST REPLY [1]

1. That there are some in England, as well as in other countries, who deny or very much corrupt even natural religion itself, is very true, and much to be lamented. But (next to the vicious affections of men) this is to be principally ascribed to the false philosophy of the materialists, to which the mathematical principles of philosophy are the most directly repugnant. That some make the souls of men, and others even God himself to be a corporeal being ; is also very true : but those who do so, are the great enemies of the mathematical principles of philosophy ; which principles, and which alone, prove matter, or body, to be the smallest and most inconsiderable part of the universe.

2. That Mr. Locke doubted whether the soul was immaterial or no, may justly be suspected from some parts of his writings : but herein he has been followed only by some materialists, enemies to the mathematical principles of philosophy ; and who approve little or nothing in Mr. Locke's writings, but his errors.

3. Sir Isaac Newton doth not say, that space is the organ which God makes use of to perceive things by ; nor that

[1] Transmitted 26th Nov. 1715 (p. 190).

he has need of any medium at all, whereby to perceive things : but on the contrary, that he, being omnipresent, perceives all things by his immediate presence to them, in all space wherever they are, without the intervention or assistance of any organ or medium whatsoever. In order to make this more intelligible, he illustrates it by a similitude : that as the mind of man, by its immediate presence to the pictures or images of things, form'd in the brain by the means of the organs of sensation, sees those pictures as if they were the things themselves ; so God sees all things, by his immediate presence to them ; he being actually present to the things themselves, to all things in the universe ; as the mind of man is present to all the pictures of things formed in his brain. Sir Isaac Newton considers the brain and organs of sensation, as the means by which those pictures are formed : but not as the means by which the mind sees or perceives those pictures, when they are so formed. And in the universe, he doth not consider things as if they were pictures, formed by certain means, or organs ; but as real things, form'd by God himself, and seen by him in all places wherever they are, without the intervention of any medium at all. And this similitude is all that he means, when he supposes infinite space [a] to be (as it were) the *sensorium* of the Omnipresent Being.

4. The reason why, among men, an artificer is justly esteemed so much the more skilful, as the machine of his composing will continue longer to move regularly without any farther interposition of the workman ; is because the skill of all human artificers consists only in composing, adjusting, or putting together certain movements, the principles of whose motion are altogether independent upon the artificer : such as are weights and springs, and the like ; whose forces are not made, but only adjusted, by

[a] The passage referred to, is as follows [Clarke then quotes the passage from *Opticks*, Query 28 : ' Is not the sensory of animals . . . that which in us perceives and thinks ', Appendix A, p. 173–174].

the workman. But with regard to God, the case is quite different ; because he not only composes or puts things together, but is himself the author and continual preserver of their original forces or moving powers : and consequently 'tis not a diminution, but the true glory of his workmanship, that nothing is done without his continual government and inspection. The notion of the world's being a great machine, going on without the interposition of God, as a clock continues to go without the assistance of a clockmaker ; is the notion of materialism and fate, and tends, (under pretence of making God a *supra-mundane intelligence*,) to exclude providence and God's government in reality out of the world. And by the same reason that a philosopher can represent all things going on from the beginning of the creation, without any government or interposition of providence ; a sceptic will easily argue still farther backwards, and suppose that things have from eternity gone on (as they now do) without any true creation or original author at all, but only what such arguers call all-wise and eternal nature. If a king had a kingdom, wherein all things would continually go on without his government or interposition, or without his attending to and ordering what is done therein ; it would be to him, merely a nominal kingdom ; nor would he in reality deserve at all the title of king or governor. And as those men, who pretend that in an earthly government things may go on perfectly well without the king himself ordering or disposing of any thing, may reasonably be suspected that they would like very well to set the king aside : so whosoever contends, that the course of the world can go on without the continual direction of God, the Supreme Governor ; his doctrine does in effect tend to exclude God out of the world.

MR. LEIBNITZ'S SECOND PAPER

being

An Answer to Dr. Clarke's First Reply

1. It is rightly observed in the paper delivered to the Princess of Wales, which Her Royal Highness has been pleased to communicate to me, that, next to corruption of manners,[1] the principles of the materialists do very much contribute to keep up impiety. But I believe the author had no reason to add, that the mathematical principles of philosophy are opposite to those of the materialists. On the contrary, they are the same ; only with this difference, that the materialists, in imitation of Democritus, Epicurus, and Hobbes, confine themselves altogether to mathematical principles, and admit only bodies ; whereas the Christian mathematicians admit also immaterial substances. Wherefore, not mathematical principles (according to the usual sense of that word) but metaphysical principles ought to be opposed to those of the materialists. Pythagoras, Plato, and Aristotle in some measure, had a knowledge of these principles ; but I pretend to have established them demonstratively in my *Theodicy*, though I have done it in a popular manner. The great foundation of mathematics is the principle of contradiction, or identity, that is, that a proposition cannot be true and false at the same time ; and that therefore A is A, and cannot be not A. This single principle is sufficient to demonstrate every part of arithmetic and geometry, that is, all mathematical principles. But in order to proceed from mathematics to natural philosophy, another principle is requisite, as I

[1] ' les passions vitieuses '.

have observed in my *Theodicy* : I mean, the principle of a sufficient reason, viz. that nothing happens without a reason why it should be so, rather than otherwise. And therefore Archimedes being to proceed from mathematics to natural philosophy, in his book *De Æquilibrio*, was obliged to make use of a particular case of the great principle of a sufficient reason. He takes it for granted, that if there be a balance, in which everything is alike on both sides, and if equal weights are hung on the two ends of that balance, the whole will be at rest. 'Tis because no reason can be given, why one side should weigh down, rather than the other. Now, by that single principle, viz. that there ought to be a sufficient reason why things should be so, and not otherwise, one may demonstrate the being of a God, and all the other parts of metaphysics or natural theology ; and even, in some measure, those principles of natural philosophy, that are independent upon mathematics : I mean, the dynamical principles, or the principles of force.

2. The author proceeds, and says, that according to the mathematical principles, that is, according to Sir Isaac Newton's philosophy, (for mathematical principles determine nothing in the present case,) matter is the most inconsiderable part of the universe. The reason is, because he admits empty space, besides matter ; and because, according to his notions, matter fills up only a very small part of space. But Democritus and Epicurus maintained the same thing : they differ'd from Sir Isaac Newton, only as to the quantity of matter ; and perhaps they believed there was more matter in the world, than Sir Isaac Newton will allow : wherein I think their opinion ought to be preferred ; for, the more matter there is, the more God has occasion to exercise his wisdom and power. Which is one reason, among others, why I maintain that there is no vacuum at all.

3. I find, in express words, in the Appendix to Sir Isaac Newton's *Opticks*, that space is the *sensorium* of God. But the

word *sensorium* hath always signified the organ of sensation. He, and his friends, may now, if they think fit, explain themselves quite otherwise : I shall not be against it.

4. The author supposes that the presence of the soul is sufficient to make it perceive what passes in the brain. But this is the very thing which Father Malebranche, and all the Cartesians deny ; and they rightly deny it. More is requisite besides bare presence, to enable one thing to perceive what passes in another. Some communication, that may be explained ; some sort of influence, is requisite for this purpose. Space, according to Sir Isaac Newton, is intimately present to the body contained in it, and commensurate with it. Does it follow from thence, that space perceives what passes in a body ; and remembers it, when that body is gone away ? Besides, the soul being indivisible, its immediate presence, which may be imagined in the body, would only be in one point. How then could it perceive what happens out of that point ? I pretend to be the first, who has shown how the soul perceives what passes in the body.

5. The reason why God perceives every thing, is not his bare presence, but also his operation. 'Tis because he preserves things by an action, which continually produces whatever is good and perfect in them. But the soul having no immediate influence over the body, nor the body over the soul ; their mutual correspondence cannot be explained by their being present to each other.

6. The true and principal reason why we commend a machine, is rather grounded upon the effects of the machine, than upon its cause. We don't enquire so much about the power of the artist, as we do about his skill in his workmanship. And therefore the reason alleged by the author for extolling the machine of God's making, grounded upon his having made it entirely, without wanting any materials to make it of ; [1] that reason, I say, is not sufficient. 'Tis

[1] ' sans avoir emprunté de la matière de dehors ', i.e. without having taken materials from elsewhere.

a mere shift the author has been forced to have recourse to : and the reason why God exceeds any other artist, is not only because he makes the whole, whereas all other artists must have matter to work upon. This excellency in God, would be only on the account of power. But God's excellency arises also from another cause, viz. wisdom : whereby his machine lasts longer, and moves more regularly, than those of any other artist whatsoever. He who buys a watch, does not mind whether the work-man made every part of it himself, or whether he got the several parts made by others, and did only put them together ; provided the watch goes right. And if the workman had received from God even the gift of creating the matter of the wheels ; yet the buyer of the watch would not be satisfied, unless the workman had also re-ceived the gift of putting them well together. In like manner, he who will be pleased with God's workmanship, cannot be so, without some other reason than that which the author has here alleged.

7. Thus the skill of God must not be inferior to that of a workman ; nay, it must go infinitely beyond it. The bare production of every thing, would indeed show the *power* of God ; but it would not sufficiently show his *wisdom*. They who maintain the contrary, will fall exactly into the error of the materialists, and of Spinoza, from whom they profess to differ. They would, in such case, acknowledge power, but not sufficient wisdom, in the principle or cause of all things.

8. I do not say, the material world is a machine, or watch, that goes without God's interposition ; and I have sufficiently insisted, that the creation wants to be con-tinually influenc'd by its creator. But I maintain it to be a watch, that goes without wanting to be mended by him : otherwise we must say, that God bethinks himself again. No ; God has foreseen every thing ; he has pro-vided a remedy for every thing before-hand ; there is in his works a harmony, a beauty, already pre-established.

9. This opinion does not exclude God's providence, or his government of the world : on the contrary, it makes it perfect. A true providence of God, requires a perfect foresight. But then it requires moreover, not only that he should have foreseen every thing ; but also that he should have provided for every thing before-hand, with proper remedies : otherwise, he must want either wisdom to foresee things, or power to provide against them. He will be like the God of the Socinians, who lives only from day to day, as Mr. Jurieu says.[1] Indeed God, according to the Socinians, does not so much as foresee inconveniences ; whereas, the gentlemen I am arguing with, who put him upon mending his work, say only, that he does not provide against them. But this seems to me to be still a very great imperfection. According to this doctrine, God must want either power, or good will.

10. I don't think I can be rightly blamed, for saying that God is *intelligentia supramundana*. Will they say, that he is *intelligentia mundana* ; that is, the soul of the world ? I hope not. However, they will do well to take care, not to fall into that notion unawares.

11. The comparison of a king, under whose reign every thing should go on without his interposition, is by no means to the present purpose ; since God preserves every thing continually, and nothing can subsist without him. His kingdom therefore is not a nominal one. 'Tis just as if one should say, that a king, who should originally have taken care to have his subjects so well educated, and should, by his care in providing for their subsistence, preserve them so well in their fitness for their several stations, and in their good affection towards him, as that he should

---

[1] This probably refers to Jurieu's *Le Tableau du Socinianisme*, The Hague 1690. The Socinians were a Protestant sect, holding a form of unitarianism, who took their name from Faustus Socinius (1539–1604). One of their doctrines was that God's foreknowledge was limited to what was necessary and did not apply to the possible ; for if it did there would be no human freedom.

have no occasion ever to be amending any thing amongst them ; would be only a nominal king.

12. To conclude. If God is oblig'd to mend the course of nature from time to time, it must be done either supernaturally or naturally. If it be done supernaturally, we must have recourse to miracles, in order to explain natural things : which is reducing an hypothesis *ad absurdum* : for, every thing may easily be accounted for by miracles. But if it be done naturally, then God will not be *intelligentia supramundana* : he will be comprehended under the nature of things ; that is, he will be the soul of the world.

DR. CLARKE'S SECOND REPLY [1]

1. When I said that the mathematical principles of philosophy are opposite to those of the materialists ; the meaning was, that whereas materialists suppose the frame of nature to be such as could have arisen from mere mechanical principles of matter and motion, of necessity and fate ; the mathematical principles of philosophy show on the contrary, that the state of things (the constitution of the sun and planets) is such as could not arise from any thing but an intelligent and free cause. As to the propriety of the name ; so far as metaphysical consequences follow demonstratively from mathematical principles, so far the mathematical principles may (if it be thought fit) be called metaphysical principles.

'Tis very true, that nothing is, without a sufficient reason why it is, and why it is thus rather than otherwise. And therefore, where there is no cause, there can be no effect. But this sufficient reason is oft-times no other, than the mere will of God. For instance : why this particular system of matter, should be created in one particular place, and that in another particular place ; when, (all

[1] Transmitted 10th Jan. 1716 (p. 193).

place being absolutely indifferent to all matter,) it would have been exactly the same thing *vice versa*, supposing the two systems (or the particles) of matter to be alike ; there can be no other reason, but the mere will of God.   Which if it could in no case act without a predetermining cause, any more than a balance can move without a preponderating weight ; this would tend to take away all power of choosing, and to introduce fatality.

2. Many ancient Greeks, who had their philosophy from the Phœnicians, and whose philosophy was corrupted by Epicurus, held indeed in general matter and vacuum ; but they knew not how to apply those principles by mathematics, to the explication of the phenomena of nature. How small soever the quantity of matter be, God has not at all the less subject to exercise his wisdom and power upon : for, other things, as well as matter, are equally subjects, on which God exercises his power and wisdom. By the same argument it might just as well have been proved, that men, or any other particular species of beings, must be infinite in number, lest God should want subjects, on which to exercise his power and wisdom.

3. The word *sensory* does not properly signify the organ, but the place of sensation. The eye, the ear, etc., are organs, but not sensoria. Besides, Sir Isaac Newton does not say, that space is the sensory ; but that it is, by way of similitude only, *as it were the sensory*, &c.

4. It was never supposed, that the presence of the soul was sufficient, but only that it is necessary in order to perception. Without being present to the images of the things perceived, it could not possibly perceive them : but being present is not sufficient, without it be also a living substance. Any inanimate substance, tho' present, perceives nothing : and a living substance can only there perceive, where it is present either to the things themselves, (as the omnipresent God is to the whole universe ;) or to the images of things, (as the soul of man is in its proper sensory.) Nothing can any more act, or be acted upon,

where it is not present ; than it can be, where it is not. The soul's being indivisible, does not prove it to be present only in a mere point. Space, finite or infinite, is absolutely indivisible, even so much as in thought ; (to imagine its parts moved from each other, is to imagine them moved out of themselves [a];) and yet space is not a mere point.

5. God perceives things, not indeed by his simple presence to them, nor yet by his operation upon them, but by his being a living and intelligent, as well as an omnipresent substance. The soul likewise, (within its narrow sphere,) not by its simple presence, but by its being a living substance, perceives the images to which it is present ; and which, without being present to them, it could not perceive.

6 and 7. 'Tis very true, that the excellency of God's workmanship does not consist in its showing the power only, but in its showing the wisdom also of its author. But then this wisdom of God appears, not in making nature (as an artificer makes a clock) capable of going on without him : (for that's impossible ; there being no powers of nature independent upon God, as the powers of weights and springs are independent upon men ;) but the wisdom of God consists, in framing originally the perfect and complete idea of a work, which begun and continues, according to that original perfect idea, by the continual uninterrupted exercise of his power and government.

8. The word *correction*, or *amendment*, is to be understood, not with regard to God, but to us only. The present frame of the solar system (for instance,) according to the present laws of motion, will in time fall into confusion ; and

---

[a] Ut partium temporis ordo est immutabilis, sic etiam ordo partium spatii. Moveantur hae de locis suis, et movebuntur (ut ita dicam) de seipsis. Newton, *Principia*, Schol. ad Defin. 8 [i.e. As the order of the parts of time is immutable, so also is the order of the parts of space. Suppose these parts to be moved out of their places, and they will be moved (if the expression be allowed) out of themselves].

perhaps, after that, will be amended or put into a new form. But this amendment is only relative, with regard to our conceptions. In reality, and with regard to God ; the present frame, and the consequent disorder, and the following renovation, are all equally parts of the design framed in God's original perfect idea. 'Tis in the frame of the world, as in the frame of man's body : the wisdom of God does not consist, in making the present frame of either of them eternal, but to last so long as he thought fit.

9. The wisdom and foresight [a] of God, do not consist in providing originally remedies, which shall of themselves cure the disorders of nature. For in truth and strictness, with regard to God, there are no disorders, and consequently no remedies, and indeed no powers of nature at all, that can do any thing of themselves, (as weights and springs work of themselves with regard to men) ; but the wisdom and foresight of God, consist (as has been said) in contriving at once, what his power and government is continually putting in actual execution.

10. God is neither a *mundane intelligence,* nor a *supra-mundane intelligence* ; but an omnipresent intelligence, both in and without the world. He is in all, and through all, as well as above all.

11. If God's conserving all things, means his actual operation and government, in preserving and continuing the beings, powers, orders, dispositions and motions of all things ; this is all that is contended for. But if his conserving things, means no more than a king's creating such subjects, as shall be able to act well enough without his intermeddling or ordering any thing amongst them ever after ; this is making him indeed a real creator, but a governor only nominal.

12. The argument in this paragraph supposes, that whatsoever God does, is supernatural or miraculous ; and consequently it tends to exclude all operation of God in

[a] See my Sermons preached at Mr. Boyle's Lecture. Part I, page 106. Fourth Edition [*Works,* vol. II, p. 566].

the governing and ordering of the natural world. But the truth is ; *natural* and *supernatural* are nothing at all different with regard to God, but distinctions merely in our conceptions of things. To cause the sun (or earth) to move regularly, is a thing we call natural : to stop its motion for a day, we call supernatural : but the one is the effect of no greater power, than the other ; nor is the one, with respect to God, more or less natural or super-natural than the other. God's being present in or to the world, does not make him to be the soul of the world.[a] A soul, is part of a compound, whereof body is the other part ; and they mutually affect each other, as parts of the same whole. But God is present to the world, not as a part, but as a governor ; acting upon all things, himself acted upon by nothing. He is not far from every one of us, for in him we (and all things) live and move and have our beings.

[a] [Clarke quotes here from the General Scholium in the *Principia*, parts of the paragraph that begins ' This Being governs all things . . .', Appendix A, p. 166.]

MR. LEIBNITZ'S THIRD PAPER [1]

being

An Answer to Dr. Clarke's Second Reply

1. According to the usual way of speaking, mathematical principles concern only mere mathematics, viz. numbers, figures, arithmetic, geometry. But metaphysical principles concern more general notions, such as are cause and effect.

2. The author grants me this important principle; that nothing happens without a sufficient reason, why it should be so, rather than otherwise. But he grants it only in words, and in reality denies it. Which shows that he does not fully perceive the strength of it. And therefore he makes use of an instance, which exactly falls in with one of my demonstrations against real absolute space, which is an idol of some modern Englishmen. I call it an idol, not in a theological sense, but in a philosophical one; as Chancellor Bacon says, that there are *idola tribus*, *idola specus*. [2]

3. These gentlemen maintain therefore, that space is a real absolute being. But this involves them in great difficulties; for such a being must needs be eternal and infinite. Hence some have believed it to be God himself, or, one of his attributes, his immensity. But since space consists of parts, it is not a thing which can belong to God.

4. As for my own opinion, I have said more than once, that I hold space to be something merely [3] relative, as time is; that I hold it to be an order of coexistences, as

---

[1] Despatched 25th Feb. 1716 (p. 193).
[2] ' idols of the tribe, idols of the cave ', *Novum Organum* I, Aphor. 38 ff.
[3] ' purement '.

time is an order of successions. For space denotes, in terms of possibility, an order of things which exist at the same time, considered as existing together ; without enquiring into their manner of existing. And when many things are seen together, one perceives that order of things among themselves.

5. I have many demonstrations, to confute the fancy of those who take space to be a substance, or at least an absolute being. But I shall only use, at the present, one demonstration, which the author here gives me occasion to insist upon. I say then, that if space was an absolute being, there would something happen for which it would be impossible there should be a sufficient reason. Which is against my axiom. And I prove it thus. Space is something absolutely uniform ; and, without the things placed in it, one point of space does not absolutely differ in any respect whatsoever from another point of space. Now from hence it follows, (supposing space to be something in itself, besides the order of bodies among themselves,) that 'tis impossible there should be a reason, why God, preserving the same situations of bodies among themselves, should have placed them in space after one certain particular manner, and not otherwise ; why every thing was not placed the quite contrary way, for instance, by changing East into West. But if space is nothing else, but that order or relation ; and is nothing at all without bodies, but the possibility of placing them ; then those two states, the one such as it now is, the other supposed to be the quite contrary way, would not at all differ from one another. Their difference therefore is only to be found in our chimerical supposition of the reality of space in itself. But in truth the one would exactly be the same thing as the other, they being absolutely indiscernible ; and consequently there is no room to enquire after a reason of the preference of the one to the other.

6. The case is the same with respect to time. Supposing any one should ask, why God did not create every thing

a year sooner ; and the same person should infer from thence, that God has done something, concerning which 'tis not possible there should be a reason, why he did it so, and not otherwise : the answer is, that his inference would be right, if time was any thing distinct from things existing in time. For it would be impossible there should be any reason, why things should be applied to such particular instants, rather than to others, their succession continuing the same. But then the same argument proves, that instants, consider'd without the things, are nothing at all ; and that they consist only in the successive order of things : which order remaining the same, one of the two states, viz. that of a supposed anticipation, would not at all differ, nor could be discerned from, the other which now is.

7. It appears from what I have said, that my axiom has not been well understood ; and that the author denies it, tho' he seems to grant it. 'Tis true, says he, that there is nothing without a sufficient reason why it is, and why it is thus, rather than otherwise : but he adds, that this sufficient reason, is often the simple or mere will of God : as, when it is asked why matter was not placed otherwhere in space ; the same situations of bodies among themselves being preserved. But this is plainly maintaining, that God wills something, without any sufficient reason for his will : against the axiom, or the general rule of whatever happens. This is falling back into the loose indifference, which I have confuted at large, and showed to be absolutely chimerical even in creatures, and contrary to the wisdom of God, as if he could operate without acting by reason.

8. The author objects against me, that if we don't admit this simple and mere will, we take away from God the power of choosing, and bring in a fatality. But the quite contrary is true. I maintain that God has the power of choosing, since I ground that power upon the reason of a choice agreeable to his wisdom. And 'tis not this fatality,

(which is only the wisest order of providence) but a blind fatality or necessity, void of all wisdom and choice, which we ought to avoid.

9. I had observed, that by lessening the quantity of matter, the quantity of objects, upon which God may exercise his goodness, will be lessen'd. The author answers, that instead of matter, there are other things in the void space, on which God may exercise his goodness. Be it so : tho' I don't grant it ; for I hold that every created substance is attended with matter. However, let it be so : I answer, that more matter was consistent with those same things ; and consequently the said objects will be still lessened. The instance of a greater number of men, or animals, is not to the purpose ; for they would fill up place, in exclusion of other things.

10. It will be difficult to make me believe, that *sensorium* does not, in its usual meaning, signify an organ of sensation. See the words of Rudolphus Goclenius, in his *Dictionarium Philosophicum* ; *v. Sensiterium. Barbarum Scholasticorum*, says he, *qui interdum sunt Simiae Graecorum. Hi dicunt αἰσθητήριον. Ex quo illi fecerunt Sensiterium pro Sensorio, id est, Organo Sensationis.*[1]

11. The mere presence of a substance, even an animated one, is not sufficient for perception. A blind man, and even a man whose thoughts are wandering, does not see. The author must explain, how the soul perceives what is without itself.

12. God is not present to things by situation, but by essence : his presence is manifested by his immediate operation. The presence of the soul, is quite of another nature. To say that it is diffused all over the body, is to make it extended and divisible. To say it is, the whole of it, in every part of the body, is to make it divided from

[1] Goclenius, *Lexicon Philosophicum*, Frankfurt, 1613. ' Sensiterium ; a barbarism used by some scholastics who ape the Greeks. They say αἰσθητήριον. From this the scholastics make sensiterium for sensorium, that is, the organ of sensation.'

itself. To fix it to a point, to diffuse it all over many points, are only abusive expressions, *idola tribus*.

13. If *active force* should diminish in the universe, by the natural laws which God has established ; so that there should be need for him to give a new impression in order to restore that force, like an artist's mending the imperfections of his machine ; the disorder would not only be with respect to us, but also with respect to God himself. He might have prevented it, and taken better measures to avoid such an inconvenience : and therefore, indeed, he has actually done it.

14. When I said that God has provided remedies beforehand against such disorders, I did not say that God suffers disorders to happen, and then finds remedies for them ; but that he has found a way before-hand to prevent any disorders happening.

15. The author strives in vain to criticize my expression, that God is *intelligentia supramundana*. To say that God is above the world, is not denying that he is in the world.

16. I never gave any occasion to doubt, but that God's conservation is an actual preservation and continuation of the beings, powers, orders, dispositions, and motions of all things : and I think I have perhaps explained it better than many others. But, says the author, *this is all that I contended for*. To this I answer ; *your humble servant for that, sir*. Our dispute consists in many other things. The question is, whether God does not act in the most regular and most perfect manner ? Whether his machine is liable to disorders, which he is obliged to mend by extraordinary means ? Whether the will of God can act without reason ? Whether space is an absolute being ? Also concerning the nature of miracles ; and many such things, which make a wide difference between us.

17. Divines will not grant the author's position against me ; viz. that there is no difference, with respect to God, between *natural* and *supernatural* : and it will be still less approved by most philosophers. There is a vast difference

between these two things ; but it plainly appears, it has not been duly consider'd. That which is supernatural, exceeds all the powers of creatures. I shall give an instance, which I have often made use of with good success. If God would cause a body to move free in the aether round about a certain fixed centre, without any other creature acting upon it : I say, it could not be done without a miracle ; since it cannot be explained by the nature of bodies. For, a free body does naturally recede from a curve in the tangent. And therefore I maintain, that the attraction of bodies, properly so called, is a miraculous thing, since it cannot be explained by the nature of bodies.

DR. CLARKE'S THIRD REPLY [1]

1. This relates only to the signification of words. The definitions here given, may well be allowed ; and yet mathematical reasonings may be applied to physical and metaphysical subjects.

2. Undoubtedly nothing is, without a sufficient reason why it is, rather than not ; and why it is thus, rather than otherwise. But in things in their own nature indifferent ; mere will, without any thing external to influence it, is alone that sufficient reason. As in the instance of God's creating or placing any particle of matter in one place rather than in another, when all places are originally alike. And the case is the same, even though space were nothing real, but only the mere order of bodies : for still it would be absolutely indifferent, and there could be no other reason but mere will, why three equal particles should be placed or ranged in the order a, b, c, rather than in the contrary order. And therefore no argument can be drawn from this indifferency of all places, to prove that no space

[1] Transmitted 15th May 1716, delayed (p. 194).

is real.   For different spaces are really different or distinct
one from another, though they be perfectly alike.   And
there is this evident absurdity in supposing space not to
be real, but to be merely the order of bodies ; that, according to that notion, if the earth and sun and moon had been
placed where the remotest fixed stars now are, (provided
they were placed in the same order and distance they now
are with regard one to another,) it would not only have
been, (as this learned author rightly says,) *la même chose,*
the same thing in effect ; which is very true : but it
would also follow, that they would then have been in the
same place too, as they are now : which is an express
contradiction.

The ancients [a] did not call all space which is void of
bodies, but only extramundane space, by the name of
imaginary space.   The meaning of which, is not, that
such space is not real ; [b] but only that we are wholly
ignorant what kinds of things are in that space.   Those
writers, who by the word, *imaginary*, meant at any time to
affirm that space was not real ; did not thereby prove,
that it was not real.

3. Space is not a being, an eternal and infinite being,
but a property, or a consequence of the existence of a
being infinite and eternal.   Infinite space, is immensity :
but immensity is not God : and therefore infinite space,
is not God.   Nor is there any difficulty in what is here
alleged about space having parts.   For infinite space is
one, absolutely and essentially indivisible : and to suppose
it parted, is a contradiction in terms ; because there
must be space in the partition itself ; which is to suppose
it parted, and yet not parted at the same time. [c]   The

[a] This was occasioned by a passage in the private letter wherein
Mr. Leibnitz's third paper came inclosed.   [Gerhardt says that there
is no trace among the Leibniz papers of this letter.   Klopp's edition
of the Leibniz-Caroline correspondence also contains nothing relevant.]

[b] Of nothing, there are no dimensions, no magnitudes, no quantity,
no properties.

[c] See above, § 4 of my Second Reply.

immensity or omnipresence of God, is no more a dividing of his substance into parts ; than his duration, or continuance of existing, is a dividing of his existence into parts. There is no difficulty here, but what arises from the figurative abuse of the word, *parts*.

4. If space was nothing but the order of things coexisting ; it would follow, that if God should remove in a straight line the whole material world entire, with any swiftness whatsoever ; yet it would still always continue in the same place : and that nothing would receive any shock upon the most sudden stopping of that motion. And if time was nothing but the order of succession of created things ; it would follow, that if God had created the world millions of ages sooner than he did, yet it would not have been created at all the sooner. Further : space and time are quantities ; which situation and order are not.

5. The argument in this paragraph, is ; that because space is uniform or alike, and one part does not differ from another ; therefore the bodies created in one place, if they had been created in another place, (supposing them to keep the same situation with regard to each other,) would still have been created in the same place as before : which is a manifest contradiction. The uniformity of space, does indeed prove, that there could be no (external) reason why God should create things in one place rather than in another : but does that hinder his own will, from being to itself a sufficient reason of acting in any place, when all places are indifferent or alike, and there be good reason to act in some place ?

6. The same reasoning takes place here, as in the foregoing.

7 and 8. Where there is any difference in the nature of things, there the consideration of that difference always determines an intelligent and perfectly wise agent. But when two ways of acting are equally and alike good, (as in the instances before mentioned ;) to affirm in such case,

that God cannot act at all, or that 'tis no perfection in him to be able to act, because he can have no external reason to move him to act one way rather than the other, seems to be a denying God to have in himself any original principle or power of beginning to act, but that he must needs (as it were mechanically) be always determined by things extrinsic.

9. I suppose, that determinate quantity of matter, which is now in the world, is the most convenient for the present frame of nature, or the present state of things : and that a greater (as well as a less) quantity of matter, would have made the present frame of the world less convenient ; and consequently would not have been a greater object for God to have exercised his goodness upon.

10. The question is not, what Goclenius, but what Sir Isaac Newton means by the word *sensorium*, when the debate is about the sense of Sir Isaac Newton's, and not about the sense of Goclenius's book. If Goclenius takes the eye, or ear, or any other organ of sensation, to be the sensorium ; he is certainly mistaken. But when any writer expressly explains what he means by any term of art ; of what use is it, in this case, to enquire in what different senses perhaps some other writers have sometimes used the same word ? Scapula [1] explains it by *domicilium*, the place where the mind resides.

11. The soul of a blind man does for this reason not see, because no images are conveyed (there being some obstruction in the way) to the sensorium where the soul is present. How the soul of a seeing man, sees the images to which it is present, we know not : but we are sure it cannot perceive what it is not present to ; because nothing can act, or be acted upon, where it is not.

12. God, being omnipresent, is really present to every

[1] This is not quite accurate. Scapula : *Lexicon Graeco-Latinum* (1639 edition) says ' αἰσθητήριον : sentienti instrumentum. Nonnulli exp. domicilium sensus ', i.e. ' instrument of sensation. Sometimes, place where the sense resides.'

thing, essentially and substantially.[a] His presence manifests itself indeed by its operation, but it could not operate if it was not there. The soul is not omnipresent to every part of the body, and therefore does not and cannot itself actually operate upon every part of the body, but only upon the brain, or certain nerves and spirits, which, by laws and communications of God's appointing, influence the whole body.

13 and 14. The *active forces*,[b] which are in the universe, diminishing themselves so as to stand in need of new impressions ; is no inconvenience, no disorder, no imperfection in the workmanship of the universe ; but is the consequence of the nature of dependent things. Which dependency of things, is not a matter that wants to be rectified. The case of a human workman making a machine, is quite another thing : because the powers or forces by which the machine continues to move, are altogether independent on the artificer.

15. The phrase, *intelligentia supramundana*, may well be allowed, as it is here explained : but without this explication, the expression is very apt to lead to a wrong notion, as if God was not really and substantially present every where.

16. To the questions here proposed, the answer is : that

[a] Deus omnipraesens est, non per virtutem solam, sed etiam per substantiam : nam virtus sine substantia subsistere non potest ; i.e. God is omnipresent, not only virtually, but substantially ; for powers cannot subsist without a substance. Newtoni, *Principia*, Scholium Generale sub finem.

[b] The word *active force*, signifies here nothing but motion, and the impetus or relative impulsive force of bodies, arising from and being proportional to their motion. For, the occasion of what has passed upon this head, was the following passage. ' . . . it appears that motion may be got or lost. But by reason of the tenacity of fluids and attrition of their parts and the weakness of elasticity in solids, motion is much more apt to be lost than got, and is always upon the decay . . . Seeing therefore the variety of motion which we find in the world is always decreasing, there is a necessity of conserving and recruiting it by active principles.' *Opticks*. Query 31 [pp. 176–178 below].

God does always act in the most regular and perfect manner : that there are no disorders in the workmanship of God ; and that there is nothing more extraordinary in the alterations he is pleased to make in the frame of things, than in his continuation of it : that in things in their own nature absolutely equal and indifferent, the will of God can freely choose and determine itself, without any external cause to impel it ; and that 'tis a perfection in God, to be able so to do : that space, does not at all depend on the order or situation or existence of bodies. And as to the notion of miracles,

17. The question is not, what it is that divines or philosophers usually allow or not allow ; but what reasons men allege for their opinions. If a miracle be that only, which surpasses the power of all created beings ; then for a man to walk on the water, or for the motion of the sun or the earth to be stopped, is no miracle ; since none of these things require infinite power to effect them. For a body to move in a circle round a centre *in vacuo* ; if it be usual (as the planets moving about the sun,) 'tis no miracle, whether it be effected immediately by God himself, or mediately by any created power : but if it be unusual, (as, for a heavy body to be suspended, and move so in the air,) 'tis equally a miracle, whether it be effected immediately by God himself, or mediately by any invisible created power. Lastly ; if whatever arises not from, and is not explicable by, the natural powers of body, be a miracle ; then every animal-motion whatsoever, is a miracle. Which seems demonstrably to show, that this learned author's notion of a miracle is erroneous.

MR. LEIBNITZ'S FOURTH PAPER [1]

being

An Answer to Dr. Clarke's Third Reply.

1. In things absolutely indifferent, there is no [foundation for] [2] choice ; and consequently no election, nor will ; since choice must be founded on some reason, or principle.

2. A mere will without any motive, is a fiction, not only contrary to God's perfection, but also chimerical and contradictory ; inconsistent with the definition of the will, and sufficiently confuted in my Theodicy.

3. 'Tis a thing indifferent, to place three bodies, equal and perfectly alike, in any order whatsoever ; and consequently they will never be placed in any order, by him who does nothing without wisdom. But then he being the author of things, no such things will be produced by him at all ; and consequently there are no such things in nature.

4. There is no such thing as two individuals indiscernible from each other. An ingenious gentleman of my acquaintance, discoursing with me, in the presence of Her Electoral Highness the Princess Sophia,[3] in the garden of Herrenhausen ; thought he could find two leaves perfectly alike. The Princess defied him to do it, and he ran all over the garden a long time to look for some ; but it was to no purpose. Two drops of water, or milk, viewed with a microscope, will appear distinguishable from each other. This is an argument against atoms ; which are confuted, as well as a vacuum, by the principles of true metaphysics.

[1] Despatched with letter dated 2nd June 1716 (p. 195).
[2] Clarke's addition.
[3] Sophia, Electress of Hanover, mother of George I of England. Herrenhausen was the residence of the Electors of Hanover.

5. Those great principles of a *sufficient reason*, and of the *identity of indiscernibles*, change the state of metaphysics. That science becomes real and demonstrative by means of these principles ; whereas before, it did generally consist in empty words.

6. To suppose two things indiscernible, is to suppose the same thing under two names. And therefore to suppose that the universe could have had at first another position of time and place, than that which it actually had ; and yet that all the parts of the universe should have had the same situation among themselves, as that which they actually had ; such a supposition, I say, is an impossible fiction.

7. The same reason, which shows that extramundane space is imaginary, proves that all empty space is an imaginary thing ; for they differ only as greater and less.

8. If space is a property or attribute, it must be the property of some substance. But what substance will that bounded empty space be an affection or property of, which the persons I am arguing with, suppose to be between two bodies ?

9. If infinite space is immensity, finite space will be the opposite to immensity, that is, 'twill be mensurability, or limited extension. Now extension must be the affection of some thing extended. But if that space be empty, it will be an attribute without a subject, an extension without any thing extended. Wherefore by making space a property, the author falls in with my opinion, which makes it an order of things, and not any thing absolute.

10. If space is an absolute reality ; far from being a property or an accident opposed to substance, it will have a greater reality than substances themselves.[1] God cannot destroy it, nor even change it in any respect. It will be not only immense in the whole, but also immutable and eternal in every part. There will be an infinite number of eternal things besides God.

[1] 'il sera plus subsistant que les substances'.

11. To say that infinite space has no parts, is to say that it does not consist of finite spaces ; and that infinite space might subsist, though all finite spaces should be reduced to nothing. It would be, as if one should say, in the Cartesian supposition of a material extended unlimited world, that such a world might subsist, though all the bodies of which it consists, should be reduced to nothing.

12. The author ascribes parts to space, p. 19. of the 3rd edition of his *Defense of the Argument against Mr. Dodwell* ; [1] and makes them inseparable one from another. But, p. 30 of his *Second Defense*,[1] he says they are parts *improperly so called* : which may be understood in a good sense.

13. To say that God can cause the whole universe to move forward in a right line, or in any other line, without making otherwise any alteration in it ; is another chimerical supposition. For, two states indiscernible from each other, are the same state ; and consequently, 'tis a change without any change. Besides, there is neither rhyme nor reason in it. But God does nothing without reason ; and 'tis impossible there should be any here. Besides, it would be *agendo nihil agere*, as I have just now said, because of the indiscernibility.

14. These are *idola tribus*, mere chimeras, and superficial imaginations. All this is only grounded upon the supposition, that imaginary space is real.

15. It is a like fiction, (that is) an impossible one, to suppose that God might have created the world some millions of years sooner. They who run into such kind of fictions, can give no answer to one that should argue for the eternity of the world. For since God does nothing without reason, and no reason can be given why he did not create the world sooner ; it will follow, either that he has created nothing at all, or that he created the world before any assignable time, that is, that the world is eternal. But when once it has been shown, that the beginning, whenever it was, is always the same thing ;

[1] Clarke, *Works*, vol. III, p. 763 and p. 794.

the question, why it was not otherwise ordered, becomes needless and insignificant.

16. If space and time were any thing absolute, that is, if they were any thing else, besides certain orders of things ; then indeed my assertion would be a contradiction. But since it is not so, the hypothesis [that space and time are any thing absolute] [1] is contradictory, that is, 'tis an impossible fiction.

17. And the case is the same as in geometry ; where by the very supposition that a figure is greater than it really is, we sometimes prove that it is not greater. This indeed is a contradiction ; but it lies in the hypothesis, which appears to be false for that very reason.

18. Space being uniform, there can be neither any external nor internal reason, by which to distinguish its parts, and to make any choice among them. For, any external reason to discern between them, can only be grounded upon some internal one. Otherwise we should discern what is indiscernible, or choose without discerning. A will without reason, would be the chance of the Epicureans. [2] A God, who should act by such a will, would be a God only in name. The cause of these errors proceeds from want of care to avoid what derogates from the divine perfections.

19. When two things which cannot both be together, are equally good ; and neither in themselves, nor by their combination with other things, has the one any advantage over the other ; God will produce neither of them.

20. God is never determined by external things, but always by what is in himself ; that is, by his knowledge of things, before any thing exists without himself.

21. There is no possible reason, that can limit the

---

[1] Clarke's addition.

[2] Epicurus held that while most atoms moved in regular courses, some occasionally made entirely uncaused swerves. Such a swerve occurring in the atoms of a man's brain gives rise to what the man regards as an act of free will.

quantity of matter ; and therefore such limitation can have no place.

22. And supposing an arbitrary limitation of the quantity of matter, something might always be added to it without derogating from the perfection of those things which do already exist ; and consequently something must always be added, in order to act according to the principle of the perfection of the divine operations.

23. And therefore it cannot be said, that the present quantity of matter is the fittest for the present constitution of things. And supposing it were, it would follow that this present constitution of things would not be the fittest absolutely, if it hinders God from using more matter. It were therefore better to choose another constitution of things, capable of something more.

24. I should be glad to see a passage of any philosopher, who takes *sensorium* in any other sense than Goclenius does.

25. If Scapula says that *sensorium* is the place in which the understanding resides, he means by it the organ of internal sensation. And therefore he does not differ from Goclenius.

26. *Sensorium* has always signified the organ of sensation. The *glandula pinealis* would be, according to Cartesius, the sensorium, in the above-mentioned sense of Scapula.

27. There is hardly any expression less proper upon this subject, than that which makes God to have a sensorium. It seems to make God the soul of the world. And it will be a hard matter to put a justifiable sense upon this word, according to the use Sir Isaac Newton makes of it.

28. Though the question be about the sense put upon that word by Sir Isaac Newton, and not by Goclenius ; yet I am not to blame for quoting the philosophical dictionary of that author, because the design of dictionaries is to show the use of words.

29. God perceives things in himself. Space is the place of things, and not the place of God's ideas : unless we look upon space as something that makes an union between

God and things, in imitation of the imagined union between the soul and the body ; which would still make God the soul of the world.

30. And indeed the author is much in the wrong, when he compares God's knowledge and operation, with the knowledge and operation of souls. The soul knows things, because God has put into it a principle representative of things without. But God knows things, because he produces them continually.

31. The soul does not act upon things, according to my opinion, any otherwise than because the body adapts itself to the desires of the soul, by virtue of the harmony, which God has pre-established between them.

32. But they who fancy that the soul can give a new force to the body ; and that God does the same in the world, in order to mend the imperfections of his machine ; make God too much like the soul, by ascribing too much to the soul, and too little to God.

33. For, none but God can give a new force to nature ; and he does it only supernaturally. If there was need for him to do it in the natural course of things ; he would have made a very imperfect work. At that rate, he would be with respect to the world, what the soul, in the vulgar notion, is with respect to the body.

34. Those who undertake to defend the vulgar opinion concerning the soul's influence over the body, by instancing in God's operating on things external ; make God still too much like a soul of the world. To which I add, that the author's affecting to find fault with the words, *intelligentia supramundana*, seems also to incline that way.

35. The images, with which the soul is immediately affected,[1] are within itself ; but they correspond to those of the body. The presence of the soul is imperfect, and can only be explained by that correspondence. But the presence of God is perfect, and manifested by his operation.

[1] ' affected ' is used here not in the sense of ' caused ' or ' influenced ' ' but rather in the sense in which a quality is an affect of an object '

36. The author wrongly supposes against me, that the presence of the soul is connected with its influence over the body ; for he knows, I reject that influence.

37. The soul's being diffused through the brain, is no less inexplicable, than its being diffused through the whole body. The difference is only in more and less.

38. They who fancy that active force lessens of itself in the world, do not well understand the principal laws of nature, and the beauty of the works of God.

39. How will they be able to prove, that this defect is a consequence of the dependence of things ?

40. The imperfection of our machines, which is the reason why they want to be mended, proceeds from this very thing, that they do not sufficiently depend upon the workman. And therefore the dependence of nature upon God, far from being the cause of such an imperfection, is rather the reason why there is no such imperfection in nature, because it depends so much upon an artist, who is too perfect to make a work that wants to be mended. 'Tis true that every particular machine of nature, is, in some measure, liable to be disordered ; but not the whole universe, which cannot diminish in perfection.

41. The author contends, that space does not depend upon the situation of bodies. I answer : 'tis true, it does not depend upon such or such a situation of bodies ; but it is that order, which renders bodies capable of being situated, and by which they have a situation among themselves when they exist together ; as time is that order, with respect to their successive position. But if there were no creatures, space and time would be only in the ideas of God.

42. The author seems to acknowledge here, that his notion of a miracle is not the same with that which divines and philosophers usually have. It is therefore sufficient for my purpose, that my adversaries are obliged to have recourse to what is commonly called a miracle.

43. I am afraid the author, by altering the sense commonly put upon the word *miracle*, will fall into an incon-

venient opinion. The nature of a miracle does not at all consist in usualness or unusualness ; for then monsters would be miracles.

44. There are miracles of an inferior sort, which an angel can work. He can, for instance, make a man walk upon the water without sinking. But there are miracles, which none but God can work ; they exceeding all natural powers. Of which kind, are creating and annihilating.

45. 'Tis also a supernatural thing, that bodies should attract one another at a distance, without any intermediate means ; and that a body should move round, without receding in the tangent, though nothing hinder it from so receding. For these effects cannot be explained by the nature of things.

46. Why should it be impossible to explain the motion of animals by natural forces ? Tho' indeed, the beginning of animals is no less inexplicable by natural forces, than the beginning of the world.

P. S.[1]

All those who maintain a vacuum, are more influenced by imagination than by reason. When I was a young man, I also gave into the notion of a vacuum and atoms ; but reason brought me into the right way. It was a pleasing imagination. Men carry their inquiries no farther than those two things : they (as it were) nail down their thoughts to them : they fancy, they have found out the first elements of things, a *non plus ultra*. We would have nature to go no farther ; and to be finite, as our minds are : but this is being ignorant of the greatness and majesty of the author of things. The least corpuscle is actually subdivided *in infinitum*, and contains a world of other creatures, which would be wanting in the universe, if that corpuscle was

---

[1] This ' postscript ' was actually written and despatched by Leibniz as a postscript to a private letter to Caroline, dated 12th May 1716. It was occasioned by Caroline's mention of experiments on the vacuum in her letter of 15th May 1716. See Appendix B, p. 194.

an atom, that is, a body of one entire piece without sub-division. In like manner, to admit a vacuum in nature, is ascribing to God a very imperfect work : 'tis violating the grand principle of the necessity of a sufficient reason ; which many have talked of, without understanding its true meaning ; as I have lately shown, in proving, by that principle, that space is only an order of things, as time also is, and not at all an absolute being. To omit many other arguments against a vacuum and atoms, I shall here mention those which I ground upon God's perfection, and upon the necessity of a sufficient reason. I lay it down as a principle, that every perfection, which God could impart to things without derogating from their other perfections, has actually been imparted to them. Now let us fancy a space wholly empty. God could have placed some matter in it, without derogating in any respect from all other things : therefore he has actually placed some matter in that space : therefore, there is no space wholly empty : therefore all is full. The same argument proves that there is no corpuscle, but what is subdivided. I shall add another argument, grounded upon the necessity of a sufficient reason. 'Tis impossible there should be any principle to determine what proportion of matter there ought to be, out of all the possible degrees from a plenum to a vacuum, or from a vacuum to a plenum.[1] Perhaps it will be said, that the one should be equal to the other : but, because matter is more perfect than a vacuum, reason requires that a geometrical proportion should be observed, and that there should be as much more matter than vacuum, as the former deserves to have the preference before the latter. But then there must be no vacuum at all ; for the perfection of matter is to that of a vacuum, as something to nothing. And the case is the same with atoms : what reason can any one assign for confining nature in the progression of subdivision ? These are fictions

[1] ' de determiner la proportion de la matière, ou du rempli au vuide, ou du vuide au plein '.

merely arbitrary, and unworthy of true philosophy.   The
reasons alleged for a vacuum, are mere sophisms.

DR. CLARKE'S FOURTH REPLY [1]

1 and 2. This notion leads to universal necessity and
fate, by supposing that motives have the same relation
to the will of an intelligent agent, as weights have to a
balance ; [a] so that of two things absolutely indifferent, an
intelligent agent can no more choose either, than a balance
can move itself when the weights on both sides are equal.
But the difference lies here.   A balance is no agent, but
is merely passive and acted upon by the weights ; so that,
when the weights are equal, there is nothing to move it.
But intelligent beings are agents ; not passive, in being
moved by the motives, as a balance is by weights ; but
they have active powers and do move themselves, sometimes upon the view of strong motives, sometimes upon
weak ones, and sometimes where things are absolutely
indifferent.   In which latter case, there may be very
good reason to act, though two or more ways of acting may
be absolutely indifferent.   This learned writer always supposes the contrary, as a principle ; but gives no proof of
it, either from the nature of things, or the perfections
of God.

3 and 4. This argument, if it was true, would prove that
God neither has created, nor can possibly create any matter
at all.   For the perfectly solid parts of all matter, if you
take them of equal figure and dimensions (which is always
possible in supposition,) are exactly alike ; and therefore it
would be perfectly indifferent if they were transposed in
place ; and consequently it was impossible (according to this

[a] See above, Mr. Leibnitz's Second Paper, § 1.

[1] Transmitted 26th June 1716 (p. 196).

learned author's argument,) for God to place them in those places wherein he did actually place them at the creation, because he might as easily have transposed their situation. 'Tis very true, that no two leaves, and perhaps no two drops of water are exactly alike ; because they are bodies very much compounded. But the case is very different in the parts of simple solid matter. And even in compounds, there is no impossibility for God to make two drops of water exactly alike. And if he should make them exactly alike, yet they would never the more become one and the same drop of water, because they were alike. Nor would the place of the one, be the place of the other ; though it was absolutely indifferent, which was placed in which place. The same reasoning holds likewise concerning the original determination of motion, this way or the contrary way.

5 and 6. Two things, by being exactly alike, do not cease to be two. The parts of time, are as exactly like to each other, as those of space : yet two points of time, are not the same point of time, nor are they two names of only the same point of time. Had God created the world but this moment, it would not have been created at the time it was created. And if God has made (or can make) matter finite in dimensions, the material universe must consequently be in its nature moveable ; for nothing that is finite, is immoveable. To say therefore that God could not have altered the time or place of the existence of matter, is making matter to be necessarily infinite and eternal, and reducing all things to necessity and fate.

7. Extra-mundane space, (if the material world be finite in its dimensions,) is not imaginary, but real. Nor are void spaces in the world, merely imaginary. In an exhausted receiver,[a] though rays of light, and perhaps some other matter, be there in an exceeding small quantity ;

---

[a] This was occasioned by a passage in the private letter wherein Mr. Leibnitz's paper came inclosed. [This was Leibniz's letter of 2nd June 1716, the relevant parts of which are given in Appendix B, p. 195.]

yet the want of resistance plainly shows, that the greatest part of that space is void of matter. For subtleness or fineness of matter, cannot be the cause of want of resistance. Quicksilver is as subtle, and consists of as fine parts and as fluid, as water ; and yet makes more than ten times the resistance : which resistance arises therefore from the quantity, and not from the grossness of the matter.

8. Space void of body, is the property of an incorporeal substance. Space is not bounded by bodies, but exists equally within and without bodies. Space is not inclosed between bodies ; but bodies, existing in unbounded space, are, themselves only, terminated by their own dimensions.

9. Void space, is not an attribute without a subject ; because, by void space, we never mean space void of every thing, but void of body only. In all void space, God is certainly present, and possibly many other substances which are not matter ; being neither tangible, nor objects of any of our senses.

10. Space is not a substance, but a property ;[1] and if it be a property of that which is necessary, it will consequently (as all other properties of that which is necessary must do,) exist more necessarily, (though it be not itself a substance,) than those substances themselves which are not necessary. Space is immense, and immutable, and eternal ; and so also is duration. Yet it does not at all from hence follow, that any thing is eternal *hors de Dieu*. For space and duration are not *hors de Dieu*, but are caused by, and are immediate and necessary consequences of his existence.[a] And without them, his eternity and ubiquity (or omnipresence) would be taken away.

[a] [Clarke quotes here from the General Scholium in the *Principia*, the passage, ' He is eternal and infinite, . . . cannot be never and nowhere. He is omnipresent not virtually only but also substantially ; for virtue cannot subsist without substance ', Appendix, pp. 167–8.]

[1] Clarke qualifies this use of the term *property* in a note contained in the preface to Des Maiseaux's editions of the Correspondence. Cf. Introduction, p. xxix.

11 and 12. Infinites are composed of finites, in no other sense, than as finites are composed of infinitesimals. In what sense space has or has not parts, has been explained before, Reply III, § 3. Parts, in the corporeal sense of the word, are separable, compounded, ununited, independent on, and moveable from, each other : but infinite space, though it may by us be partially apprehended, that is, may in our imagination be conceived as composed of parts ; yet those parts (improperly so called) being essentially indiscernible and immoveable from each other, and not partable without an express contradiction in terms, (see above, Reply II, § 4 and Reply III, § 3 ;) space consequently is in itself essentially one, and absolutely indivisible.

13. If the world be finite in dimensions, it is moveable by the power of God and therefore my argument drawn from that moveableness is conclusive. Two places, though exactly alike, are not the same place. Nor is the motion or rest of the universe, the same state ; any more than the motion or rest of a ship, is the same state, because a man shut up in the cabin cannot perceive whether the ship sails or not, so long as it moves uniformly. The motion of the ship, though the man perceives it not, is a real different state, and has real different effects ; and, upon a sudden stop, it would have other real effects ; and so likewise would an indiscernible motion of the universe. To this argument, no answer has ever been given. It is largely insisted on by Sir Isaac Newton in his *Mathematical Principles*, (Definit. 8.) where, from the consideration of the properties, causes, and effects of motion, he shows the difference between real motion, or a body's being carried from one part of space to another ; and relative motion, which is merely a change of the order or situation of bodies with respect to each other. This argument is a mathematical one ; showing, from real effects, that there may be real motion where there is none relative ; and relative motion, where there is none real : and is not to be answered, by barely asserting the contrary.

14. The reality of space is not a supposition, but is proved by the foregoing arguments, to which no answer has been given. Nor is any answer given to that other argument, that space and time are quantities, which situation and order are not.

15. It was no impossibility for God to make the world sooner or later than he did : nor is it at all impossible for him to destroy it sooner or later than it shall actually be destroyed. As to the notion of the world's eternity ; they who suppose matter and space to be the same, must indeed suppose the world to be not only infinite and eternal, but necessarily so ; even as necessarily as space and duration, which depend not on the will, but on the existence of God. But they who believe that God created matter in what quantity, and at what particular time, and in what particular spaces he pleased, are here under no difficulty. For the wisdom of God may have very good reasons for creating this world, at that particular time he did ; and may have made other kinds of things before this material world began, and may make other kinds of things after this world is destroyed.

16 and 17. That space and time are not the mere order of things, but real quantities (which order and situation are not ;) has been proved above, (See Third Reply, § 4 ; and in this paper, § 13,) and no answer yet given to those proofs. And till an answer be given to those proofs, this learned author's assertion is (by his own confession in this place) a contradiction.

18. The uniformity of all the parts of space, is no argument against God's acting in any part, after what manner he pleases. God may have good reasons to create finite beings, and finite beings can be but in particular places. And, all places being originally alike, (even though place were nothing else but the situation of bodies ;) God's placing one cube of matter behind another equal cube of matter, rather than the other behind that ; is a choice no way unworthy of the perfections of God, though both these

situations be perfectly equal : because there may be very good reasons why both the cubes should exist and they cannot exist but in one or other of equally reasonable situations. The Epicurean chance, is not a choice of will, but a blind necessity of fate.

19. This argument, (as I now observed, § 3,) if it proves anything, proves that God neither did nor can create any matter at all ; because the situation of equal and similar parts of matter, could not but be originally indifferent : as was also the original determination of their motions, this way, or the contrary way.

20. What this tends to prove, with regard to the argument before us ; I understand not.

21. That God cannot limit the quantity of matter, is an assertion of too great consequence, to be admitted without proof. If he cannot limit the duration of it neither, then the material world is both infinite and eternal necessarily and independently upon God.

22 and 23. This argument, if it were good, would prove that whatever God can do, he cannot but do ; and consequently that he cannot but make every thing infinite and every thing eternal. Which is making him no governor at all, but a mere necessary agent, that is, indeed no agent at all, but mere fate and nature and necessity.

24–28. Concerning the use of the word, *sensory* ; (though Sir Isaac Newton says only, *as it were the sensory* ;) enough has been said in my Third Reply, § 10 ; and Second Reply, § 3 ; and First Reply, § 3.

29. Space is the place of all things, and of all ideas : just as duration is the duration of all things, and of all ideas. That this has no tendency to make God the soul of the world, see above, Reply II, § 12. There is no union between God and the world. The mind of man might with greater propriety be styled the soul of the images of things which it perceives, than God can be styled the soul of the world, to which he is present throughout, and acts upon it as he pleases, without being acted upon by it.

Though this answer was given before, (Reply II, § 12.) yet the same objection is repeated again and again, without taking any notice of the answer.

30. What is meant by *representative principle*, I understand not. The soul discerns things, by having the images of things conveyed to it through the organs of sense : God discerns things, by being present to and in the substances of the things themselves. Not by producing them continually ; (for he rests now from his work of creation :) but by being continually omnipresent to every thing which he created at the beginning.

31. That the soul should not operate upon the body ; and yet the body, by mere mechanical impulse of matter, conform itself to the will of the soul in all the infinite variety of spontaneous animal-motion ; is a perpetual miracle. *Pre-established harmony*, is a mere word or term of art, and does nothing towards explaining the cause of so miraculous an effect.

32. To suppose that in spontaneous animal-motion, the soul gives no new motion or impression to matter ; but that all spontaneous animal-motion is performed by mechanical impulse of matter ; is reducing all things to mere fate and necessity. God's acting in the world upon every thing, after what manner he pleases, without any union, and without being acted upon by any thing ; shows plainly the difference between an omnipresent governor, and an imaginary soul of the world.

33. Every action is (in the nature of things) the giving of a new force to the thing acted upon. Otherwise 'tis not really action, but mere passiveness ; as in the case of all mechanical and inanimate communications of motion. If therefore the giving a new force, be supernatural ; then every action of God is supernatural and he is quite excluded from the government of the natural world : and every action of man, is either supernatural, or else man is as mere a machine as a clock.

34 and 35. The difference between the true notion of

God, and that of a soul of the world, has been before shown : Reply II, § 12, and in this Paper, § 29 and 32.

36. This has been answered just above, § 31.

37. The soul is not diffused through the brain ; but is present to that particular place, which is the sensorium.

38. This is a bare assertion, without proof. Two bodies, void of elasticity, meeting each other with equal contrary forces, both lose their motion. And Sir Isaac Newton has given a mathematical instance, (p. 341 of the Latin Edition of his *Opticks* [1]), wherein motion is continually diminishing and increasing in quantity, without any communication thereof to other bodies.

39. This is no defect, as is here supposed ; but 'tis the just and proper nature of inert matter.

40. This argument (if it be good,) proves that the material world must be infinite, and that it must have been from eternity, and must continue to eternity : and that God must always have created as many men, and as many of all other things, as 'twas possible for him to create ; and for as long a time also, as it was possible for him to do it.

41. What the meaning of these words is ; *an order,* (or situation,) *which makes bodies to be situable* ; I understand not. It seems to me to amount to this, that situation is the cause of situation. That space is not merely the order of bodies, has been shown before ; and that no answer has been given to the arguments there offered, has been shown in this Paper, § 13 and 14. Also that time is not merely the order of things succeeding each other, is evident ; because the quantity of time may be greater or less, and yet that order continue the same. The order of things succeeding each other in time, is not time itself : for they may succeed each other faster or slower in the same order of succession, but not in the same time. If no creatures existed, yet the ubiquity of God, and the continuance of his existence, would make space and duration to be exactly the same as they are now.

[1] p. 176 below.

42. This is appealing from reason to vulgar opinion ; which philosophers should not do, because it is not the rule of truth.

43. Unusualness is necessarily included in the notion of a miracle. For otherwise there is nothing more wonderful, nor that requires greater power to effect, than some of those things we call natural. Such as, the motions of the heavenly-bodies, the generation and formation of plants and animals etc. Yet these are for this only reason not miracles, because they are common. Nevertheless, it does not follow, that every thing which is unusual, is therefore a miracle. For it may be only the irregular and more rare effect of usual causes : of which kind are eclipses, monstrous births, madness in men, and innumerable things which the vulgar call prodigies.

44. This is a concession of what I alleged. And yet 'tis contrary to the common opinion of divines, to suppose that an angel can work a miracle.

45. That one body should attract another without any intermediate means, is indeed not a miracle, but a contradiction : for 'tis supposing something to act where it is not. But the means by which two bodies attract each other, may be invisible and intangible, and of a different nature from mechanism ; and yet, acting regularly and constantly, may well be called natural ; being much less wonderful than animal-motion, which yet is never called a miracle.

46. If the word *natural forces*, means here mechanical ; then all animals, and even men, are as mere machines as a clock. But if the word does not mean, mechanical forces ; then gravitation may be effected by regular and natural powers, though they be not mechanical.

N.B. The arguments alleged in the postscript to Mr. Leibnitz's fourth paper, have been already answered in the foregoing replies. All that needs here to be observed, is, that his notion concerning the impossibility of physical atoms, (for the question is not about mathematical atoms) is a manifest absurdity. For either there are, or there are not, any perfectly solid particles of matter. If there are any such ; then the parts of such perfectly solid particles, taken of equal figure and dimensions (which is always possible in supposition) are physical atoms perfectly alike. But if there be no such perfectly solid particles, then there is no matter at all in the universe. For, the further the division and subdivision of the parts of any body is carried, before you arrive at parts perfectly solid and without pores ; the greater is the proportion of pores to solid matter in that body. If therefore, carrying on the division *in infinitum*, you never arrive at parts perfectly solid and without pores ; it will follow that all bodies consist of pores only, without any matter at all : which is a manifest absurdity. And the argument is the same with regard to the matter of which any particular species of bodies is composed, whether its pores be supposed empty, or always full of extraneous matter.[1]

[1] In the 1717 edition of the Correspondence, this sentence is added in the Errata.

MR. LEIBNITZ'S FIFTH PAPER [1]

being

An Answer to Dr. Clarke's Fourth Reply [2]

1. I shall at this time make a larger answer; to clear the difficulties; and to try whether the author be willing to hearken to reason, and to show that he is a lover of truth; or whether he will only cavil, without clearing any thing.

2. He often endeavours to impute to me necessity and fatality; though perhaps no one has better and more fully explained, than I have done in my *Theodicy*, the true difference between liberty, contingency, spontaneity, on the one side; and absolute necessity, chance, coaction, on the other. I know not yet, whether the author does this, because he will do it, whatever I may say; or whether he does it, (supposing him sincere in those imputations,) because he has not yet duly considered my opinions. I shall soon find what I am to think of it, and I shall take my measures accordingly.

3. It is true, that reasons in the mind of a wise being, and motives in any mind whatsoever, do that which answers to the effect produced by weights in a balance. The author objects, that this notion leads to necessity and

---

[1] Despatched in part with letter dated 18th August 1716 (p. 196).

[2] In the 1717 edition there occurs the following note in French at the beginning of the French version of Leibniz's Fifth Paper: ' The variant readings printed in the margin of the following paper, are changes made in Mr. Leibnitz's own hand in another copy of this paper which he sent to one of his friends in England a short time before his death.' In this edition they have been inserted in the text within square brackets.

fatality. But he says so, without proving it, and without taking notice of the explications I have formerly given, in order to remove the difficulties that may be raised upon that head.

4. He seems also to play with equivocal terms. There are necessities, which ought to be admitted. For we must distinguish between an absolute and an hypothetical necessity. We must also distinguish between a necessity, which takes place because the opposite implies a contradiction ; (which necessity is called logical, metaphysical, or mathematical ;) and a necessity which is moral, whereby, a wise being chooses the best, and every mind follows the strongest inclination.

5. Hypothetical necessity is that, which the supposition or hypothesis of God's foresight and pre-ordination lays upon future contingents. And this must needs be admitted, unless we deny, as the Socinians do, God's foreknowledge of future contingents, and his providence which regulates and governs every particular thing.

6. But neither that foreknowledge, nor that pre-ordination, derogate from liberty. For God, being moved by his supreme reason to choose, among many series of things or worlds possible, that, in which free creatures should take such or such resolutions, though not without his concourse ; has thereby rendered every event certain and determined [1] once for all ; without derogating thereby from the liberty of those creatures : that simple decree of choice, not at all changing, but only actualizing their free natures, which he saw in his ideas.

7. As for moral necessity, this also does not derogate from liberty. For when a wise being, and especially God, who has supreme wisdom, chooses what is best, he is not the less free upon that account : on the contrary, it is the most perfect liberty, not to be hindered from acting in the best manner. And when any other chooses according to the

[1] ' a rendu, par là, leur évènement certain et determiné ', i.e. has thereby rendered their future certain and determined.

most apparent and the most strongly inclining good, he imitates therein the liberty of a truly wise being, in proportion to his disposition. Without this, the choice would be a blind chance.

8. But good, either true or apparent; in a word, the motive, inclines without necessitating; that is, without imposing an absolute necessity. For when God (for instance) chooses the best; what he does not choose, and is inferior in perfection, is nevertheless possible. But if what he chooses, was absolutely necessary; any other way would be impossible: which is against the hypothesis. For God chooses among possibles, that is, among many ways, none of which implies a contradiction.

9. But to say, that God can only choose what is best; and to infer from thence, that what he does not choose, is impossible; this, I say, is confounding of terms: 'tis blending power and will, metaphysical necessity and moral necessity, essences and existences. For, what is necessary, is so by its essence, since the opposite implies a contradiction; but a contingent which exists, owes its existence to the principle of what is best, which is a sufficient reason for the existence of things. And therefore I say, that motives incline without necessitating; and that there is a certainty and infallibility, but not an absolute necessity in contingent things. Add to this, what will be said hereafter, Numb. 73, and 76.

10. And I have sufficiently shown in my *Theodicy*, that this moral necessity is a good thing, agreeable to the divine perfection; agreeable to the great principle or ground of existences, which is that of the want of a sufficient reason: whereas absolute and metaphysical necessity, depends upon the other great principle of our reasonings, viz., that of essences; that is, the principle of identity or contradiction: for, what is absolutely necessary, is the only possible way, and its contrary implies a contradiction.

11. I have also shown, that our will does not always exactly follow the practical understanding; because it

may have or find reasons to suspend its resolution till a further examination.

12. To impute to me after this, the notion of an absolute necessity, without having any thing to say against the reasons which I have just now alleged and which go to the bottom of things, perhaps beyond what is to be seen elsewhere ; this, I say, will be an unreasonable obstinacy.

13. As to the notion of fatality, which the author lays also to my charge ; this is another ambiguity. There is a *fatum mahometanum*, a *fatum stoicum*, and a *fatum christianum*. The Turkish fate will have an effect to happen, even though its cause should be avoided ; as if there was an absolute necessity. The stoical fate will have a man to be quiet, because he must have patience whether he will or not,[1] since 'tis impossible to resist the course of things. But 'tis agreed, that there is *fatum christianum*, a certain destiny of every thing, regulated by the foreknowledge and providence of God. *Fatum* is derived from *fari* ; that is, *to pronounce, to decree* ; and in its right sense, it signifies the decree of providence. And those who submit to it through a knowledge of the divine perfections, whereof the love of God is a consequence [since it consists in the pleasure which this knowledge gives] ; have not only patience like the heathen philosophers, but are also contented with what is ordained by God, knowing he does every thing for the best ; and not only for the greatest good in general, but also for the greatest particular good of those who love him.

14. I have been obliged to enlarge, in order to remove ill-grounded imputations once for all ; as I hope I shall be able to do by these explications, so as to satisfy equitable persons. I shall now come to an objection raised here, against my comparing the weights of a balance with the motives of the will. 'Tis objected, that a balance is merely passive, and mov'd by the weights ; whereas agents intelligent, and endowed with will, are active. To this I answer, that the principle of the want of a sufficient reason is

[1] 'patience par force ', i.e. patience perforce.

common both to agents and patients : they want a sufficient reason of their action, as well as of their passion. A balance does not only not act, when it is equally pulled on both sides ; but the equal weights likewise do not act when they are in an equilibrium, so that one of them cannot go down without the others rising up as much.

15. It must also be considered, that, properly speaking, motives do not act upon the mind, as weights do upon a balance ; but 'tis rather the mind that acts by virtue of the motives, which are its dispositions to act. And therefore to pretend, as the author does here, that the mind prefers sometimes weak motives to strong ones, and even that it prefers that which is indifferent before motives : this, I say, is to divide the mind from the motives, as if they were without the mind, as the weight is distinct from the balance ; and as if the mind had, besides motives, other dispositions to act, by virtue of which it could reject or accept the motives. Whereas, in truth, the motives comprehend all the dispositions, which the mind can have to act voluntarily ; for they include not only the reasons, but also the inclinations arising from passions, or other preceding impressions. Wherefore, if the mind should prefer a weak inclination to a strong one, it would act against itself, and otherwise than it is disposed to act. Which shows that the author's notions, contrary to mine, are superficial, and appear to have no solidity in them, when they are well considered.

16. To assert also, that the mind may have good reasons to act, when it has no motives, and when things are absolutely indifferent, as the author explains himself here ; this, I say, is a manifest contradiction. For if the mind has good reasons for taking the part it takes, then the things are not indifferent to the mind.

17. And to affirm that the mind will act, when it has reasons to act, even though the ways of acting were absolutely indifferent ; this, I say, is to speak again very superficially, and in a manner that cannot be defended.

For a man never has a sufficient reason to act, when he has not also a sufficient reason to act in a certain particular manner ; every action being individual, and not general, nor abstract from its circumstances, but always needing some particular way of being put in execution Wherefore, when there is a sufficient reason to do any particular thing, there is also a sufficient reason to do it in a certain particular manner ; and consequently, several manners of doing it are not indifferent. As often as a man has sufficient reasons for a single action, he has also sufficient reasons for all its requisites. See also what I shall say below, Numb. 66.

18. These arguments are very obvious ; and 'tis very strange to charge me with advancing my principle of the want of a sufficient reason, without any proof drawn either from the nature of things, or from the divine perfections. For the nature of things requires, that every event should have beforehand its proper conditions, requisites, and dispositions, the existence whereof makes the sufficient reason of such an event.

19. And God's perfection requires, that all his actions should be agreeable to his wisdom ; and that it may not be said of him, that he has acted without reason ; or even that he has prefer'd a weaker reason before a stronger.

20. But I shall speak more largely at the conclusion of this paper, concerning the solidity and importance of this great principle, of the want of a sufficient reason in order to every event ; the overthrowing of which principle, would overthrow the best part of all philosophy. 'Tis therefore very strange that the author should say, I am herein guilty of a *petitio principii* ; and it plainly appears he is desirous to maintain indefensible opinions, since he is reduced to deny that great principle, which is one of the most essential principles of reason.

To Paragraph 3, and 4.

21. It must be confessed, that though this great principle

has been acknowledged, yet it has not been sufficiently made use of. Which is, in great measure, the reason why the *prima philosophia* has not been hitherto so fruitful and demonstrative, as it should have been. I infer from that principle, among other consequences, that there are not in nature two real, absolute beings, indiscernible from each other ; because if there were, God and nature would act without reason, in ordering the one otherwise than the other ; and that therefore God does not produce two pieces of matter perfectly equal and alike. The author answers this conclusion, without confuting the reason of it ; and he answers with a very weak objection. *That argument,* says he, *if it was good, would prove that it would be impossible for God to create any matter at all. For, the perfectly solid parts of matter, if we take them of equal figure and dimensions, (which is always possible in supposition,) would be exactly alike.* But 'tis a manifest *petitio principii* to suppose that perfect likeness which, according to me, cannot be admitted. This supposition of two indiscernibles, such as two pieces of matter perfectly alike, seems indeed to be possible in abstract terms ; but it is not consistent with the order of things, nor with the divine wisdom, by which nothing is admitted without reason. The vulgar fancy such things, because they content themselves with incomplete notions. And this is one of the faults of the atomists.

22. Besides ; I don't admit in matter, parts perfectly solid, or that are the same throughout, without any variety or particular motion in their parts, as the pretended atoms are imagined to be. To suppose such bodies, is another popular opinion ill-grounded. According to my demonstrations, every part of matter is actually subdivided into parts differently moved, and no one of them is perfectly like another.

23. I said, that in sensible things, two, that are indiscernible from each other, can never be found ; that (for instance) two leaves in a garden, or two drops of water, perfectly alike, are not to be found. The author

acknowledges it as to leaves, and perhaps as to drops of water. But he might have admitted it, without any hesitation, without a perhaps, (an Italian would say, *senza forse*,) as to drops of water likewise.

24. I believe that these general observations in things sensible, hold also in proportion in things insensible, and that one may say, in this respect, what Harlequin says in the *Emperor of the Moon*; [1] 'tis there, just as 'tis here. And 'tis a great objection against indiscernibles, that no instance of them is to be found. But the author opposes this consequence, because (says he) sensible bodies are compounded; whereas he maintains there are insensible bodies, which are simple. I answer again, that I don't admit simple bodies. There is nothing simple, in my opinion, but true monads, which have neither parts nor extension. Simple bodies, and even perfectly similar ones, are a consequence of the false hypothesis of a vacuum and of atoms, or of lazy philosophy, which does not sufficiently carry on the analysis of things, and fancies it can attain to the first material elements of nature, because our imagination would be therewith satisfied.

25. When I deny that there are two drops of water perfectly alike, or any two other bodies indiscernible from each other; I don't say, 'tis absolutely impossible to suppose them; but that 'tis a thing contrary to the divine wisdom, and which consequently does not exist.

To Paragraph 5 and 6.

26. I own, that if two things perfectly indiscernible from each other did exist, they would be two; but that supposition is false, and contrary to the grand principle of reason. The vulgar philosophers were mistaken, when they believed that there are things different *solo numero*, or only because they are two; and from this error have

[1] *Arlequin, L'Empereur dans la Lune* was one of the many Harlequinades performed in France in the second half of the seventeenth century. It may have been based on Cyrano de Bergerac's *Voyages dans la Lune*.

arisen their perplexities about what they called the *principle of individuation*. Metaphysics have generally been handled like a science of mere words, like a philosophical dictionary, without entering into the discussion of things. Superficial philosophy, such as is that of the atomists and vacuists, forges things, which superior reasons do not admit. I hope my demonstrations will change the face of philosophy, notwithstanding such weak objections as the author raises here against me.

27. The parts of time or place, considered in themselves, are ideal things ; and therefore they perfectly resemble one another like two abstract units. But it is not so with two concrete ones, or with two real times, or two spaces filled up, that is, truly actual.

28. I don't say that two points of space are one and the same point, nor that two instants of time are one and the same instant, as the author seems to charge me with saying. But a man may fancy, for want of knowledge, that there are two different instants, where there is but one : in like manner as I observed in the 17th paragraph of the foregoing answer, that frequently in geometry we suppose two, in order to represent the error of a gainsayer, when there is really but one. If any man should suppose that a right line cuts another in two points ; it will be found after all, that those two pretended points must coincide, and make but one point.

29. I have demonstrated, that space is nothing else but an order of the existence of things, observed as existing together ; [1] and therefore the fiction of a material finite universe, moving forward [2] in an infinite empty space, cannot be admitted. It is altogether unreasonable and impracticable. For, besides that there is no real space out of the material universe ; such an action would be without any design in it : it would be working without doing any thing, *agendo nihil agere*. There would happen no

[1] ' dans leur simultaneité '.
[2] ' qui se promène tout entier '.

change, which could be observed by any person whatsoever. These are imaginations of philosophers who have incomplete notions, who make space an absolute reality. Mere mathematicians, who are only taken up with the conceits of imagination, are apt to forge such notions; but they are destroyed by superior reasons.

30. Absolutely speaking, it appears that God can make the material universe finite in extension; but the contrary appears more agreeable to his wisdom.

31. I don't grant, that every finite is moveable. According to the hypothesis of my adversaries themselves, a part of space, though finite, is not moveable. What is moveable, must be capable of changing its situation with respect to something else, and to be in a new state discernible from the first: otherwise the change is but a fiction. A moveable finite, must therefore make part of another finite, that any change may happen which can be observed.

32. Cartesius maintains, that matter is unlimited; and I don't think he has been sufficiently confuted. And though this be granted him, yet it does not follow that matter would be necessary, nor that it would have existed from all eternity; since that unlimited diffusion of matter, would only be an effect of God's choice, judging that to be the better.

To Paragraph 7.

33. Since space in itself is an ideal thing, like time; space out of the world must needs be imaginary, as the schoolmen themselves have acknowledged. The case is the same with empty space within the world; which I take also to be imaginary, for the reasons before alleged.

34. The author objects against me the vacuum discovered by Mr. Guerike [1] of Magdeburg, which is made

[1] Guericke (1602–86). Inventor of the air pump. He is said to have performed an experiment before the Emperor Ferdinand III in which he took two hollow copper hemispheres, exhausted the air from them with his pump, and then showed that thirty horses, fifteen pulling on each hemisphere, could not separate them. Leibniz corresponded with Guericke about the air-pump in 1671–2 (G.I.193).

by pumping the air out of a receiver ; and he pretends that there is truly a perfect vacuum, or a space without matter, (at least in part,) in that receiver. The Aristotelians and Cartesians, who do not admit a true vacuum, have said in answer to that experiment of Mr. Guerike, as well as to that of Torricellius [1] of Florence, (who emptied the air out of a glass-tube by the help of quicksilver,) that there is no vacuum at all in the tube or in the receiver ; since glass has small pores, which the beams of light, the effluvia of the load-stone, and other very thin fluids may go through. I am of their opinion : and I think the receiver may be compared to a box full of holes in the water, having fish or other gross bodies shut up in it ; which being taken out, their place would nevertheless be filled up with water. There is only this difference ; that though water be fluid and more yielding than those gross bodies, yet it is as heavy and massive, if not more, than they : whereas the matter which gets into the receiver in the room of the air is much more subtile. The new sticklers for a vacuum allege in answer to this instance, that it is not the grossness of matter, but its mere quantity, that makes resistance ; and consequently that there is of necessity more vacuum, where there is less resistance. They add, that the subtleness of matter has nothing to do here ; and that the particles of quicksilver are as subtle and fine as those of water ; and yet that quicksilver resists about ten times more. To this I reply, that it is not so much the quantity of matter, as its difficulty of giving place, that makes resistance. For instance, floating timber contains less of heavy matter, than an equal bulk of water does ; and yet it makes more resistance to a boat, than the water does.

---

[1] Torricelli (1608–47). Pupil of Galileo, and inventor of the barometer. In his most famous experiment he took a long tube closed at one end, filled it with mercury and closing the open end with his finger, inverted it in a basin of mercury. When he removed his finger, the level of mercury in the tube fell to thirty inches above the surface, leaving an apparent vacuum at the top of the tube.

35. And as for quicksilver ; 'tis true, it contains about fourteen times more of heavy matter, than an equal bulk of water does ; but it does not follow, that it contains fourteen times more matter absolutely. On the contrary, water contains as much matter ; if we include both its own matter, which is heavy ; and the extraneous matter void of heaviness, which passes through its pores. For, both quicksilver and water, are masses of heavy matter, full of pores, through which there passes a great deal of matter void of heaviness [and which makes no sensible resistance] ; such as is probably that of the rays of light, and other insensible fluids ; and especially that which is itself the cause of the gravity of gross bodies, by receding from the centre towards which it drives those bodies. For, it is a strange imagination to make all matter gravitate, and that towards all other matter, as if each body did equally attract every other body according to their masses and distances ; and this by an attraction properly so called, which is not derived from an occult impulse of bodies ; whereas the gravity of sensible bodies towards the centre of the earth, ought to be produced by the motion of some fluid. And the case must be the same with other gravities, such as is that of the planets towards the sun, or towards each other. [A body is never moved naturally, except by another body which touches it and pushes it ; after that it continues until it is prevented by another body which touches it. Any other kind of operation on bodies is either miraculous or imaginary.]

To Paragraphs 8, and 9.

36. I objected, that space taken for something real and absolute without bodies, would be a thing eternal, impassible, and independent upon God. The author endeavours to elude this difficulty, by saying that space is a property of God. In answer to this, I have said, in my foregoing paper, that the property of God is immensity ;

but that space (which is often commensurate with bodies,) and God's immensity, are not the same thing.

37. I objected further, that if space be a property, and infinite space be the immensity of God ; finite space will be the extension or mensurability of something finite. And therefore, the space taken up by a body, will be the extension of that body. Which is an absurdity ; since a body can change space but cannot leave its extension.

38. I asked also ; if space is a property, what thing will an empty limited space, (such as that which my adversary imagines in an exhausted receiver,) be the property of ? It does not appear reasonable to say, that this empty space, either round or square, is a property of God. Will it be then perhaps the property of some immaterial, extended, imaginary substances which the author seems to fancy in the imaginary spaces ?

39. If space is the property or affection of the substance, which is in space ; the same space will be sometimes the affection of one body, sometimes of another body, sometimes of an immaterial substance, and sometimes perhaps of God himself, when it is void of all other substance material or immaterial. But this is a strange property or affection, which passes from one subject to another. Thus subjects will leave off their accidents, like clothes ; that other subjects may put them on. At this rate, how shall we distinguish accidents and substances ?

40. And if limited spaces are the affections of limited substances, which are in them ; and infinite space be a property of God ; a property of God must (which is very strange,) be made up of the affections of creatures ; for all finite spaces, taken together, make up infinite space.

41. But if the author denies, that limited space is an affection of limited things ; it will not be reasonable neither, that infinite space should be the affection or property of an infinite thing. I have suggested all these difficulties in my foregoing paper ; but it does not appear that the author has endeavoured to answer them.

42. I have still other reasons against this strange imagination, that space is a property of God. If it be so, space belongs to the essence of God. But space has parts : therefore there would be parts in the essence of God. *Spectatum admissi.*[1]

43. Moreover, spaces are sometimes empty, and sometimes filled up. Therefore there will be in the essence of God, parts sometimes empty, and sometimes full, and consequently liable to a perpetual change. Bodies, filling up space, would fill up part of God's essence, and would be commensurate with it ; and in the supposition of a vacuum, part of God's essence will be within the receiver. Such a God having parts, will very much resemble the Stoics' God, which was the whole universe considered as a divine animal.

44. If infinite space is God's immensity, infinite time will be God's eternity ; and therefore we must say, that what is in space, is in God's immensity, and consequently in his essence ; and that what is in time, [is in the eternity of God and] is also in the essence of God. Strange expressions ; which plainly show, that the author makes a wrong use of terms.

45. I shall give another instance of this. God's immensity makes him actually present in all spaces. But now if God is in space, how can it be said that space is in God, or that it is a property of God ? We have often heard that a property is in its subject ; but we never heard, that a subject is in its property. In like manner, God exists in all time. How then can time be in God ; and how can it be a property of God ? These are perpetual *alloglossies.*[2]

46. It appears that the author confounds immensity, or the extension of things, with the space according to which

---

[1] Spectatum admissi risum teneatis amici, i.e. If you saw such a thing, friends, could you restrain your laughter ? Horace, *De Arte Poetica*, I.

[2] ' alloglossies ', ἀλλογλωσσία : use of a strange tongue (Liddell and Scott).

that extension is taken. Infinite space, is not the immensity of God ; finite space, is not the extension of bodies : as time is not their duration. Things keep their extension ; but they do not always keep their space. Every thing has its own extension, its own duration ; but it has not its own time, and does not keep its own space.

47. I will here show, how men come to form to themselves the notion of space. They consider that many things exist at once and they observe in them a certain order of co-existence, according to which the relation of one thing to another is more or less simple. This order, is their *situation* or distance. When it happens that one of those co-existent things changes its relation to a multitude of others, which do not change their relation among themselves ; and that another thing, newly come, acquires the same relation to the others, as the former had ; we then say, it is come into the place of the former ; and this change, we call a motion in that body, wherein is the immediate cause of the change. And though many, or even all the co-existent things, should change according to certain known rules of direction and swiftness ; yet one may always determine the relation of situation, which every co-existent acquires with respect to every other co-existent ; and even that relation which any other co-existent would have to this, or which this would have to any other, if it had not changed, or if it had changed any otherwise. And supposing, or feigning, that among those co-existents, there is a sufficient number of them, which have undergone no change ; then we may say, that those which have such a relation to those fixed existents, as others had to them before, have now the *same place* which those others had. And that which comprehends all those places, is called *space*. Which shows, that in order to have an idea of place, and consequently of space, it is sufficient to consider these relations, and the rules of their changes, without needing to fancy any absolute reality out of the things whose situation we consider. And, to give a kind of a definition :

place is that, which we say is the same to A and, to B, when
the relation of the co-existence of B, with C, E, F, G, etc.
agrees perfectly with the relation of the co-existence, which
A had with the same C, E, F, G, etc. supposing there has
been no cause of change in C, E, F, G, etc. It may
be said also, without entering into any further particularity,
that *place* is that, which is the same in different moments
to different existent things, when their relations of co-
existence with certain other existents, which are supposed
to continue fixed from one of those moments to the other,
agree entirely together. And *fixed existents* are those, in
which there has been no cause of any change of the order
of their co-existence with others ; or (which is the same
thing,) in which there has been no motion. Lastly, *space*
is that, which results from places taken together. And
here it may not be amiss to consider the difference between
place, and the relation of situation, which is in the body
that fills up the place. For, the place of A and B, is the
same ; whereas the relation of A to fixed bodies, is not
precisely and individually the same, as the relation which
B (that comes into its place) will have to the same fixed
bodies ; but these relations agree only. For, two different
subjects, as A and B, cannot have precisely the same
individual affection ; it being impossible, that the same
individual accident should be in two subjects, or pass
from one subject to another. But the mind not contented
with an agreement, looks for an identity, for something that
should be truly the same ; and conceives it as being extrinsic to the subjects : and this is what we call *place* and
space. But this can only be an ideal thing ; containing a
certain order, wherein the mind conceives the application
of relations. In like manner, as the mind can fancy to
itself an order made up of genealogical lines, whose bigness
would consist only in the number of generations, wherein
every person would have his place : and if to this one
should add the fiction of a *metempsychosis*, and bring in the
same human souls again ; the persons in those lines might

change place ; he who was a father, or a grandfather, might become a son, or a grandson, etc. And yet those genealogical places, lines, and spaces, though they should express real truth, would only be ideal things. I shall allege another example, to show how the mind uses, upon occasion of accidents which are in subjects, to fancy to itself something answerable to those accidents, out of the subjects. The ratio or proportion between two lines L and M, may be conceived three several ways ; as a ratio of the greater L, to the lesser M ; as a ratio of the lesser M, to the greater L ; and lastly, as something abstracted from both, that is, as the ratio between L and M, without considering which is the antecedent, or which the consequent ; which the subject, and which the object. And thus it is, that proportions are considered in music. In the first way of considering them, L the greater ; in the second, M the lesser, is the subject of that accident, which philosophers call relation. But, which of them will be the subject, in the third way of considering them ? It cannot be said that both of them, L and M together, are the subject of such an accident ; for if so, we should have an accident in two subjects, with one leg in one, and the other in the other ; which is contrary to the notion of accidents. Therefore we must say, that this relation, in this third way of considering it, is indeed out of the subjects ; but being neither a substance, nor an accident, it must be a mere ideal thing, the consideration of which is nevertheless useful. To conclude : [1] I have here done much like Euclid, who not being able to make his readers well understand what *ratio* is absolutely in the sense of geometricians ; defines what are the *same ratios*. Thus, in like manner, in order to explain what *place* is, I have been content to define what is the *same place*. Lastly ; I observe, that the traces of moveable bodies, which they leave sometimes upon the immoveable ones on which they are moved ; have given men occasion to form in their imagination

[1] 'au reste'.

such an idea, as if some trace did still remain, even when there is nothing unmoved. But this is a mere ideal thing, and imports only, that if there was any unmoved thing there, the trace might be marked out upon it. And 'tis this analogy, which makes men fancy places, traces and spaces ; though those things consist only in the truth of relations, and not at all in any absolute reality.

48. To conclude.[1] If the space (which the author fancies) void of all bodies, is not altogether empty ; what is it then full of ? Is it full of extended spirits perhaps, or immaterial substances, capable of extending and contracting themselves ; which move therein, and penetrate each other without any inconveniency, as the shadows of two bodies penetrate one another upon the surface of a wall ? Methinks I see the revival of the odd imaginations of Dr. Henry More (otherwise a learned and well-meaning man,) and of some others who fancied that those spirits can make themselves impenetrable whenever they please. Nay, some have fancied, that man, in the state of innocency, had also the gift of penetration ; and that he became solid, opaque, and impenetrable by his fall. Is it not over-throwing our notions of things, to make God have parts, to make spirits have extension ? The principle of the want of a sufficient reason does alone drive away all these spectres of imagination. Men easily run into fictions, for want of making a right use of that great principle.

To Paragraph 10.

49. It cannot be said that [a certain] duration is eternal but [it can be said] that the things which continue always are eternal, [gaining always a new duration.] Whatever exists of time and of duration, [being successive] perishes continually : and how can a thing exist eternally, which (to speak exactly,) does never exist at all ? For, how can a thing exist, whereof no part does ever exist ? Nothing of time does ever exist, but instants ; and an instant is not

[1] 'au reste'.

72

even itself a part of time. Whoever considers these observations, will easily apprehend that time can only be an ideal thing. And the analogy between time and space, will easily make it appear, that the one is as merely ideal as the other. [But, if in saying that the duration of a thing is eternal, it is only meant that the thing endures eternally, I have nothing to say against it.]

50. If the reality of space and time, is necessary to the immensity and eternity of God; if God must be in space; if being in space, is a property of God; he will in some measure, depend upon time and space, and stand in need of them. For I have already prevented that subterfuge, that space and time are [in God and like] properties of God. [Could one maintain the opinion that bodies move in the parts of the divine essence?]

To Paragraph 11, and 12.

51. I objected that space cannot be in God, because it has parts. Hereupon the author seeks another subterfuge, by departing from the received sense of words; maintaining that space has no parts, because its parts are not separable, and cannot be removed from one another by discerption. But 'tis sufficient that space has parts, whether those parts be separable or not; and they may be assigned in space, either by the bodies that are in it, or by lines and surfaces that may be drawn and described in it.

To Paragraph 13.

52. In order to prove that space, without bodies, is an absolute reality; the author objected, that a finite material universe might move forward in space. I answered, it does not appear reasonable that the material universe should be finite; and, though we should suppose it to be finite; yet 'tis unreasonable it should have motion any otherwise, than as its parts change their situation among themselves; because such a motion would produce no

change that could be observed, and would be without design. 'Tis another thing, when its parts change their situation among themselves ; for then there is a motion in space ; but it consists in the order of relations which are changed. The author replies now, that the reality of motion does not depend upon being observed ; and that a ship may go forward, and yet a man, who is in the ship, may not perceive it. I answer, motion does not indeed depend upon being observed ; but it does depend upon being possible to be observed. There is no motion, when there is no change that can be observed. And when there is no change that can be observed, there is no change at all. The contrary opinion is grounded upon the supposition of a real absolute space, which I have demonstratively confuted by the principle of the want of a sufficient reason of things.

53. I find nothing in the Eighth Definition of the *Mathematical Principles of Nature*, nor in the Scholium belonging to it, that proves, or can prove, the reality of space in itself. However, I grant there is a difference between an absolute true motion of a body, and a mere relative change of its situation with respect to another body. For when the immediate cause of the change is in the body, that body is truly in motion ; and then the situation of other bodies, with respect to it, will be changed consequently, though the cause of that change be not in them. 'Tis true that, exactly speaking, there is not any one body, that is perfectly and entirely at rest ; but we frame an abstract notion of rest, by considering the thing mathematically. Thus have I left nothing unanswered, of what has been alleged for the absolute reality of space. And I have demonstrated the falsehood of that reality, by a fundamental principle, one of the most certain both in reason and experience ; against which, no exception or instance can be alleged. Upon the whole,[1] one may judge from what has been said that I ought not to admit

[1] 'au reste'.

a moveable universe ; nor any place out of the material universe.

To Paragraph 14.

54. I am not sensible of any objection, but what I think I have sufficiently answered. As for the objection that space and time are quantities, or rather things endowed with quantity ; and that situation and order are not so : I answer, that order also has its quantity ; there is in it, that which goes before, and that which follows ; there is distance or interval. Relative things have their quantity, as well as absolute ones. For instance, ratios or proportions in mathematics, have their quantity, and are measured by logarithms ; and yet they are relations. And therefore though time and space consist in relations, yet they have their quantity.

To Paragraph 15.

55. As to the question, whether God could have created the world sooner ; 'tis necessary here to understand each other rightly. Since I have demonstrated, that time, without things, is nothing else but a mere ideal possibility ; 'tis manifest, if any one should say that this same world, which has been actually created, might have been created sooner, without any other change ; he would say nothing that is intelligible. For there is no mark or difference, whereby it would be possible to know, that this world was created sooner. And therefore, (as I have already said,) to suppose that God created the same world sooner, is supposing a chimerical thing. 'Tis making time a thing absolute, independent upon God ; whereas time does only co-exist with creatures, and is only conceived by the order and quantity of their changes.

56. But yet, absolutely speaking, one may conceive that an universe began sooner, than it actually did. Let us suppose our universe, or any other, to be represented by the Figure A F ; and that the ordinate A B represents

its first state ; and the ordinates C D, E F, its following

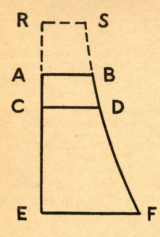

states : I say, one may conceive that such a world began sooner, by conceiving the figure prolonged backwards, and by adding to it S R A B S. For thus, things being increased, time will be also increased. But whether such an augmentation be reasonable and agreeable to God's wisdom, is another question, to which we answer in the negative ; otherwise God would have made such an augmentation. It would be like as

Humano capiti cervicem pictor equinam
Jungere si velit.[1]

The case is the same with respect to the destruction of the universe. As one might conceive something added to the beginning, so one might also conceive something taken off towards the end. But such a retrenching from it, would be also unreasonable.

57. Thus it appears how we are to understand, that God created things at what time he pleased ; for this depends upon the things, which he resolved to create. But things being once resolved upon, together with their relations ; there remains no longer any choice about the time and the place, which of themselves have nothing in them real, nothing that can distinguish them, nothing that is at all discernible.

58. One cannot therefore say, as the author does here, that the wisdom of God may have good reasons to create

[1] 'If a painter wished to join the neck of a horse to a human head . . .' Horace, *De Arte Poetica*, I.

this world at such or such a particular time : that particular time, considered without the things, being an impossible fiction ; and good reasons for a choice, being not to be found, where every thing is indiscernible.

59. When I speak of *this world*, I mean the whole universe of material and immaterial creatures taken together, from the beginning of things. But if any one mean only the beginning of the material world, and suppose immaterial creatures before it; he would have somewhat more reason for his supposition. For time then being marked by things that existed already, it would be no longer indifferent ; and there might be room for choice. And yet indeed, this would be only putting off the difficulty. For, supposing the whole universe of immaterial and material creatures together, to have a beginning ; there is no longer any choice about the time, in which God would place that beginning.

60. And therefore, one must not say, as the author does here, that God created things in what particular space, and at what particular time he pleased. For, all time and all spaces being in themselves perfectly uniform and indiscernible from each other, one of them cannot please more than another.

61. I shall not enlarge here upon my opinion explained elsewhere, that there are no created substances wholly destitute of matter. For I hold with the ancients, and according to reason, that angels or intelligences, and souls separated from a gross body, have always subtile bodies, though they themselves be incorporeal. The vulgar philosophy easily admits all sorts of fictions : mine is more strict.

62. I don't say that matter and space are the same thing. I only say, there is no space, where there is no matter ; and that space in itself is not an absolute reality. Space and matter differ, as time and motion. However, these things, though different, are inseparable.

63. But yet it does not at all follow, that matter is eternal

and necessary ; unless we suppose space to be eternal and necessary : a supposition ill grounded in all respects.

To Paragraph 16 and 17.

64. I think I have answered every thing ; and I have particularly replied to that objection, that space and time have quantity, and that order has none. See above, Number 54.

65. I have clearly shown that the contradiction lies in the hypothesis of the opposite opinion, which looks for a difference where there is none. And it would be a manifest iniquity to infer from thence, that I have acknowledged a contradiction in my own opinion.

To Paragraph 18.

66. Here I find again an argument, which I have overthrown above, Numb. 17. The author says, God may have good reasons to make two cubes perfectly equal and alike : and then (says he) God must needs assign them their places, though every other respect be perfectly equal. But things ought not to be separated from their circumstances. This argument consists in incomplete notions. God's resolutions are never abstract and imperfect : as if God decreed, first, to create the two cubes ; and then, made another decree where to place them. Men, being such limited creatures as they are, may act in this manner. They may resolve upon a thing, and then find themselves perplexed about means, ways, places, and circumstances. But God never takes a resolution about the ends, without resolving at the same time about the means, and all the circumstances. Nay, I have shown in my *Theodicy*, that properly speaking, there is but one decree for the whole universe, whereby God resolved to bring it out of possibility into existence. And therefore God will not choose a cube, without choosing its place at the same time ; and he will never choose among indiscernibles.

67. The parts of space are not determined and dis-

tinguished, but by the things which are in it : and the diversity of things in space, determines God to act differently upon different parts of space. But space without things, has nothing whereby it may be distinguished ; and indeed not any thing actual.

68. If God is resolved to place a certain cube of matter at all, he is also resolved in what particular place to put it. But 'tis with respect to other parts of matter ; and not with respect to bare space itself, in which there is nothing to distinguish it.

69. But wisdom does not allow God to place at the same time two cubes perfectly equal and alike, because there is no way to find any reason for assigning them different places. At this rate, there would be a will without a motive.

70. A will without motive, (such as superficial reasoners suppose to be in God,) I compar'd to Epicurus's chance. The author answers : Epicurus's chance is a blind necessity, and not a choice of will. I reply, that Epicurus's chance is not a necessity, but something indifferent. Epicurus brought it in on purpose to avoid necessity. 'Tis true, chance is blind ; but a will without motive would be no less blind, and no less owing to mere chance.

To Paragraph 19.

71. The author repeats here, what has been already confuted above, Numb. 21 ; that matter cannot be created, without God's choosing among indiscernibles. He would be in the right, if matter consisted of atoms, similar particles, or other the like fictions of superficial philosophy. But that great principle, which proves there is no choice among indiscernibles, destroys also these ill-contrived fictions.

To Paragraph 20.

72. The author objected against me in his Third Paper, (Numb. 7, and 8 ;) that God would not have in himself

a principle of acting, if he was determined by things external. I answered, that the ideas of external things are in him ; and that therefore he is determined by internal reasons, that is, by his wisdom. But the author here will not understand, to what end I said it.

To Paragraph 21.

73. He frequently confounds, in his objections against me, what God will not do, with what he cannot do. See above, Numb. 9 [and below Numb. 76]. For example ; God can do every thing that is possible, but he will do only what is best. And therefore I don't say, as the author here will have it, that God cannot limit the extension of matter ; but 'tis likely [1] he will not do it, and that he has thought it better to set no bounds to matter.

74. From extension to duration, *non valet consequentia*. Though the extension of matter were unlimited, yet it would not follow that its duration would be also unlimited ; nay, even *a parte ante*, it would not follow, that it had no beginning. If it is the nature of things in the whole, to grow uniformly in perfection ; the universe of creatures must have had a beginning. And therefore, there will be reasons to limit the duration of things, even though there were none to limit their extension. Besides, the world's having a beginning, does not derogate from the infinity of its duration *a parte post* ; but bounds of the universe would derogate from the infinity of its extension. And therefore it is more reasonable to admit a beginning of the world, than to admit any bounds of it ; that the character of its infinite author, may be in both respects preserved.

75. However, those who have admitted the eternity of the world, or at least, (as some famous divines have done,) the possibility of its eternity ; did not, for all that, deny its dependence upon God ; as the author here lays to their charge, without any ground.

---

[1] 'il y a de l'apparence '.

To Paragraph 22 and 23.

76. He here further objects, without any reason, that, according to my opinion, whatever God can do, he must needs have done. As if he was ignorant, that I have solidly confuted this notion in my *Theodicy* ; and that I have overthrown the opinion of those, who maintain that there is nothing possible but what really happens ; as some ancient philosophers did, and among others Diodorus in Cicero.[1]   The author confounds moral necessity, which proceeds from the choice of what is best, with absolute necessity : he confounds the will of God, with his power. God can produce every thing that is possible, or whatever does not imply a contradiction ; but he wills only to produce what is the best among things possible.   See what has been said above, Numb. 9 [and Numb. 74].

77. God is not therefore a necessary agent in producing creatures, since he acts with choice.   However, what the author adds here, is ill-grounded, viz. that a necessary agent would not be an agent at all.   He frequently affirms things boldly, and without any ground ; advancing [against me] notions which cannot be proved.

To Paragraph 24–28.

78. The author alleges, it was not affirmed that *space is God's sensorium*, but only *as it were his sensorium*.   The latter seems to be as improper, and as little intelligible as the former.

To Paragraph 29.

79. Space is not the place of all things ; for it is not the place of God.   Otherwise there would be a thing co-eternal with God, and independent upon him ; nay, he himself would depend upon it, if he has need of place.

80. Nor do I see, how it can be said, that space is the place of ideas ; for ideas are in the understanding.

[1] Cicero, *De Fato*.

81. 'Tis also very strange to say, that the soul of man is the soul of the images it perceives. The images, which are in the understanding, are in the mind : but if the mind was the soul of the images, they would then be extrinsic to it. And if the author means corporeal images, how then will he have a human mind to be the soul of those images, they being only transient impressions in a body belonging to that soul ?

82. If 'tis by means of a sensorium that God perceives what passes in the world ; it seems that things act upon him ; and that therefore he is what we mean by a soul of the world. The author charges me with repeating objections, without taking notice of the answers ; but I don't see that he has answered this difficulty. They had better wholly lay aside this pretended sensorium.

To Paragraph 30.

83. The author speaks, as if he did not understand, how, according to my opinion, the soul is a representative principle. Which is, as if he had never heard of my pre-established harmony.

84. I don't assent to the vulgar notions, that the images of things are conveyed by the organs (of sense) to the soul. For, it is not conceivable by what passage, or by what means of conveyance, these images can be carried from the organ to the soul. This vulgar notion in philosophy is not intelligible, as the new Cartesians have sufficiently shown. It cannot be explained, how immaterial substance is affected by matter : and to maintain an unintelligible notion thereupon, is having recourse to the scholastic chimerical notion of I know not what inexplicable *species intentionales*,[1] passing from the organs to

---

[1] In medieval scholasticism, the doctrine of the *species intentionales* as opposed to the *species reales* which were the actual forms of things, arose in an attempt to explain sense perception. The *species intentionales* were usually thought of as modifications of the mind caused by the action of an external object, the mind being likened or conformed to the object

the soul. Those Cartesians saw the difficulty ; but they could not explain it. They had recourse to a [very particular] concourse of God, which would really be miraculous. But, I think, I have given the true solution of that enigma.

85. To say that God perceives what passes in the world, because he is present to the things, and not by [the dependence on him of the continuation of their existence, which may be said to involve] a continual production of them ; is saying something unintelligible. A mere presence or proximity of co-existence, is not sufficient to make us understand, how that which passes in one being, should answer to what passes in another.

86. Besides ; this is exactly falling into that opinion, which makes God to be the soul of the world ; seeing it supposes God to perceive things, not by their dependence upon him, that is, by a continual production of what is good and perfect in them ; but by a kind of perception, such as that by which men fancy our soul perceives what passes in the body. This is a degrading of God's knowledge very much.

87. In truth and reality, this way of perception is wholly chimerical, and has no place even in human souls. They perceive what passes without them, by what passes within them, answering to the things without : in virtue of the harmony which God has pre-established by the most beautiful and most admirable of all his productions ; whereby every simple substance is by its nature, (if one may so say,) a concentration, and a living mirror of the whole universe, according to its point of view. Which is likewise one of the most beautiful and most undeniable proofs of the existence of God ; since none but God, viz. the universal cause, can produce such a harmony of things.

and thus enabled to know it. (cf. Aristotle, *De Anima*, 424^a 17–24.) At times among the later scholastics, they were, however, regarded almost as images, or forms, intermediate between and thus different from both the mind and the object.

But God himself cannot perceive things by the same means whereby he makes other beings perceive them. He perceives them, because he is able to produce that means. And other beings would not be caused to perceive them, if he himself did not produce them all harmonious, and had not therefore in himself a representation of them ; not as if that representation came from the things, but because the things proceed from him, and because he is the efficient and exemplary cause of them. He perceives them, because they proceed from him ; if one may be allowed to say, that he *perceives* them : which ought not to be said, unless we divest that word of its imperfection ; for else it seems to signify, that things act upon him. They exist, and are known to him, because he understands and wills them ; and because what he wills, is the same as what exists. Which appears so much the more, because he makes them to be perceived by one another ; and makes them perceive one another in consequence of the natures which he has given them once for all, and which he keeps up only, according to the laws of every one of them severally ; which, though different one from another, yet terminate in an exact correspondence of the results of the whole. This surpasses all the ideas, which men have generally framed concerning the divine perfections, and the works of God ; and raises [our notion of] [1] them, to the highest degree ; as Mr. Bayle has acknowledged,[2] though he believed, without any ground, that it exceeded possibility.

88. To infer from that passage of Holy Scripture, wherein God is said to have rested from his works, that there is no longer a continual production of them ; would be to make a very ill use of that text. 'Tis true, there is no production of new simple substances : but it would be wrong to infer from thence, that God is now in the world,

---

[1] Clarke's addition.

[2] This probably refers to the article *Rorarius* in the second edition of Bayle's *Historical and Critical Dictionary*.

only as the soul is conceived to be in the body, governing it merely by his presence, without any concourse being necessary to continue its existence.

To Paragraph 31.

89. The harmony or correspondence between the soul and the body, is not a perpetual miracle ; but the effect or consequence of an original miracle, worked at the creation of things ; as all natural things are. Though indeed it is a perpetual wonder, as many natural things are.

90. The word, *pre-established harmony*, is a term of art, I confess ; but 'tis not a term that explains nothing, since it is made out very intelligibly ; and the author alleges nothing, that shows there is any difficulty in it.

91. The nature of every simple substance, soul, or true monad, being such, that its following state is a consequence of the preceding one ; here now is the cause of the harmony found out. For God needs only to make a simple substance become once and from the beginning, a representation of the universe, according to its point of view ; since from thence alone it follows, that it will be so perpetually ; and that all simple substances will always have a harmony among themselves, because they always represent the same universe.

To Paragraph 32.

92. 'Tis true, that, according to me, the soul does not disturb the laws of the body, nor the body those of the soul ; and that the soul and body do only agree together ; the one acting freely, according to the rules of final causes ; and the other acting mechanically, according to the laws of efficient causes. But this does not derogate from the liberty of our souls ; as the author here will have it. For, every agent which acts according to final causes, is free, though it happens to agree with an agent acting only by efficient causes without knowledge, or mechanically ;

because God, foreseeing what the free cause would do, did from the beginning regulate the machine in such manner, that it cannot fail to agree with that free cause. Mr. Jaquelot [1] has very well resolved this difficulty, in one of his books against Mr. Bayle ; and I have cited the passage, in my *Theodicy*, Part. I, Paragraph 63.[2] I shall speak of it again below, Numb. 124.

To Paragraph 33.

93. I don't admit, that every action gives a new force to the patient. It frequently happens in the concourse of bodies, that each of them preserves its force ; as when two equal hard bodies meet directly. Then the direction only is changed, without any change in the force ; each of the bodies receiving the direction of the other, and going back with the same swiftness it came.

94. However, I am far from saying that it is supernatural to give a new force to a body ; for I acknowledge that one body does frequently receive a new force from another, which loses as much of its own. But I say only, 'tis supernatural that the whole universe of bodies should receive a new force ; and consequently that one body should acquire any new force, without the loss of as much in others. And therefore I say likewise, 'tis an indefensible opinion to suppose the soul gives force to the body ; for then the whole universe of bodies would receive a new force.

95. The author's dilemma here, is ill grounded ; viz. that according to me, either a man must act supernaturally, or be a mere machine, like a watch. For, man does not act supernaturally : and his body is truly a machine, acting only mechanically ; and yet his soul is a free cause.

---

[1] Jaquelot, *Conformité de la Foi avec la Raison*, Amsterdam, 1705. Isaac Jaquelot (1647–1708) was a French Protestant theologian, the author of three controversial books written against Bayle's dictionary.
[2] See Clarke's appendix, p. 134 below.

To Paragraph 34 and 35.

96. I here refer to what has been or shall be said in this Paper, Numb. 82, 86, and 111 ; concerning the comparison between God and a soul of the world ; and how the opinion contrary to mine, brings the one of these too near to the other.

To Paragraph 36.

97. I here also refer to what I have before said, concerning the harmony between the soul and the body, Numb. 89, &c.

To Paragraph 37.

98. The author tells us, that the soul is not in the brain, but in the sensorium ; without saying what that sensorium is. But supposing that sensorium to be extended, as I believe the author understands it ; the same difficulty still remains, and the question returns, whether the soul be diffused through that whole extension, be it great or small. For, more or less in bigness, is nothing to the purpose here.

To Paragraph 38.

99. I don't undertake here to establish my dynamics, or my doctrine of forces ; this would not be a proper place for it. However, I can very well answer the objection here brought against me. I have affirmed that active forces are preserved in the world *a* [without diminution] [1]. The author objects, that two soft or un-elastic bodies meeting together, lose some of their force. I answer, no. 'Tis true, their wholes lose it with respect to their total motion ; but their parts receive it, being shaken [internally] by the force of the concourse. And therefore that

a See above the note on § 13, of Dr. Clarke's Third Reply [Clarke's note].

[1] Clarke's addition.

loss of force, is only in appearance. The forces are not destroyed, but scattered among the small parts. The bodies do not lose their forces ; but the case here is the same, as when men change great money into small. However, I agree that the quantity of motion does not remain the same ; and herein I approve what Sir Isaac Newton says, page 341 of his *Opticks*,[1] which the author here quotes. But I have shown elsewhere, that there is a difference between the quantity of motion, and the quantity of force.

To Paragraph 39.

100. The author maintained against me, that force does naturally lessen in the material universe ; and that this arises from the dependence of things. (Third Reply, Paragraph 13 and 14.) In my third answer,[a] I desired him to prove that this imperfection is a consequence of the dependence of things. He avoids answering my demand ; by falling upon an incident, and denying this to be an imperfection. But whether it be an imperfection, or not, he should have proved that 'tis a consequence of the dependence of things.

101. However ; that which would make the machine of the world as imperfect, as that of an unskilful watchmaker ; surely must needs be an imperfection.

102. The author says now, that it is a consequence of the inertia of matter. But this also, he will not prove. That inertia, alleged here by him, mentioned by Kepler, repeated by Cartesius [in his letters] and made use of by me in my *Theodicy*, in order to give a notion [and at the same time an example] of the natural imperfection of creatures ; has no other effect, than to make the velocities diminish, when the quantities of matter are increased : but this is without any diminution of the forces.

[a] Which is Mr. Leibnitz's Fourth Paper in this collection [Clarke's note].

---

[1] p. 176 below.

To Paragraph 40.

103. I maintained, that the dependence of the machine of the world upon its divine author, is rather a reason why there can be no such imperfection in it ; and that the work of God does not want to be set right again ; that it is not liable to be disordered ; and lastly, that it cannot lessen in perfection. Let any one guess now, how the author can hence infer against me, as he does, that, if this be the case, then the material world must be infinite and eternal, without any beginning ; and that God must always have created as many men and other kinds of creatures, as can possibly be created.

To Paragraph 41.

104. I don't say, that space is an order or situation, which makes things capable of being situated : this would be nonsense. Any one needs only consider my own words, and add them to what I said above, (Numb. 47) in order to show how the mind comes to form to itself an idea of space, and yet that there need not be any real and absolute being answering to that idea, distinct from the mind, and from all relations. I don't say therefore, that space is an order or situation, but an order of situations ; or (an order) according to which, situations are disposed ; and that abstract space is that order of situations, when they are conceived as being possible. Space is therefore something [merely] [1] ideal. But, it seems, the author will not understand me. I have already, in this paper, (Numb. 54,) answered the objection, that order is not capable of quantity.

105. The author objects here, that time cannot be an order of successive things, because the quantity of time may become greater or less, and yet the order of successions continue the same. I answer ; this is not so. For if the time is greater, there will be more successive and like states

---

[1] Clarke's addition.

interposed ; and if it be less, there will be fewer ; seeing there is no vacuum, nor condensation, or penetration, (if I may so speak), in times, any more than in places.

106. 'Tis true, the immensity and eternity of God would subsist, though there were no creatures ; but those attributes would have no dependence either on times or places. If there were no creatures, there would be neither time nor place, and consequently no actual space. The immensity of God is independent upon space, as his eternity is independent upon time. These attributes signify only, [with regard to these two orders of things] that God would be present and co-existent with all the things that should exist. And therefore I don't admit what's here alleged, that if God existed alone, there would be time and space as there is now : whereas then, in my opinion, they would be only in the ideas of God as mere possibilities. The immensity and eternity of God, are things more transcendent,[1] than the duration and extension of creatures ; not only with respect to the greatness, but also to the nature of the things. Those divine attributes do not imply the supposition of things [2] extrinsic to God, such as are actual places and times. These truths have been sufficiently acknowledged by divines and philosophers.

To Paragraph 42.

107. I maintained, that an operation of God, by which he should mend the machine of the material world,[a] tending in its nature (as this author pretends) to lose all its motion, would be a miracle. His answer was ; that it would not be a miraculous operation, because it would be usual, and must frequently happen. I reply'd ; that 'tis not usualness or unusualness, that makes a miracle properly

---

[a] See above, the note on § 13 of Dr. Clarke's Third Reply [Clarke's note].

[1] ' éminent '.

[2] ' n'ont point besoin de choses ', i.e. have no need of things.

so called, or a miracle of the highest sort ; but it's sur-
passing the powers of creatures ; and this is the [general] [1]
opinion of divines and philosophers : and that therefore
the author acknowledges at least, that the thing he introduces, and I disallow, is, according to the received notion,
a miracle of the highest sort, that is, one which surpasses
all created powers : and that this is the very thing which
all men endeavour to avoid in philosophy. He answers
now, that this is appealing from reason to vulgar opinion.
But I reply again, that this vulgar opinion, according to
which we ought in philosophy to avoid, as much as possible,
what surpasses the natures of creatures ; is a very reasonable opinion. Otherwise nothing will be easier than to
account for any thing by bringing in the deity, *Deum ex
machina*, without minding the natures of things.

108. Besides ; the common opinion of divines, ought
not to be looked upon merely as vulgar opinion. A man
should have weighty reasons, before he ventures to contradict it ; and I see no such reasons here.

109. The author seems to depart from his own notion,
according to which a miracle ought to be unusual ; when,
in Paragraph 31, he objects to me, (though without any
ground,) that the pre-established harmony would be a
perpetual miracle. Here, I say, he seems to depart from
his own notion ; unless he had a mind to argue against
me *ad hominem*.

To Paragraph 43.

110. If a miracle differs from what is natural only in
appearance, and with respect to us ; so that we call that
only a miracle, which we seldom see ; there will be no
internal real difference, between a miracle and what is
natural, and at the bottom, every thing will be either
equally natural, or equally miraculous. Will divines like
the former, or philosophers the latter ?

[1] Clarke's addition.

111. Will not this doctrine, moreover, tend to make God the soul of the world ; if all his operations are natural, like those of our souls upon our bodies ? And so God will be a part of nature.

112. In good philosophy, and sound theology, we ought to distinguish between what is explicable by the natures and powers of creatures, and what is explicable only by the powers of the infinite substance. We ought to make an infinite difference between the operation of God, which goes beyond the extent of natural powers ; and the operations of things that follow the law which God has given them, and which he has enabled them to follow by their natural powers, though not without his assistance.

113. This overthrows attractions, properly so called, and other operations inexplicable by the natural powers of creatures ; which kinds of operations, the assertors of them must suppose to be effected by miracles or else have recourse to absurdities, that is, to the occult qualities of the schools ; which some men begin to revive under the specious name of forces ; but they bring us back again into the kingdom of darkness. This is, *inventa fruge, glandibus vesci*.[1]

114. In the time of Mr. Boyle, and other excellent men, who flourished in England under Charles II, [in the early part of his reign] no body would have ventured to publish such chimerical notions. I hope that happy time will return under so good a government as the present [and that minds a little too much distracted by the misfortunes of the times will return to cultivate sound knowledge better]. Mr. Boyle made it his chief business to inculcate, that every thing was done mechanically in natural philosophy. But it is men's misfortune to grow, at last, out of conceit with reason itself, and to be weary of light. Chimeras begin to appear again, and they are pleasing because they have something in them that is

---

[1] ' to feed on acorns when corn has been discovered '. Probably adapted from Cicero, *Orationes*, 31.

wonderful. What has happened in poetry, happens also in the philosophical world. People are grown weary of rational romances, such as were the French *Clelia*, or the German *Aramene* ;[1] and they are become fond again of the tales of fairies.

115. As for the motions of the celestial bodies, and even the formation of plants and animals ; there is nothing in them that looks like a miracle, except their beginning. The organism of animals is a mechanism, which supposes a divine preformation. What follows upon it, is purely natural, and entirely mechanical.

116. Whatever is performed in the body of man, and of every animal, is no less mechanical, than what is performed in a watch. The difference is only such, as ought to be between a machine of divine invention, and the workmanship of such a limited artist as man is.

To Paragraph 44.

117. There is no difficulty among divines, about the miracles of angels. The question is only about the use of that word. It may be said that angels work miracles ; but less properly so called, or of an inferior order. To dispute about this, would be a mere question about a word. It may be said that the angel, who carried Habakkuk through the air,[2] and he who troubled the water of the pool of Bethesda,[3] worked a miracle. But it was not a miracle of the highest order ; for it may be explained by the natural powers of angels, which surpass those of man.

---

[1] *Clélie*—a six-volume novel by M[lle.] de Scudéry (1607–1701), published in 1656 and reprinted several times.

Aramene—Die durchleuchtige Syrerin Aramena, a five-volume novel by Anton Ulrich, Herzog von Braunschweig-Wolfenbüttel (1663–1714), published 1669–73.

[2] In the Apocryphal book *Bel and the Dragon*, vv. 33–42, Habakkuk is described as being carried by an angel to take dinner to Daniel in the lions' den at Babylon.

[3] John v. 2.

To Paragraph 45.

118. I objected, that an attraction, properly so called, or in the scholastic sense, would be an operation at a distance, without any means intervening. The author answers here, that an attraction without any means intervening, would be indeed a contradiction. Very well ! But then what does he mean, when he will have the sun to attract the globe of the earth through an empty space ? Is it God himself that performs it ? [1] But this would be a miracle, if ever there was any. This would surely exceed the powers of creatures.

119. Or, are perhaps some immaterial substances, or some spiritual rays, or some accident without a substance, or some kind of *species intentionalis*, or some other I know not what, the means by which this is pretended to be performed ? Of which sort of things, the author seems to have still a good stock in his head, without explaining himself sufficiently.

120. That means of communication (says he) is invisible, intangible, not mechanical. He might as well have added, inexplicable, unintelligible, precarious, groundless, and unexampled.

121. But it is regular, (says the author,) it is constant, and consequently natural. I answer ; it cannot be regular, without being reasonable ; nor natural, unless it can be explained by the natures of creatures.

122. If the means, which causes an attraction properly so called, be constant, and at the same time inexplicable by the powers of creatures, and yet be true ; it must be a perpetual miracle : and if it is not miraculous, it is false. 'Tis a chimerical thing, a scholastic occult quality.

123. The case would be the same, as in a body going round without receding in the tangent, though nothing that can be explained, hindered it from receding. Which is an instance I have already alleged ; and the author

[1] ' sert de moyen '.

has not thought fit to answer it, because it shows too clearly the difference between what is truly natural on the one side, and a chimerical occult quality of the schools on the other.

To Paragraph 46.

124. All the natural forces of bodies, are subject to mechanical laws ; and all the natural powers of spirits, are subject to moral laws. The former follow the order of efficient causes ; and the latter follow the order of final causes. The former operate without liberty, like a watch ; the latter operate with liberty, though they exactly agree with that machine,[1] which another cause, free and superior, has adapted to them before-hand. I have already spoken of this, above, No. 92.

125. I shall conclude with what the author objected against me at the beginning of this Fourth Reply : to which I have already given an answer above, (Numb. 18, 19, 20.) But I deferred speaking more fully upon that head, to the conclusion of this paper. He pretended, that I have been guilty of a *petitio principii*. But, of what principle, I beseech you ? Would to God, less clear principles had never been laid down. The principle in question, is the principle of the want of a sufficient reason ; in order to any thing's existing, in order to any event's happening, in order to any truth's taking place. Is this a principle, that wants to be proved ? The author granted it, or pretended to grant it, Numb. 2, of his Third Paper ; possibly, because the denial of it would have appeared too unreasonable. But either he has done it only in words, or he contradicts himself, or retracts his concession.

126. I dare say, that without this great principle, one cannot prove the existence of God, nor account for many other important truths.

127. Has not everybody made use of this principle, upon a thousand occasions ? 'Tis true, it has been neglected, out of carelessness, on many occasions : but

[1] ' espèce de montre ', i.e. sort of watch.

that neglect, has been the true cause of chimeras ; such as are (for instance,) an absolute real time or space, a vacuum, atoms, attraction in the scholastic sense, a physical influence of the soul over the body, [and of the body over the soul] and a thousand other fictions, either derived from erroneous opinions of the ancients, or lately invented by modern philosophers.

128. Was it not upon account of Epicurus's violating this great principle, that the ancients derided his groundless declination of atoms ? And I dare say, the scholastic attraction, revived in our days, and no less derided about thirty years ago, is not at all more reasonable.

129. I have often defied people to allege an instance against that great principle, to bring any one uncontested example wherein it fails. But they have never done it, nor ever will. 'Tis certain, there is an infinite number of instances, wherein it succeeds [or rather it succeeds] in all the known cases in which it has been made use of. From whence one may reasonably judge, that it will succeed also in unknown cases, or in such cases as can only by its means become known : according to the method of experimental philosophy, which proceeds *a posteriori* ; though the principle were not perhaps otherwise justified by bare reason, or *a priori*.

130. To deny this great principle, is likewise to do as Epicurus did ; who was reduced to deny that other great principle, viz. the principle of contradiction ; which is, that every intelligible enunciation must be either true, or false. Chrysippus [1] undertook to prove that principle against Epicurus ; but I think I need not imitate him. I have already said, what is sufficient to justify mine : and I might say something more upon it ; but perhaps it would be too abstruse for this present dispute. And I believe, reasonable and impartial men will grant me, that having

[1] Chrysippus (*c.* 280–206 B.C.), third leader of the Stoic school, and one of the most eminent Greek logicians. The reference here is to Cicero, *De Fato*, X.

forced an adversary to deny that principle, is reducing him *ad absurdum.*

DR. CLARKE'S FIFTH REPLY [1]

As multitudes of words are neither an argument of clear ideas in the writer, nor a proper means of conveying clear notions to the reader ; I shall endeavour to give a distinct answer to this Fifth Paper, as briefly as I can.

1–20. There is no (§ 3) similitude between a balance being moved by weights or impulse, and a mind moving itself, or acting upon the view of certain motives. The difference is, that the one is entirely passive ; which is being subject to absolute necessity : the other not only is acted upon, but acts also ; which is the essence of liberty. To (§ 14) suppose that an equal apparent goodness in different ways of acting, takes away from the mind all power of acting at all, as an equality of weights keeps a balance necessarily at rest ; is denying the mind to have in itself a principle of action ; and is confounding the power of acting, with the impression made upon the mind by the motive, wherein the mind is purely passive. The motive, or thing considered as in view, is something extrinsic to the mind : the impression made upon the mind by that motive, is the perceptive quality, in which the mind is passive : the doing of any thing, upon and after, or in consequence of, that perception ; this is the power of self-motion or action : which in all animate agents, is spontaneity ; and, in moral agents, is what we properly call liberty. The not carefully distinguishing these things, but confounding (§ 15) the motive with the principle of action, and denying the mind to have any principle of action besides the motive, (when indeed in receiving the impression of the motive, the mind is purely passive ;) this, I say,

[1] Transmitted 29th Oct. 1716 (p. 198). Leibniz died 14th Nov. 1716.

is the ground of the whole error ; and leads men to think that the mind is no more active, than a balance would be with the addition of a power of perception : which is wholly taking away the very notion of liberty. A balance pushed on both sides with equal force, or pressed on both sides with equal weights, cannot move at all : and supposing the balance endued with a power of perception, so as to be sensible of its own incapacity to move ; or so as to deceive itself with an imagination that it moves itself, when indeed it is only moved ; it would be exactly in the same state, wherein this learned author supposes a free agent to be in all cases of absolute indifference. But the fallacy plainly lies here : the balance, for want of having in itself a principle or power of action, cannot move at all when the weights are equal : but a free agent, when there appear two, or more, perfectly alike reasonable ways of acting, has still within itself, by virtue of its self-motive principle, a power of acting : and it may have very strong and good reasons, not to forbear acting at all ; when yet there may be no possible reason to determine one particular way of doing the thing, to be better than another. To affirm therefore, (§ 16–19, 69) that supposing two different ways of placing certain particles of matter were equally good and reasonable, God could neither wisely nor possibly place them in either of those ways, for want of a sufficient weight to determine him which way he should choose ; is making God not an active, but a passive being : which is, not to be a God, or governor, at all. And for denying the possibility of the supposition, that there may be two equal parts of matter, which may with equal fitness be transposed in situation ; no other reason can be alleged, but this (§ 20) *petitio principii*, that then this learned writer's notion of a sufficient reason would not be well-grounded. For otherwise, how can any man say, that 'tis (§ 16, 17, 69, 66) impossible for God to have wise and good reasons to create many particles of matter exactly alike in different parts of the universe ? In which case, the parts of space being alike, 'tis evident there can be no reason, but mere will, for not having originally transposed their situations. And yet even this cannot be reasonably said to be a (§ 16, 69) will without motive ; for as much as the wise reasons God may possibly have to create many particles of matter exactly alike, must consequently be a motive to him to take (what a balance could not do,) one out of two absolutely indifferents ; that is, to place them in one situation, when the transposing of them could not but have been exactly alike good.

Necessity, in philosophical questions, always signifies absolute necessity, (§ 4–13). *Hypothetical necessity,*[a] and *moral necessity,* are only figurative ways of speaking, and in philosophical strictness of truth, are no necessity at all. The question is not, whether a thing must be, when it is supposed that it is, or that it is to be ; (which is hypothetical necessity :) neither is it the question whether it be true that a good being, continuing to be good, cannot do evil ; or a wise being, continuing to be wise, cannot act unwisely ; or a veracious person, continuing to be veracious, cannot tell a lie ; (which is moral necessity :) but the true and only question in philosophy concerning liberty, is, whether the immediate physical cause or principle of action be indeed in him whom we call the agent ; or whether it be some other reason sufficient, which is the real cause of the action, by operating upon the agent, and making him to be, not indeed an agent, but a mere patient.

It may here be observed, by the way ; that this learned author contradicts his own hypothesis, when he says, that (§ 11) the will does not always precisely follow the practical understanding, because it may sometimes find reasons to suspend its resolution. For are not those very reasons, the last judgment of the practical understanding ?

21–25. If it is possible for God to make or to have made two pieces of matter exactly alike, so that the transposing in situation would be perfectly indifferent ; this learned

[a] See my Sermons at Mr. Boyle's Lecture, Part I, p. 106, Edit. 4 [*Works,* II, p. 566].

author's notion of a sufficient reason falls to the ground.
To this he answers ; not, (as his argument requires,) that
'tis impossible for God to make two pieces exactly alike ; [a]
but, that 'tis not wise for him to do so. But how does he
know, it would not be wise for God to do so ? Can he
prove that it is not possible God may have wise reasons
for creating many parts of matter exactly alike in different
parts of the universe ? The only argument he alleges, is
that then there would not be a sufficient reason to determine
the will of God, which piece should be placed in which
situation. But if, for ought that any otherwise appears to
the contrary, God may possibly have many wise reasons for
creating many pieces exactly alike ; will the indifference
alone of the situation of such pieces, make it impossible
that he should create, or impossible that it should be wise
in him to create them ? I humbly conceive, this is an
(§ 20) express begging of the question. To the like argument drawn by me from the absolute indifference of the
original particular determination of motion, no answer has
been returned.

26-32. In these articles, there seem to be contained
many contradictions. It is allowed (§ 26) that two things
exactly alike, would really be two ; and yet it is still
alleged, that they would want the *principle of individuation* ;
and in Paper 4th, Paragraph 6, it was expressly affirmed,
that they would be only the same thing under two names.
A (§ 26) supposition is allowed to be possible, and yet I
must not be allowed to make the supposition. The (§ 27)
parts of time and space are allowed to be exactly alike in
themselves, but not so when bodies exist in them. Different
co-existent parts of space, and different successive parts of
time, are (§ 28) compared to a straight line cutting another
straight line in two coincident points, which are but one
point only. 'Tis affirmed, that (§ 29) space is nothing but
the order of things co-existing ; and yet it is (§ 30) confessed
that the material universe may possibly be finite ; in which

---

[a] See Mr. Leibnitz's Fourth Paper, §2, 3, 6, 13, 15.

case there must necessarily be an empty extra-mundane space. 'Tis (§ 30, 8, 73) allowed, that God could make the material universe finite : and yet the supposing it to be possibly finite, is styled not only a supposition unreasonable and void of design, but also an (§ 29) impracticable fiction ; and 'tis affirmed, there can be no possible reason which can limit the quantity of matter.[a] 'Tis affirmed, that the motion of the material universe would produce (§ 29) no change at all ; and yet no answer is given to the argument I alleged, that a sudden increase or stoppage of the motion of the whole, would give a sensible shock to all the parts : and 'tis as evident, that a circular motion of the whole, would produce a *vis centrifuga* in all the parts. My argument, that the material world must be moveable, if the whole be finite ; is (§ 31) denied, because the parts of space are immoveable, of which the whole is infinite and necessarily existing. It is affirmed, that motion necessarily implies a (§ 31) relative change of situation in one body, with regard to other bodies : and yet no way is shown to avoid this absurd consequence, that then the mobility of one body depends on the existence of other bodies ; and that any single body existing alone, would be incapable of motion ; or that the parts of a circulating body, (suppose the sun,) would lose the *vis centrifuga* arising from their circular motion, if all the extrinsic matter around them were annihilated. Lastly, 'tis affirmed that the (§ 32) infinity of matter is an effect of the will of God ; and yet Cartesius's notion is (ibid.) approved as irrefragable ; the only foundation of which, all men know to have been this supposition, that matter was infinite necessarily in the nature of things, it being a contradiction to suppose it finite : his words are, *puto implicare contradictionem, ut mundus sit finitus.*[b] Which if it be true, it never was in the power of

---

[a] Fourth Paper, § 21.

[b] Epist. 69, Partis primae. [*Letter to Henry More*, 15/4/1649, Clersélier, I, 69, Adam & Tannery, V, p. 345, i.e. ' I think it implies a contradiction that the world should be finite.']

God to determine the quantity of matter ; and consequently he neither was the creator of it, nor can destroy it.

And indeed there seems to run a continual inconsistency through the whole of what this learned author writes concerning matter and space. For sometimes he argues against a vacuum (or space void of matter,) as if it was (§ 29, 33-5, 62-3) absolutely impossible in the nature of things ; space and matter being (§ 62) inseparable : and yet frequently he allows the quantity of matter in the universe, to depend upon the (§ 30, 32, 73) will of God.

33-35. To the argument drawn against a plenum of matter, from the want of resistance in certain spaces ; this learned author answers, that those spaces are filled with a matter which has no (§ 35) gravity. But the argument was not drawn from gravity, but from resistance ; which must be proportionable to the quantity of matter, whether the matter had any gravity or no.[a]

To obviate this reply, he alleges that (§ 34) resistance does not arise so much from the quantity of matter, as from its difficulty of giving place. But this allegation is wholly wide of the purpose ; because the question related only to such fluid bodies which have little or no tenacity, as water and quicksilver, whose parts have no other difficulty of giving place, but what arises from the quantity of the matter they contain. The instance of a (ibid.) floating piece of wood, containing less of heavy matter than an equal bulk of water, and yet making greater resistance ; is wonderfully unphilosophical : for an equal bulk of water shut up in a vessel, or frozen into ice, and floating, makes a greater resistance than the floating wood ; the resistance then arising from the whole bulk of the water : but when the water is loose and at liberty in its state of fluidity, the resistance is then not made by the whole, but by part only, of the equal bulk of water ; and then it is no wonder that it seems to make less resistance than the wood.

[a] Otherwise, what makes the body of the earth more difficult to be moved (even the same way that its gravity tends) than the smallest ball ?

36–48. These paragraphs do not seem to contain serious arguments, but only represent in an ill light the notion of the immensity or omnipresence of God ; who is not a mere *intelligentia supramundana*, (semota a nostris rebus sejunct-aque longe ;) *is not far from every one of us ; for in him we* (and all things) *live and move and have our being.*[a]

The space occupied by a body, is not the (§ 36–7) extension of the body ; but the extended body exists in that space.

There is no such thing in reality, as (§ 38) bounded space ; but only we in our imagination fix our attention upon what part or quantity we please, of that which itself is always and necessarily unbounded.

Space is not an (§ 39) affection of one body, or of another body, or of any finite being ; nor passes from subject to subject ; but is always invariably the immensity of one only and always the same *immensum.*

Finite spaces are not at all the (§ 40) affections of finite substances ; but they are only those parts of infinite space, in which finite substances exist.

If matter was infinite, yet infinite space would no more be an (§ 41) affection of that infinite body, than finite spaces are the affections of finite bodies ; but, in that case, the infinite matter would be, as finite bodies now are, in the infinite space.

Immensity, as well as eternity, is (§ 42) essential to God. The parts of immensity [b] (being totally of a different kind from corporeal, partable, separable, divisible, moveable parts which are the ground of corruptibility ;) do no more hinder immensity from being essentially one, than the parts of duration hinder eternity from being essentially one.

God himself suffers no (§ 43) change at all, by the variety and changeableness of things which live and move and have their being in him.

This (§ 44) strange doctrine, is the express assertion

[a] Acts xvii. 27, 28.
[b] See above in my Third Reply, § 3 ; and Fourth Reply, § 11.

of St. Paul,[a] as well as the plain voice of nature and reason.

God does not exist (§ 45) in space, and in time ; but his existence [b] causes space and time. And when, according to the analogy of vulgar speech, we say that he exists in all space and in all time ; the words mean only that he is omnipresent and eternal, that is, that boundless space and time are necessary consequences of his existence ; and not, that space and time are beings distinct from him, and IN which he exists.

(§ 46) How [1] finite space is not the extension of bodies, I have shown just above, on Paragraph 40. And the two following paragraphs also, (Paragraphs 47 and 48), need only to be compared with what hath been already said.

49–51. These seem to me, to be only a quibbling upon words. Concerning the question about space having parts, see above ; Reply 3, Paragraph 3 ; and Reply 4, Paragraph 11.

52, and 53. My argument here, for the notion of space being really independent upon body, is founded on the possibility of the material universe being finite and moveable : 'tis not enough therefore for this learned writer to reply, that he thinks it would not have been wise and reasonable for God to have made the material universe finite and moveable. He must either affirm, that 'twas impossible for God to make the material world finite and moveable ; or else he must of necessity allow the strength of my argument, drawn from the possibility of the world's being finite and moveable. Neither is it sufficient barely to repeat his assertion, that the motion of a finite material universe would be nothing, and (for want of other bodies to compare it with) would (§ 52) produce no discoverable

---

[a] Acts xvii. 27, 28.
[b] See above, the note on my Fourth Reply, § 10.

---

[1] There occurs at this point a long footnote on the nature of space, which in this edition is printed at the end of this paper (p. 120 below).

change : unless he could disprove the instance which I gave of a very great change that would happen ; viz. that the parts would be sensibly shocked by a sudden acceleration, or stopping of the motion of the whole : to which instance, he has not attempted to give any answer.

53. Whether this learned author's being forced here to acknowledge the difference between absolute real motion and relative motion, does not necessarily infer that space is really a quite different thing from the situation or order of bodies ; I leave to the judgment of those who shall be pleased to compare what this learned writer here alleges, with what Sir Isaac Newton has said in his *Principia*, Lib. 1, Defin. 8.[1]

54. I had alleged that time and space were QUANTITIES, which situation and order were not. To this, it is replied ; that *order has its quantity ; there is that which goes before, and that which follows ; there is distance or interval.* I answer : going before, and following, constitutes situation or order : but the distance, interval, or quantity of time or space, wherein one thing follows another, is entirely a distinct thing from the situation or order, and does not constitute any quantity of situation or order : the situation or order may be the same, when the quantity of time or space intervening is very different. This learned author further replies, that ratios or proportions, (§ 54) have their quantity ; and therefore so may time and space, though they be nothing but relations. I answer 1st ; if it had been true, that some particular sorts of relations, such as ratios or proportions were quantities ; yet it would not have followed, that situation and order, which are relations of a quite different kind, would have been quantities too. But 2dly ; proportions are not quantities, but the proportions of quantities. If they were quantities, they would be the quantities of quantities ; which is absurd. Also, if they were quantities, they would (like all other quantities) increase always by addition : but the addition of the proportion of

[1] pp. 150–160 below.

1 to 1, to the proportion of 1 to 1, makes still no more than the proportion of 1 to 1 ; and the addition of the proportion of half to 1, to the proportion of 1 to 1, does not make the proportion of 1 and a half to 1, but the proportion only of half to 1. That which mathematicians sometimes inaccurately call the quantity of proportion, is (accurately and strictly speaking), only the quantity of the relative or comparative magnitude of one thing with regard to another : and proportion is not the comparative magnitude itself, but the comparison or relation of the magnitude to another. The proportion of 6 to 1, with regard to that of 3 to 1, is not a double quantity of proportion, but the proportion of a double quantity. And in general, what they call bearing a greater or less proportion, is not bearing a greater or less quantity of proportion or relation, but, bearing the proportion or relation of a greater or less quantity to another : 'tis not a greater or less quantity of comparison, but the comparison of a greater or less quantity. The (§ 54) logarithmic expression of a proportion, is not (as this learned author styles it) a measure, but only an artificial index or sign of proportion : 'tis not the expressing a quantity of proportion, but barely a denoting the number of times that any proportion is repeated or complicated. The logarithm of the proportion of equality, is 0 ; and yet 'tis as real and as much a proportion, as any other : and when the logarithm is negative, as $\bar{1}$; yet the proportion of which it is the sign or index, is itself affirmative. Duplicate or triplicate proportion, does not denote a double or triple quantity of proportion, but the number of times that the proportion is repeated. The tripling of any magnitude or quantity once, produces a magnitude or quantity, which to the former bears the proportion of 3 to 1. The tripling it a second time, produces (not a double quantity of proportion, but a magnitude or quantity, which to the former bears the proportion (called duplicate) of 9 to 1. The tripling it a third time, produces (not a triple quantity of proportion, but) a

magnitude or quantity, which to the former bears the proportion (called triplicate) of 27 to 1 : and so on.   3dly, time and space are not of the nature of proportions at all, but of the nature of absolute quantities to which proportions belong. As for example : the proportion of 12 to 1, is a much greater proportion, (that is, as I now observed, not a greater quantity of proportion, but the proportion of a greater comparative quantity,) than that of 2 to 1 ; and yet one and the same unvaried quantity, may to one thing bear the proportion of 12 to 1, and to another thing at the same time the proportion of 2 to 1. Thus the space of a day, bears a much greater proportion to an hour, than it does to half a day ; and yet it remains, notwithstanding both the proportions, the same unvaried quantity of time.   Time therefore, (and space likewise by the same argument,) is not of the nature of a proportion, but of an absolute and unvaried quantity, to which different proportions belong.   Unless this reasoning can be shown to be false, our learned author's opinion still remains, by his own confession,[a] a contradiction.

55–63. All this, seems to me to be a plain contradiction ; and I am willing to leave it to the judgment of the learned. In one paragraph (§ 56), there is a plain and distinct supposition, that the universe might be created as much sooner or later as God pleased.   In the rest (§ 55, 57–63), the very terms (sooner or later) are treated as unintelligible terms and impossible suppositions.[b]   And the like, concerning the space in which matter subsists ; see above, on Paragraphs 26–32.

64 and 65. See above upon Paragraph 54.

66–70. See above, on Paragraphs 1–20 ; and on Paragraphs 21–25.   I shall here only add, that (§ 70) comparing the will of God, when it chooses one out of many equally good ways of acting, to Epicurus's chance, who allowed no will, no intelligence, no active principle at all in the formation of the universe ; is comparing together two

[a] Fourth Paper, § 16.   [b] Fourth Paper, § 15.

things, than which no two things can possibly be more different.

71. See above, on Paragraphs 21-25.

72. See above, on Paragraphs 1-20.

73-75. In the consideration whether space be independent upon matter, and whether the material universe can be finite and moveable, (see above, on Paragraphs 1-20, and on 26-32 ;) the question is not concerning the wisdom or (§ 73) will of God, but concerning the absolute and necessary nature of things. If the material universe CAN possibly, by the will of God, be finite and moveable ; (which this learned author here finds himself necessitated to grant, though he perpetually treats it as an impossible supposition ;) then space, (in which that motion is performed,) is manifestly independent upon matter. But if, on the contrary, the material universe cannot be finite and moveable,[a] and space cannot be independent upon matter ; then (I say) it follows evidently, that God neither can nor ever could set bounds to matter ; and consequently the material universe must be not only boundless, but (§ 74) eternal also, both *a parte ante* and *a parte post*, necessarily and independently on the will of God. For, the opinion of those who contend, that the world (§ 75) might possibly be eternal, by the will of God exercising his eternal power ; this has no relation at all, to the matter at present in question.

76 and 77. See above, on Paragraphs 73-75 ; and on Paragraphs 1-20, and below, on Paragraph 103.

78. This paragraph contains no new objection. The aptness and intelligibleness of the similitude made use of by Sir Isaac Newton, and here excepted against, has been abundantly explained in the foregoing Papers.

79-82. All that is objected in the (§ 79, 80) two former of these paragraphs, is a mere quibbling upon words. The existence of God, (as has often been already observed,) causes space ; and in that space, all other things exist. It

[a] Fourth Paper, § 21, and Fifth Paper, § 29.

is therefore (§ 80) the place of ideas likewise ; because it is the place of the substances themselves, in whose under- standings ideas exist.

The soul of man being (§ 81) the soul of the images of the things which it perceives, was alleged by me, in way of comparison, as an instance of a ridiculous notion : and this learned writer pleasantly argues against it, as if I had affirmed it to be my own opinion.

God perceives every thing, not (§ 82) by means of any organ, but by being himself actually present everywhere. This everywhere therefore, or universal space, is the place of his perception. The notion of *sensorium*, and of the soul of the world, has been abundantly explained before. 'Tis too much to desire to have the conclusion given up, without bringing any further objection against the premises.

83–88 : and 89–91. That (§ 83) the soul is a *repre- sentative principle* ; that (§ 87) *every simple substance is by its nature a concentration and living mirror of the whole universe* ; that (§ 91) *it is a representation of the universe, according to its point of view* ; and that *all simple substances will always have a harmony between themselves, because they always represent the same universe* : all this, I acknowledge, I understand not at all.

Concerning the (§ 83, 87, 89, 90) *harmonia praestabilita*, by which the affections of the soul, and the mechanic motions of the body, are affirmed to agree, without at all influencing each other ; see below, on Paragraphs 110–116.

That the images of things are conveyed by the organs of sense into the sensory, where the soul perceives them ; is affirmed, but not proved, to be an (§ 84) unintelligible notion.

Concerning (§ 84) immaterial substance affecting, or being affected by, material substance ; see below, on Paragraphs 110–116.

That God (§ 85) perceives and knows all things, not by being present to them, but by continually producing them anew ; is a mere fiction of the schoolmen, without any proof.

The objection concerning God's being (§ 86–88, 82) the soul of the world, has been abundantly answered above ; Reply II, Paragraph 12 ; and Reply IV, Paragraph 32.

92. To suppose, that all the motions of our bodies are necessary, and caused entirely (§ 92, 95, 116) by mere mechanical impulses of matter, altogether independent on the soul ; is what (I cannot but think) tends to introduce necessity and fate. It tends to make men be thought as mere machines, as Descartes imagined beasts to be ; by taking away all arguments drawn from phenomena, that is, from the actions of men, to prove that there is any soul, or any thing more than mere matter in men at all. See below, on Paragraphs 110–116.

93–95. I alleged, that every action is the giving of a new force to the thing acted upon. To this it is objected, that two equal hard bodies striking each other, return with the same force ; and that therefore their action upon each other, gives no new force. It might be sufficient to reply, that the bodies do neither of them return with their own force, but each of them loses its own force, and each returns with a new force impressed by the other's elasticity : for if they are not elastic, they return not at all. But indeed, all mere mechanical communications of motion, are not properly action, but mere passiveness, both in the bodies that impel, and that are impelled. Action, is the beginning of a motion where there was none before, from a principle of life or activity : and if God or man, or any living or active power, ever influences any thing in the material world ; and every thing be not mere absolute mechanism ; there must be a continual increase and decrease of the whole quantity of motion in the universe. Which this learned gentleman [1] frequently denies.

96 and 97. Here this learned author refers only to what he has said elsewhere : and I also am willing to do the same.

---

[1] There occurs at this point a very long footnote on the question of force ; in this edition this note is printed at the end of this paper (pp. 121–125 below).

98. If the soul be a substance which fills the sensorium, or place wherein it perceives the images of things conveyed to it ; yet it does not thence follow, that it must consist of corporeal parts, (for the parts of body are distinct substances independent on each other ;) but the whole soul sees, and the whole hears, and the whole thinks, as being essentially one individual.

99. In order to show that the *active forces* in the world (meaning the quantity of motion or impulsive force given to bodies,) do not naturally diminish ; this learned writer urges, that two soft un-elastic bodies meeting together with equal and contrary forces, do for this only reason lose each of them the motion of their whole, because it is communicated and dispersed into a motion of their small parts. But the question is ; when two perfectly HARD un-elastic bodies lose their whole motion by meeting together, what then becomes of the motion or active impulsive force ? It cannot be dispersed among the parts, because the parts are capable of no tremulous motion for want of elasticity. And if it be denied, that the bodies would lose the motion of their wholes ; I answer : then it would follow, that elastic hard bodies would reflect with a double force ; viz. the force arising from the elasticity, and moreover all (or at least part of) the original direct force : which is contrary to experience.

At length, (upon the demonstration I cited from Sir Isaac Newton,) he is obliged to (§ 99) allow, that the quantity of motion in the world, is not always the same ; and goes to another refuge, that motion and force are not always the same in quantity. But this is also contrary to experience. For the force here spoken of, is not the *vis inertiae* [a] of matter, (which continues indeed always the same,

---

[a] The *vis inertiae* of matter, is that passive force, by which it always continues of itself in the state 'tis in ; and never changes that state, but in proportion to a contrary power acting upon it. 'Tis that passive force, not by which (as Mr. Leibnitz from Kepler understands it,) matter resists motion ; but by which it equally resists any change from

so long as the quantity of matter continues the same :) but the force here meant, is relative active impulsive force ; which is always proportional to the quantity of relative motion [a] : as is constantly evident in experience ; except where some error has been committed, in not rightly computing and subducting the contrary or impeding force, which arises from the resistance of fluids to bodies moved any way, and from the continual contrary action of gravitation upon bodies thrown upwards.

100–102. That active force, in the sense above-defined, does naturally diminish continually in the material universe ; hath been shown in the last paragraph. That this is no defect, is evident ; because 'tis only a consequence of matter being lifeless, void of motivity, unactive and inert. For the inertia of matter, causeth, not only (as this learned author observes,) that velocity decreases in proportion as quantity of matter increases, (which is indeed no decrease of the quantity of motion ;) but also that solid and perfectly hard bodies, void of elasticity, meeting together with equal and contrary forces, lose their whole motion and active force, (as has been shown above,) and must depend upon some other cause for new motion.

the state 'tis in, either of rest or motion : so that the very same force, which is requisite to give any certain velocity to any certain quantity of matter at rest, is always exactly requisite to reduce the same quantity of matter from the same degree of velocity to a state of rest again. This *vis inertiae* is always proportional to the quantity of matter ; and therefore continues invariably the same, in all possible states of matter, whether at rest or in motion ; and is never transferred from one body to another. Without this *vis*, the least force would give any velocity to the greatest quantity of matter at rest ; and the greatest quantity of matter in any velocity of motion, would be stopped by the least force, without any the least shock at all. So that, properly and indeed, all force in matter either at rest or in motion, all its action and reaction, all impulse and all resistance, is nothing but this *vis inertiae* in different circumstances.

[a] That is ; proportional to the quantity of matter and the velocity ; not (as Mr. Leibnitz affirms, *Acta Erudit.* ad Ann 1695, pag. 156,) to the quantity of matter and the square of the velocity. See above, the Note on Paragraphs 93–95.

103. That none of the things here referred to are defects ; I have largely shown in my former papers. For why was not God at liberty to make a world, that should continue in its present form as long or as short a time as he thought fit, and should then be altered (by such changes as may be very wise and fit, and yet impossible perhaps to be performed by mechanism,) into whatever other form he himself pleased ? Whether my inference from this learned author's affirming *a* that the universe cannot diminish in perfection, that there is no possible reason which can limit the quantity of matter, that God's perfections oblige him to produce always as much matter as he can, and that a finite material universe is an impracticable fiction *b* ; whether (I say) my inferring, that (according to these notions) the world must needs have been both infinite and eternal, be a just inference or no, I am willing to leave to the learned, who shall compare the papers, to judge.

104–106. We are now told, that (§ 104) space is not an order or situation but an order of situations. But still the objection remains ; that an order of situations is not quantity, as space is. He refers therefore to Paragraph 54, where he thinks he has proved that order is a quantity : and I refer to what I have said above in this paper, upon that section ; where I think I have proved, that it is not a quantity. What he alleges concerning (§ 105) time likewise, amounts plainly to the following absurdity : that time is only the order of things successive, and yet is truly a quantity ; because it is, not only the order of things successive, but also the quantity of duration intervening between each of the particulars succeeding in that order. Which is an express contradiction.

To say that (§ 106) *immensity* does not signify boundless space, and that *eternity* does not signify duration or time without beginning and end, is (I think) affirming that words have no meaning. Instead of reasoning upon this

---

a Fourth Paper, § 40, 20, 21, 22, and Fifth Paper, § 29.
b See above, Mr. Leibnitz's postscript to his Fourth Paper.

point, we are referred to what certain divines and philosophers (that is, such as were of this learned author's
opinion,) have acknowledged : which is not the matter in
question.

107–109. I affirmed, that, with regard to God, no one
possible thing is more miraculous than another ; and that
therefore a miracle does not consist in any difficulty in the
nature of the thing to be done, but merely in the unusualness of God's doing it. The terms, *nature*, and *powers of
nature*, and *course of nature*, and the like, are nothing but
empty words ; and signify merely, that a thing usually or
frequently comes to pass. The raising of a human body
out of the dust of the earth, we call a miracle ; the generation of a human body in the ordinary way, we call natural ;
for no other reason, but because the power of God effects
one usually, the other unusually. The sudden stopping of
the sun (or earth,) we call a miracle ; the continual motion
of the sun (or earth,) we call natural ; for the very same
reason only, of the one's being usual and the other unusual.
Did man usually arise out of the grave, as corn grows out
of seed sown, we should certainly call that also natural ;
and did the sun (or earth,) constantly stand still, we should
then think that to be natural, and its motion at any time
would be miraculous. Against these evident reasons, (*ces*
(§ 108) *grandes raisons*) this learned writer offers nothing at
all ; but continues barely to refer us to the vulgar forms of
speaking of certain philosophers and divines : which (as
I before observed) is not the matter in question.

110–116. It is here very surprising, that, in a point of
reason and not of authority, we are still again (§ 110)
remitted to the opinions of certain philosophers and divines.
But, to omit this : what does this learned writer mean by
a (§ 110) *real internal difference* between what is miraculous,
and not miraculous ; or between (§ 111) operations natural,
and not natural ; absolutely, and with regard to God ?
Does he think there are in God two different and really
distinct principles or powers of acting, and that one thing

is more difficult to God than another ?   If not : then either a *natural* and a *super-natural action* of God, are terms whose signification is only relative to us ; we calling an usual effect of God's power, *natural* ; and an unusual one, *super-natural* ; the (§ 112) *force of nature* being, in truth, nothing but an empty word : or else, by the one must be meant that which God does immediately himself ; and by the other, that which he does mediately by the instrumentality of second causes.   The former of these distinctions, is what this learned author is here professedly opposing : the latter is what he expressly disclaims, (§ 117) where he allows that angels may work true miracles.   And yet besides these two, I think no other distinction can possibly be imagined.

It is very unreasonable to call (§ 113) attraction a miracle, and an unphilosophical term ; after it has been so often distinctly declared [1] that by that term we do not mean to express the cause of bodies tending towards each other, but barely the effect, or the phenomenon itself, and the laws or proportions of that tendency discovered by experience ; whatever be or be not the cause of it.   And it seems still more unreasonable, not to admit gravitation or attraction in this sense, in which it is manifestly an actual phenomenon of nature ; and yet at the same time to expect that there should be admitted so strange an hypothesis, as the (§ 109, 92, 87, 89, 90) *harmonia praestabilita* ; which is, that the soul and body of a man have no more influence upon each other's motions and affections, than two clocks, which, at the greatest distance from each other, go alike,

---

[1] Clarke quotes the following passages in Newton, where it is denied that gravity is regarded as an occult quality.

' How these attractions may be performed, I do not here consider . . . attraction is performed ', *Opticks*, Query 31 (p. 174 below).

' These principles I consider not as occult qualities . . . though the causes of these principles were not yet discovered ', Query 31 (printed in 1717 version, pp. 179-180 below).

' Hitherto . . . I frame no hypotheses ', *Principia*, General Scholium (pp. 169-170 below).

without at all affecting each other. It is alleged indeed that God, (§ 92) foreseeing the inclinations of every man's soul, so contrived at first the great machine of the material universe, as that by the mere necessary laws of mechanism, suitable motions should be excited in human bodies, as parts of that great machine. But is it possible, that such kinds of motion, and of such variety, as those in human bodies are ; should be performed by mere mechanisms, without any influence of will and mind upon them ? Or is it credible, that when a man has it in his power to resolve and know a month before-hand, what he will do upon such a particular day or hour to come ; is it credible, I say, that his body shall by the mere power of mechanism, impressed originally upon the material universe at its creation, punctually conform itself to the resolutions of the man's mind at the time appointed ? According to this hypothesis, all arguments in philosophy, taken from phenomena and experiments, are at an end. For, if the *harmonia praestabilita* be true, a man does not indeed see, nor hear, nor feel any thing, nor moves his body ; but only dreams that he sees, and hears, and feels, and moves his body. And if the world can once be persuaded, that a man's body is a mere machine ; and that all his seemingly voluntary motions are performed by the mere necessary laws of corporeal mechanism, without any influence, or operation, or action at all of the soul upon the body ; they will soon conclude, that this machine is the whole man ; and that the harmonical soul, in the hypothesis of an *harmonia praestabilita,* is merely a fiction and a dream. Besides : what difficulty is there avoided, by so strange an hypothesis ? This only ; that it cannot be conceived (it seems) how immaterial substance should act upon matter. But is not God an immaterial substance ? And does not he act upon matter ? And what greater difficulty is there in conceiving how an immaterial substance should act upon matter, than in conceiving how matter acts upon matter ? Is it not as easy to conceive, how certain parts of matter may be obliged to follow the motions and affections of the soul, without corporeal contact ; as that certain portions of matter should be obliged to follow each other's motions by the adhesion of parts, which no mechanism can account for ; or that rays of light should reflect regularly from a surface which they never touch ? [a] Of which, Sir Isaac Newton in his *Opticks* has given us several evident and ocular experiments.

Nor is it less surprising, to find this assertion again repeated in express words, that, after the first creation of things, (§ 115–6) the continuation of the motions of the heavenly bodies, and the formation of plants and animals, and every motion of the bodies both of men and all other animals, is as mechanical as the motions of a clock. Whoever entertains this opinion, is (I think) obliged in reason to be able to explain particularly, by what laws of mechanism the planets and comets can continue to move in the orbs they do, thro' unresisting spaces ; and by what mechanical laws, both plants and animals are formed ; and how the infinitely various spontaneous motions of animals and men, are performed. Which, I am fully persuaded, is as impossible to make out, as it would be to show how a house or city could be built, or the world itself have been at first formed by mere mechanism, without any intelligent and active cause. That things could not be at first produced by mechanism, is expressly allowed : and, when this is once granted ; why, after that, so great concern should be shown, to exclude God's actual government of the world, and to allow his providence to act no further than barely in concurring (as the phrase is) to let all things

[a] See Sir Isaac Newton's *Opticks*, Latin edition, p. 224, English edition, Book 2, page 65.[1]

---

[1] Newton here gives several reasons for his theory that reflection, refraction etc. are caused by a repulsive force acting on the rays of light, cf. Query 1 of the *Opticks*, ' Do not bodies act upon light at a distance and by their action bend its rays, and is not this action (*ceteris paribus*) strongest at the least distance ? '

do only what they would do of themselves by mere mechanism ; and why it should be thought that God is under any obligation or confinement either in nature or wisdom, never to bring about any thing in the universe, but what is possible for a corporeal machine to accomplish by mere mechanic laws, after it is once set a going ; I can no way conceive.

117. This learned author's allowing in this place, that there is greater and less in true miracles, and that angels are capable of working some true miracles ; is perfectly contradictory to that notion of the nature of a miracle,[a] which he has all along pleaded for in these papers.

118–123. That the sun attracts the earth, through the intermediate void space ; that is, that the earth and sun gravitate towards each other, or tend (whatever be the cause of that tendency) towards each other, with a force which is in a direct proportion to their masses, or magnitudes and densities together, and in an inverse duplicate proportion of their distances ; and that the space betwixt them is void, that is, hath nothing in it which sensibly resists the motion of bodies passing transversely through : all this, is nothing but a phenomenon, or actual matter of fact, found by experience. That this phenomenon is not produced (§ 118) *sans moyen*, that is without some cause capable of producing such an effect ; is undoubtedly true. Philosophers therefore may search after and discover that cause, if they can ; be it mechanical, or not mechanical. But if they cannot discover the cause ; is therefore the effect itself, the phenomenon, or the matter of fact discovered by experience, (which is all that is meant by the words attraction and gravitation,) ever the less true ? Or is a manifest quality to be called (§ 122) *occult*, because the immediate efficient cause of it (perhaps) is occult, or not yet discovered ? When a body (§ 123) moves in a circle, without flying off in the tangent ; 'tis certain there is something that hinders it : but if in some cases it be not mechanically

[a] See above, Mr. Leibnitz's Third Paper, § 17.

(§ 123) explicable, or be not yet discovered, what that something is ; does it therefore follow, that the phenomenon itself is false ? This is very singular arguing indeed.

124–130. The phenomenon itself, the attraction, gravitation, or tendency of bodies towards each other, (or whatever other name you please to call it by ;) and the laws, or proportions, of that tendency, are now sufficiently known by observations and experiments. If this or any other learned author can by (§ 124) the laws of mechanism explain these phenomena, he will not only not be contradicted, but will moreover have the abundant thanks of the learned world. But, in the mean time, to (§ 128) compare gravitation, (which is a phenomenon or actual matter of fact,) with Epicurus's declination of atoms, (which, according to his corrupt and atheistical perversion of some more ancient and perhaps better philosophy, was an hypothesis or fiction only, and an impossible one too, in a world where no intelligence was supposed to be present ;) seems to be a very extraordinary method of reasoning.

As to the grand principle of a (§ 125) sufficient reason ; all that this learned writer here adds concerning it, is only by way of affirming and not proving, his conclusion ; and therefore needs no answer. I shall only observe, that the phrase is of an equivocal signification ; and may either be so understood, as to mean necessity only, or so as to include likewise will and choice. That in general there (§ 125) is a sufficient reason why every thing is, which is ; is undoubtedly true, and agreed on all hands. But the question is, whether, in some cases, when it may be highly reasonable to act, yet different possible ways of acting may not possibly be equally reasonable ; and whether, in such cases, the bare will of God be not itself a sufficient reason for acting in this or the other particular manner ; and whether in cases where there are the strongest possible reasons altogether on one side, yet in all intelligent and free agents, the principle of action (in which I think the essence of liberty consists,) be not a distinct thing from the motive or reason which the agent has in his view. All these are constantly denied by this learned writer. And his (§ 20, 25, etc.) laying down his grand principle of a sufficient reason in such a sense as to exclude all these ; and expecting it should be granted him in that sense, without proof ; this is what I call his *petitio principii*, or begging of the question : than which, nothing can be more unphilosophical.

N.B. Mr. Leibnitz was prevented by death, from returning any answer to this last paper.

[*Footnote to* § 36–48]

The principal occasion or reason of the confusion and inconsistencies, which appear in what most writers have advanced concerning the nature of space, seems to be this : that (unless they attend carefully,) men are very apt to neglect that necessary distinction, (without which there can be no clear reasoning,) which ought always to be made between abstracts and concretes, such as are *immensitas* and *immensum* ; and also between ideas and things, such as are the notion (which is within our own mind) of immensity, and the real immensity actually existing without us.

All the conceptions (I think) that ever have been or can be framed concerning space, are these which follow. That it is either absolutely nothing, or a mere idea, or only a relation of one thing to another, or that it is body, or some other substance, or else a property of a substance.

That it is not absolutely nothing, is most evident. For of nothing there is no quantity, no dimensions, no properties. This principle is the first foundation of all science whatsoever ; expressing the only difference between what does, and what does not, exist.

That it is not a mere idea, is likewise most manifest. For no idea of space, can possibly be framed larger than finite ; and yet reason demonstrates that 'tis a contradiction for space itself not to be actually infinite.

That it is not a bare relation of one thing to another, arising from their situation or order among themselves, is no less apparent : because space is a quantity, which relations (such as situation and order) are not ; as I have largely shown below, on Paragraph 54. Also because, if the material universe is, or can possibly be, finite ; there cannot but be, actual or possible, extramundane space : see on Paragraphs 31, 52 and 73.

That space is not body, is also most clear. For then body would be necessarily infinite ; and no space could be void of resistance to motion. Which is contrary to experience.

That space is not any kind of substance, is no less plain. Because infinite space is *immensitas*, not *immensum* ; whereas infinite substance is *immensum* not *immensitas*. Just as duration is not a substance : because infinite duration is *aeternitas*, not *aeternum* ; but infinite substance is *aeternum*, not *aeternitas*.

It remains therefore, by necessary consequence, that space is a property, in like manner as duration is. *Immensitas* is τοῦ *immensi* ; just as *aeternitas* is τοῦ *aeterni*.

[*Footnote to* § 93-95]

There appears a great confusion and inconsistency in Mr. Leibnitz's whole notion of this matter. For the word, *force*, and *active force*, signifies in the present question, the impetus, or relative impulsive force of bodies in motion : see my Third Reply, Paragraph 13. Mr. Leibnitz constantly uses the word in this sense : as when he speaks (Paragraphs 93, 94, 99, and 107, of this last answer,) of bodies not changing their force after reflexion, because they return with the same swiftness: of a body's receiving a new force from another body, which loses as much of its own : of the impossibility, that one body should acquire any new force, without the loss of as much in others : of the new force which the whole material universe would receive, if the soul of man communicated any force to the body : and of active forces continuing always the same in the universe, because the force which un-elastic bodies lose in their whole, is communicated to and dispersed among their small parts. Now this impetus, or relative impulsive active force of bodies in motion, is evidently both in reason and experience, always proportional to the quantity of motion. Therefore, according to Mr. Leibnitz's principles, this impulsive active force being always the same in quantity, the quantity of motion also must of necessity be always the same in the universe. Yet elsewhere, he consistently acknowledges, (Paragraph 99,) that the quantity of motion is not always the same : and in the *Acta Eruditorum ad Ann.* 1686, pag. 161,[1] he endeavours to prove that the quantity of motion in the universe is not always the same, from that very argument, and from that single argument only, (of the quantity of impulsive force being always the same,) which, if it was true, would necessarily infer on the contrary, that the quantity of motion could not but be always the same. The reason of his inconsistency in this matter, was his computing, by a wonderfully unphilosophical error, the quantity of impulsive force in

---

[1] G.M. VI, pp. 117-19. *Brevis Demonstratio erroris memorabilis erroris Cartesii* . . .

an ascending body, from the quantity of its matter and of the space described by it in ascending, without considering the time of its ascending.

He says (*Act Erudit.* 1686, p. 162) :

' I suppose the same force is requisite to raise a body A of one pound weight, to the height of four yards ; which will raise the body B, of four pounds weight, to the height of one yard. This is granted both by the Cartesians, and other philosophers and mathematicians of our times. And from hence it follows, that the body A, by falling from the height of four yards, acquires exactly the same force, as the body B by falling from the height of one yard.'

But in this supposition, Mr. Leibnitz is greatly mistaken. Neither the Cartesians, nor any other philosophers or mathematicians ever grant this, but in such cases only, where the times of ascent or descent are equal. If a pendulum oscillates in a cycloid ; the arch of the cycloid described in ascending, will be as the force with which the pendulous body begins to ascend from the lowest point ; because the times of ascending are equal. And if equal bodies librate upon the arm of a balance, at various distances from the axis of the balance ; the forces of the bodies will be in proportion as the arcs described by them in librating, because they librate in the same time. And if two equal globes lying upon an horizontal plane, be impelled by unequal forces, they will in equal times describe spaces proportioned to the forces impelling them. Or if unequal globes be impelled with equal forces, they will in equal times describe spaces reciprocally proportional to their masses. And in all these cases, if equal bodies be impelled by unequal forces, the forces impressed, the velocities generated, and the spaces described in equal times, will be proportional to one another. And if the bodies be unequal, the velocity of the bigger bodies will be so much less, as the bodies are bigger ; and therefore the motion (arising from the mass and velocity together) will be in all these cases, and in all other cases consequently, proportional to the force imprest. (From whence by the way, it plainly follows, that if there be always the same impulsive force in the world, as Mr. Leibnitz affirms ; there must be always the same motion in the world, contrary to what he affirms.)

But Mr. Leibnitz confounds these cases where the times are equal with the cases where the times are unequal : and chiefly that of bodies rising and falling at the ends of the unequal arms of a balance, (*Acta Erudit. ad. Ann.* 1686, Pag. 162 ; & *ad. Ann.* 1690, Pag. 234 ; & *ad. Ann.* 1691, Pag. 439 ; & *ad. Ann.* 1695, Pag. 155 ;) [1] is by him confounded with that of bodies falling downwards and thrown upwards,

---

[1] G.M. VI, pp. 117-19 ; pp. 193-203, *De Causa Gravitatis* ; pp. 204-211, *De Legibus Naturae* . . . ; p. 234, *Specimen Dynamicum.*

without allowing for the inequality of the time. For a body with one and the same force, and one and the same velocity, will in a longer time describe a greater space ; and therefore the time is to be considered ; and the forces are not to be reckoned proportional to the spaces, unless where the times are equal. Where the times are unequal, the forces of equal bodies are as the spaces applied to the times. And in this, the Cartesians and other philosophers and mathematicians agree ; all of them making the impulsive forces of bodies proportional to their motions, and measuring their motions by their masses and velocities together, and their velocities by the spaces which they describe, applied to the times in which they describe them. If a body thrown upwards does, by doubling its velocity, ascend four times higher in twice the time ; its impulsive force will be increased, not in the proportion of the space described by its ascent, but in the proportion of that space applied to the time ; that is, in the proportion of $\frac{4}{2}$ to $\frac{1}{1}$ or 2 to 1. For if, in this case, the force should be increased in the proportion of 4 to 1 ; and, in oscillating in a cycloid, the same body, with the same velocity doubled, describes only a doubled arc, and its force is therefore only doubled : this body, with one and the same degree of velocity, would have twice as much force when thrown upwards, as when thrown horizontally : which is a plain contradiction. And there is the same contradiction in affirming, that although a body at the end of the unequal arms of a balance, by doubling its velocity, acquires only a double impulsive force, yet, by being thrown upwards with the same doubled velocity, it acquires a quadruple impulsive force ; in this assertion, I say, there is the same contradiction : for equal bodies with equal velocities, cannot have unequal impulsive forces.

Upon the supposition of gravity being uniform, Galileo demonstrated the motion of projectiles in mediums void of resistance ; and his propositions are allowed by all mathematicians, not excepting Mr. Leibnitz himself. Now, supposing the time of a falling body to be divided into equal parts ; since gravity is uniform, and, by being so, acts equally in equal parts of time, it must by its action impress and communicate to the falling body, equal impulsive forces, velocities, and motions, in equal times. And therefore the impulsive force, the velocity, and the motion of the falling body, will increase in proportion to the time of falling. But the space described by the falling body, arises partly from the velocity of the body, and partly from the time of its falling ; and so is in a compound ratio of them both, or as the square of either of them ; and consequently as the square of the impulsive force. And by the same way of arguing, it may be proved, that when a body is thrown upwards with any impulsive force, the height to which it will ascend, will be as the square of that force : and that the force requisite to make the body B, of four pounds weight, rise up one yard, will make the body A, of one pound weight, rise up, (not four yards, as Mr. Leibnitz represents, but) sixteen yards, in quadruple the time. For the gravity of four pounds weight in one part of time, acts as much as the gravity of one pound weight in four parts of time.

But Mr. Herman, in his *Phoronomia*,[1] Pag. 113, (arguing for Mr. Leibnitz against those who hold that the forces acquired by falling bodies are proportional to the times of falling ; or to the velocities acquired,) represents that this is founded upon a false supposition, that bodies thrown upwards receive from the gravity which resists them, an equal number of impulses in equal times. Which is as much as to say, that gravity is not uniform ; and, by consequence, to overthrow the theory of Galileo concerning projectiles, allowed by all geometers. I suppose, he means that the swifter the motion of bodies is upwards, the more numerous are the impulses ; because the bodies meet the (imaginary) gravitating particles. And thus the weight of bodies will be greater when they move upwards, and less when they move downwards. And yet Mr. Leibnitz and Mr. Herman themselves allow, that gravity in equal times generates equal velocities in descending bodies, and takes away equal velocities in ascending bodies ; and therefore is uniform. In its action upon bodies for generating velocity, they allow it to be uniform ; in its action upon them for generating impulsive force, they deny it to be uniform : and so are inconsistent with themselves.

If the force acquired by a body in falling, be as the space described : let the time be divided into equal parts ; and if in the first part of time it gain one part of force, in the two first parts of time it will gain four parts of force, in the three first parts of time it will gain nine parts of force, and so on. And by consequence, in the second part of time it will gain three parts of force, in the third part of time it will gain five parts of force, in the fourth part of time it will gain seven parts of force, and so on. And therefore if the action of gravity for generating these forces, be supposed in the middle of the first part of time, to be of one degree ; it will, in the middle of the second, third, and fourth parts of time, be of three, five, and seven degrees, and so on ; that is, it will be proportional to the time and to the velocity acquired : and, by consequence, in the beginning of the time it will be none at all ; and so the body, for want of gravity, will not fall down. And by the same way of arguing, when a body is thrown upwards, its gravity will decrease as its velocity decreases, and cease when the body ceases to ascend : and then for want of gravity, it will rest in the air, and fall

---

[1] Jacob Hermann (1678–1733) : *Phoronomia, sive de viribus et motibus corporum solidorum et fluidorum libri duo.* Amsterdam, 1716. Although the book is dedicated to Leibniz, Hermann starts by postulating the existence of absolute space and time in the same way as Newton.

down no more. So full of absurdities is the notion of this learned author in this particular.

To decide this question demonstratively ; let two pendulous globes of hardened steel, be suspended by equal radii or threads of equal length ; so that when they hang down and touch each other, the radii or threads may be parallel. Let one of the globes be constantly the same, and be drawn aside from the other to one and the same distance in all the subsequent trials. Let the other be of any bigness, and be drawn aside the contrary way to a distance reciprocally proportional to its weight. Let both of them then be let go at one and the same moment of time, so that they may meet each other at the lowest place of their descent, where they hung before they were drawn aside : and the first globe will always rebound alike from the other. Wherefore the force of the other is always the same, when its velocity is reciprocally proportional to its weight. And by consequence, if its weight remains the same, its force will be proportional to its velocity.

Q.E.D.

THE APPENDIX

being

A Collection of Passages out of Mr. LEIBNITZ'S
Printed Works, which may give Light to many
Parts of the fore-going Papers.

No. 1

[C.I.4, L.II.10, L.II.12, C.II.10, L.III.15] [1]

God, according to my opinion, is an extramundane
Intelligence, as Martianus Capella [2] styles him ; or rather,
a supramundane Intelligence.

Theodicy, pag. 396. [§ 217, G.VI.248]

No. 2

[L.I.4, L.II.1, C.II.9, L.V.87, L.V.91, C.V.83-91]

We must know, that a spontaneity strictly speaking, is
common to us with all simple substances ; and that this,
in an intelligent or free substance, amounts to a dominion
over its own actions. . . . Naturally, every simple substance has perception etc.

Theodicy, pag. 479. [§ 291, G.VI.289]

But active force contains a certain act or [3] efficacy, and
is something of a middle nature between the faculty of
acting and action itself : it involves a *conatus* or endeavour,
and is of itself carried towards action ; and stands in need

[1] These are the paragraphs in the Correspondence to which Clarke,
in the 1717 edition, attached marginal notes referring to this section
of the appendix.

[2] Martianus Capella. A Latin author of the late fifth century,
known as the author of a sort of encyclopaedia written in verse.

[3] Leibniz uses the Greek ' ἐντελέχειαν '.

of no help, but only that the impediment be taken away. This may be illustrated by the examples of a heavy body stretching the string it is hung by, and of a bow bent. For though gravity or elasticity may and ought to be explained mechanically by the motion of aether ; yet the ultimate cause of the motion in matter, is a force impressed at the creation : which is in every part of matter, but, according to the course of nature, is variously limited and restrained by bodies striking against each other. And this active faculty I affirm to be in all substance, and that some action is always arising from it : so that not even corporeal substance, any more than spiritual, ever ceases acting. Which seems not to have been apprehended by those, who have placed the essence of matter in extension alone, or even in impenetrability ; and fancied they could conceive a body absolutely at rest. It will appear also from what I have advanced, that one created substance does not receive from another the active force itself, but only the limits and determination of the endeavour or active faculty already pre-existing in it.

> Acta Erud. Ann. 1694. Pag. 112. [De Prima Philosophiae Emendatione et de Notione substantiae ; G.IV.468–70]

To act, is the characteristic of substances.

> Ibid. ad Ann. 1695. Pag. 145. [Specimen Dynamicum . . . ; G.M.VI.234–46]

Which primitive active power, is of itself in all corporeal substance : for, I think a body absolutely at rest, is inconsistent with the nature of things.

> Ibid. Pag. 146.

Every part of matter is, by its form, continually acting.

> Ibid. Pag. 147.

The active power, which is in the form ; and the inertia, or repugnance to motion, which is in the matter.

> Ibid. Pag. 151.

Though I admit everywhere in bodies, a principle superior to the (common) notion of matter ; a principle active, and (if I may so speak), vital.

Ibid. Pag. 153.

I have elsewhere explained, though it is a thing perhaps not yet well understood by all ; that the very substance of things, consists in the power of acting and being acted upon.

> Ibid. *ad Ann.* 1698. Pag. 432. [De Ipsa Natura, sive de vi insita, actionibus creaturarum ; G.IV.504–16]

So that, not only every thing which acts, is a single substance ; but also every single substance does perpetually act : not excepting even matter itself ; in which there never is any absolute rest.

Ibid.

If we ascribe to our own minds an intrinsic power of producing immanent actions, or (which is the same thing) of acting immanently : 'tis no way unreasonable, nay 'tis very reasonable, to allow that there is the same power in other souls or forms, or (if that be a better expression) in the natures of substances.   Unless a man will imagine, that, in the whole extent of nature within the compass of our knowledge, our own minds are the only things endued with active powers ; or that all power of acting immanently and vitally (if I may so speak,) is connected with understanding.   Which kind of assertions, certainly, are neither founded on any reason ; nor can be maintained, but in opposition to truth.

Ibid. Pag. 433.

Hence we may gather, that there must needs be in corporeal substance an original efficacy, or (as it were) prime recipient [1] of active force : that is, there must be in it a primitive motive power : which being added over and

---

[1] Leibniz uses the Greek ' πρῶτον δεκτικὸν '.

above the extension (or that which is merely geometrical,) and over and above the bulk (or that which is merely material ;) acts indeed continually, but yet is variously modified by the conatus's and impetus's of bodies striking against each other. And this is that substantial principle, which in living substances, is styled soul ; in others, the substantial form.

Ibid. Pag. 434.

The *materia prima* is indeed merely passive, but 'tis not a complete substance. To make it complete substance, there must be moreover a soul, or a form analogous to soul, or an original efficacy,[1] that is, a certain endeavour, or primitive power of acting ; which is an innate law, impressed by the decree of God. Which opinion I think is not different from that of an eminent ingenious gentleman, who has lately maintained,[2] that body consists of matter and spirit ; meaning by the word *spirit*, not (as usually) an intelligent thing, but a soul or form analogous to soul ; and not a simple modification, but a substantial permanent constituent, which I used to call a monad, in which is as it were perception and desire.

Ibid. Pag. 435.

On the contrary, I am rather of opinion, that 'tis neither agreeable to the order, nor beauty, nor reason of things, that there should be a vital principle or power of acting immanently, only in a very small part of matter ; when it would be an argument of greater perfection, for it to be in all matter ; and nothing hinders but that there may everywhere be souls, or at least something analogous to souls ; though souls endued with dominion and understanding, such as are human souls, cannot be everywhere.

Ibid. Pag. 436.

What doth not act, what wants active power, what is

---

[1] ' ἐντελέχειαν τὴν πρώτην '.

[2] Perhaps van Helmont (1618–1698) or Henry More (1614–1687), cf. *New Essays*, I. 1.

void of discernibility, what wants the whole ground and foundation of subsistence ; can no way be a substance.

Ibid. Pag. 439.

See below, No. 11.

No. 3
[L.II.1, C.IV.1–2, L.V.3, L.V.14]

Mr. Bayle has shown at large (in his *Answer to a Provincial*, ch. 139, p. 748 etc.) that a man's soul may be compared to a balance, wherein reasons and inclinations are in the place of weights : and, according to him, the manner of our forming our resolutions may be explained by this hypothesis, that the will of man is like a balance, which stands always unmoved when the weights in both scales are equal, and always turns on one side or the other, in proportion as one scale has more weight in it than the other. A new reason, makes an overpoise of weight. A new idea strikes the mind more vigorously than a foregoing one. The fear of a great pain, determines more strongly than the expectation of a pleasure. When two passions contend against each other, the stronger always remains master of the field, unless the other be assisted either by reason, or by some other passion conspiring with it.

Theodicy, Pag. 514. [§ 324, G.VI.308]

A man has always so much the more difficulty of determining himself, as the opposite reasons draw nearer to an equality : just as we see a balance turn so much the more readily, as the weights in each scale are more different from one another. However, since there are often more than two ways which a man may take ; we may therefore, instead of this similitude of a balance, compare the soul to a force, which has at one and the same time a tendency many ways, but acts on that part only where it finds the greatest ease, or the least resistance. For example : air strongly compressed in a glass-receiver, will break the glass to get out.

It presses upon every part, but at last makes its way where the glass is weakest. Thus the inclinations of the soul, tend towards all apparent goods ; and these are the antecedent volitions : but the consequent volition, which is the last result, determines itself towards that good which affects us the most strongly.

Ibid. Pag. 515. [§ 324–5, G.VI.309]

See below, No. 4 and 9.

No. 4

[C.II.1, L.III.5, C.III.7–8, L.IV.3, L.IV.19, C.IV.1–2,
C.IV.3–4, C.IV.19, L.V.69, C.V.1–20]

There is never any such thing as an indifference *in aequilibrio* ; that is, such an one, where every circumstance is perfectly equal on both sides, so that there is no inclination to one side rather than the other.

Theodicy, Pag. 158. [§ 46, G.VI. 129]

'Tis true, if the case (of the ass standing between two green fields, and equally liking both of them) was possible, we must say he would suffer himself to be starved to death. But at the bottom, the case is impossible to happen ; unless God should order circumstances so on purpose.

Ibid. Pag. 161. [§ 49, G.VI.129]

See above, No. 3 ; and below, No. 9.

No. 5

[L.II.4, L.II.5, L.IV.31, C.IV.31, L.V.83, L.V.87, L.V.92,
C.V.33–9, C.V.110–116]

This is a consequence of my system of a pre-established harmony ; which it may be necessary here to give some account of. The scholastic philosophers were of opinion that the soul and body mutually affected each other by

a natural [1] influence : but since it has been well considered, that *a* thought and extended substance have no
connexion with each other, and are beings that differ *toto
genere* ; many modern philosophers have acknowledged,
that there is no physical communication between the soul
and the body, though a metaphysical communication there
always is, by means of which the soul and the body make
up one *suppositum*, or what we call a person. If there was
any physical communication between them, then the soul
could change the degree of swiftness, and the line of
direction of certain motions in the body ; and, on the other
side, the body could cause a change in the series of
thoughts which are in the soul. But now, such an effect
as this, cannot be deduced from the notion of any thing
we can conceive in the body and soul ; though nothing be
better known to us *b* than the soul, because 'tis intimate to
us, that is, to itself.

Theodicy, Pag. 172. [§ 59, G.VI.135]

I cannot help coming into this notion, that God created
the soul in such a manner at first, as that it produces within
itself, and represents in itself successively, what passes in the
body, and that he has made the body also in such manner,
as that it must of itself do what the soul wills. So that the
laws which make the thoughts of the soul follow each other
successively in the order of final causes, and in the order of
its perceptions arising within itself ; must produce images,
which shall be coincident, and go hand in hand with the
impressions made by bodies upon our organs of sense : and
the laws by which the motions of the body follow each other

---

a The thinking substance, he should have said : for thought, or the
act of thinking is not a substance. [*Clarke's note.*]

b Note. As the eye sees not itself; and if a man had never seen
another's eye, nor the image of his own in a glass, he could never
have had any notion what an eye is : so the soul differs not in its
substance. [*Clarke's note.*]

---

[1] ' physique '.

successively in the order of efficient causes, are likewise coincident and go hand in hand with the thoughts of the soul, in such manner as that these laws of motion make the body act at the same time that the soul wills.

Ibid. Pag. 176. [§ 62, G.VI.137]

Mr. Jaquelot has very well shown in his book concerning the agreement of reason and faith, that this is just as if one who knew before-hand every particular thing that I should order my footman to do to-morrow all the day long, should make a machine to resemble my footman exactly, and punctually to perform all day to-morrow every thing I directed. Which would not at all hinder my freely ordering whatever I pleased, though the actions of my machine-footman had no liberty at all.

Ibid. Pag. 176. [§ 63, G.VI.137]

The true means by which God causes the soul to have a perception of what passes in the body, is this; that he has made the nature of the soul to be representative of bodies, and to be before-hand so constituted, as that the representations which shall arise in it, one following another according to the natural succession of thoughts shall be coincident with such change as happens in bodies.

Ibid. Page. 550. [§ 355, G.VI.326]

See above, No. 2; and below, No. 11.

No. 6

[L.II.12]

In like manner, should it be the will of God, that the organs of human bodies should move conformably to the volitions of the soul, considering those volitions as occasional causes; such a law could not be put in execution, but by perpetual miracles.

Theodicy, Pag. 383. [§ 207, G.VI.241]

See below, No. 8.

No. 7

[C.V.99. Footnote]

Nay rather, matter resists motion, by a certain natural inertia, very properly so styled by Kepler ; so that matter is not indifferent to motion and rest, as is vulgarly supposed ; but needs a greater active force, in proportion to the magnitude of the body, to put it in motion.

Acta Erudit. ad Ann. 1698, Pag. 434.
[G.IV.504–516]

A natural inertia, repugnant to motion.

Ibid.

A certain sluggishness, if I may so speak, that is, a repugnancy to motion.

Acta Erudit. ad Ann. 1695. Pag. 147.
[G.M.VI.234–246]

A sluggishness, or resistance to motion, in matter.

Ibid. Pag. 151.

The experiments of bodies striking against each other, as well as reason, show that twice as much force is required to give the same velocity [a] to a body of the same kind of matter, double in bigness. Which would not be needful, if matter was absolutely indifferent to rest and motion, and had not that natural inertia I spoke of, which gives it a sort of repugnancy to motion.

Theodicy, Pag. 142. [§ 30, G.VI.120]

It might be expected, supposing matter indifferent to motion and rest, that the largest body at rest, might be carried away without any resistance, by the least body in motion. In which case, there would be action without reaction, and an effect greater than its cause.

Ibid. Pag. 538. [§ 347, G.VI.320]

---

[a] Note. The author did not consider, that twice as much force is requisite likewise to stop the same velocity in a body of the same kind of matter, double in bigness. [*Clarke's note.*]

No. 8
[L.III.17, L.V.113]

Wherefore if God made a general law, that bodies should attract each other ; it could not be put in execution, but by perpetual miracles.

Theodicy, Pag. 382. [§ 207, G.VI.241]

See above, No. 6.

No. 9
[L.IV.3, L.IV.19, C.IV.3-4, C.IV.19]

The same may be said concerning perfect wisdom, (which is no less regular than mathematics) ; that if there was not a best among all the worlds that were possible to have been made, God would not have made any at all.

Theodicy, Pag. 116. [§ 8, G.VI.107]

See above, No. 4, and No. 3.

No. 10
[L.IV.13, C.IV.13, L.V.29, L.V.52, C.V.26-32]

If we imagine two perfect spheres concentrical, and perfectly similar both in the whole and in every part, to be enclosed one in the other, so as that there shall not be the least interstice between them ; then, whether the enclosed sphere be supposed to revolve, or to continue at rest ; an angel himself (not to say more) could discover no difference between the state of these globes at different times, nor find any way of discerning whether the enclosed globe continued at rest, or turned about ; or with what law of motion it turned.[1]

Acta Erudit. ad Ann. 1698. Pag. 437.

[G.IV.504-516]

[1] *This passage continues* ' Whence it must be considered as certain . . . that such things are foreign to the nature and order of things and (what is one of my new and more important axioms) that there is nowhere any perfect similarity.'

No. 11

[L.IV.30, C.IV.30, L.V.87, L.V.91, C.V.63–91]

In my doctrine of a pre-established harmony, I show that every single [1] substance, is naturally endued with perception; and that its individuality consists in that perpetual law, which causes its appointed succession of perceptions, arising naturally in order one from another, so as to represent to it its own body, and, by the same means, the whole universe, according to the point of view proper to that single [2] substance; without its needing to receive any physical influence from the body. And the body likewise, on its part, acts correspondingly to the volitions of the soul, by its own proper laws; and consequently does not obey the soul, any otherwise than as those laws are correspondent.

Theodicy, Pag. 479. [§ 291, G.VI.289]

It must also be confessed, that every soul represents to itself the universe, according to its point of view, and by a relation peculiar to it: but there is always a perfect harmony between them.

Ibid. Pag. 552. [§ 357, G.VI.327]

The operation of spiritual machines, that is, of souls, is not mechanical; but it contains eminently, whatever is excellent in mechanism; the motions which appear actually in bodies, being concentrated by representation in the soul, as in an ideal world, which represents the laws of the actual world, and the series of their being put in execution; differing in this from the perfect ideal world which is in God, that most of the perceptions in human souls are but confused. For we must know, that every single [3] substance includes the universe in its indistinct perceptions; [4] and that the succession of these perceptions is regulated by the particular nature of the substance; but yet in a manner which always represents whole universal nature. And

---

[1] 'simple'.   [2] 'simple'.   [3] 'simple'.
[4] 'perceptions confuses ou sentimens'.

every present perception tends towards a new perception ; as every motion, which such perception represents, tends towards a new motion. But 'tis impossible the soul should be able to understand distinctly its own whole nature, and to apprehend how this numberless number of little perceptions, heaped up, or rather concentred together, are produced. In order to this, it would be requisite that the soul understood perfectly the whole universe, which is included within it ; that is, it must be a God.

Ibid. Pag. 603. [§ 403, G.IV.356]

See above, No. 2 and 5.

No. 12
[C.V.1–20, C.V.92, C.V.110–116]

The chain of causes connected one with another, reaches very far. Wherefore the reason alleged by Descartes, to prove by a pretended vigorous inward sense, the independence of our free actions ; is altogether inconclusive. We cannot, strictly speaking, be sensible of our not depending on other causes : for we cannot always perceive the causes, (they being often imperceptible,) on which our resolutions depend. 'Tis as if a needle touched with a loadstone, was sensible of, and pleased with its turning towards the North. For it would believe that it turned itself, independently on any other cause ; not perceiving the insensible motions of the magnetic matter.

Theodicy, Pag. 162. [§ 49–50, G.VI.130]

See below, No. 13.

No. 13
[L.V.92, L.V.116, C.V.92, C.V.110–116]

An infinite number of great and small motions internal and external, concur with us, which generally we are not sensible of. And I have already said, that, when a man walks out of a room, there are such reasons which determine him to set one foot forward rather than the other, though he observes it not.

Theodicy, Pag. 158. [§ 46, G.VI.128]

See above, No. 12.

APPENDICES

APPENDIX A

EXTRACTS FROM NEWTON

FROM THE *PRINCIPIA* [1]

Newton's Preface to the first edition.

Definitions, from the beginning of Book I, including the scholium to Definition 8.

Axioms or Laws of Motion.

Rules of Reasoning in Philosophy, from the end of Book II.

General Scholium, from the end of Book III (first appeared in second edition, 1713).

FROM THE *OPTICKS* [2]

Query 15 (1704).

Beginning of Query 21 (1717).

End of Query 28 (1706).

Beginning of Query 31 (1706).

End of Query 31 (mainly 1706).

---

[1] *The extracts here are taken, except for some very minor revisions, from Motte's English translation of 1729. This was based on the 3rd edition of 1727.*

[2] *The four English editions of the ' Opticks ' appeared in 1704, 1717, 1721, and 1730, the Latin translation by Clarke, in 1706. The differences between these editions lie almost entirely in the queries at the end of the book. The first edition has sixteen queries which are chiefly concerned with optics ; the Latin edition contains seven new queries ranging considerably wider ; the second English edition contains these together with eight more, seven on particular scientific points, the eighth on gravity. Here they are numbered as in the 1717 and subsequent editions.*

FROM THE *PRINCIPIA*

Since the ancients (as we are told by Pappus) made great account of the science of mechanics in the investigation of natural things, and the moderns, rejecting substantial forms and occult qualities, have endeavoured to subject the phenomena of nature to the laws of mathematics, I have in this treatise cultivated mathematics as far as it relates to philosophy. The ancients considered mechanics in a twofold respect ; as rational, which proceeds accurately by demonstration, and practical. To practical mechanics all the manual arts belong, from which mechanics took its name. But as artificers do not work with perfect accuracy, it comes to pass that mechanics is so distinguished from geometry that what is perfectly accurate is called geometrical ; what is less so, is called mechanical. But the errors are not in the art, but in the artificers. He that works with less accuracy is an imperfect mechanic ; and if any could work with perfect accuracy, he would be the most perfect mechanic of all. For the description of right lines and circles, upon which geometry is founded, belongs to mechanics. Geometry does not teach us to draw these lines, but requires them to be drawn ; for it requires that the learner should first be taught to describe these accurately before he enters upon geometry, then it shows how by these operations problems may be solved. To describe right lines and circles are problems, but not geometrical problems. The solution of these problems is required from mechanics, and by geometry the use of them, when so solved, is shown ; and it is the glory of geometry that from those few principles, fetched from without, it is able to produce so many things. Therefore geometry is founded in mechanical practice, and is nothing but that part of universal mechanics which accurately proposes and demonstrates the art of measuring. But since the manual arts are chiefly conversant in the moving bodies, it comes to pass that geometry is commonly referred to their magnitude, and mechanics to their motion. In this sense rational mechanics will be the science of motions resulting from any forces whatsoever, and of the forces required to produce any motions, accurately proposed and demonstrated. This part of mechanics, as far as it extended to the five powers [1] which relate to manual arts, was cultivated by the ancients, who considered gravity (it not being a manual power) no otherwise than as it moved weights by those powers. Our design not respecting arts but philosophy and our subject not manual but natural powers, we consider chiefly those things which relate to gravity, levity, elastic force, the resistance of fluids, and the like forces, whether attractive or impulsive ; and therefore we offer this work as the mechanical principles of philosophy. For all the difficulty of philosophy seems to consist in this, from the phenomena of motions to investigate the forces of nature, and then from these forces to demonstrate the other phenomena. And to this end the general propositions in the first and second books are directed. In the third book we give an example of this in the explication of the System of the World ; for by the propositions mathematically demonstrated in the former books, in the third we derive from the celestial phenomena the forces of gravity with which bodies tend to the sun and the several planets. Then from these forces, by other propositions which are also mathematical, we deduce the motions of the planets, the comets, the moon, and the sea. I wish we could derive

---

[1] This refers to what are sometimes called the mechanical powers. Most authors, e.g. Pemberton, *A View of Sir Isaac Newton's Philosophy* 1728, p. 69 f., give six : the lever, wheel and axis, pulley, wedge, screw and inclined plane.

the rest of the phenomena of nature by the same kind of reasoning from mechanical principles, for I am induced by many reasons to suspect that they may all depend upon certain forces by which the particles of bodies, by some causes hitherto unknown, are either mutually impelled towards one another, and cohere in regular figures, or are repelled and recede from one another ; which forces being unknown, philosophers have hitherto attempted the search of nature in vain. But I hope the principles here laid down will afford some light either to this or some truer method of philosophy.

In the publication of this work the most acute and universally learned Mr. Edmund Halley not only assisted me in correcting the errors of the press and preparing the geometrical figures, but it was through his solicitations that it came to be published. For when he had obtained of me my demonstrations of the figure of the celestial orbits, he continually pressed me to communicate the same to the Royal Society, who afterwards, by their kind encouragement and entreaties, engaged me to think of publishing them. But after I had begun to consider the inequalities of the lunar motions, and had entered upon some other things relating to the laws and measures of gravity and other forces ; and the figures that would be described by bodies attracted according to given laws ; and the motion of several bodies moving among themselves ; the motion of bodies in resisting mediums ; the forces, densities, and motions, of mediums ; the orbits of the comets, and such like ; I deferred the publication until I had made a search into those matters, and could put forth the whole together. What relates to the lunar motions (being imperfect), I have put altogether in the corollaries of Prop. LXVI, to avoid being obliged to propose and distinctly demonstrate the several things there contained in a method more prolix than the subject deserved, and interrupt the series of the other propositions. Some things, found out after the rest, I chose to insert in places less suitable, rather than change the number of the propositions and the citations. I heartily beg that what I have here done may be read with candour ; and that the defects I have been guilty of in so difficult a subject may be not so much censured as investigated anew by the efforts of my readers.

Is. Newton.

Cambridge, Trinity College, May 8, 1686.

DEFINITIONS

DEFINITION I

The quantity of matter is the measure of the same, arising from its density and bulk conjunctly.

Thus air of a double density, in a double space, is quadruple in quantity ; in a triple space, sextuple in quantity. The same thing is to be understood of snow, and fine dust or powders, that are condensed by compression or liquefaction, and of all bodies that are by any causes whatever differently condensed. I have no regard in this place to a medium, if any such there is, that freely pervades the interstices between the parts of bodies. It is this quantity that I mean hereafter everywhere under the name of body or mass. And the same is known by the weight of each body ; for it is proportional to the weight, as I have found by experiments on pendulums, very accurately made, which shall be shown hereafter.

DEFINITION II

The quantity of motion is the measure of the same, arising from the velocity and quantity of matter conjunctly.

The motion of the whole is the sum of the motions of all the parts ; and therefore in a body double in quantity, with equal velocity, the motion is double ; with twice the velocity, it is quadruple.

DEFINITION III

The vis insita, *or innate force of matter, is a power of resisting, by which every body, as much as in it lies, perseveres in its present state, whether it be of rest, or of moving uniformly forward in a right line.*

This force is always proportional to the body whose force it is, and differs nothing from the inertia of the mass, but in our manner of conceiving it. A body, from the inertia of matter, is not without difficulty put out of its state of rest or motion. Upon which account, this *vis insita* may, by a most significant name, be called inertial force (*vis inertiae*). But a body exerts this force only when another force, impressed upon it, endeavours to change its condition ; and the exercise of this force may be considered as both resistance and impulse ; it is resistance in so far as the body, for maintaining its present state, opposes the force impressed ; it is impulse in so far as the body, by not easily giving way to the impressed force of another, endeavours to change the state of that other. Resistance is usually ascribed to bodies at rest, and impulse to those in motion ; but motion and rest, as commonly conceived, are only relatively distinguished ; nor are those bodies always truly at rest, which commonly are taken to be so.

DEFINITION IV

An impressed force is an action exerted upon a body, in order to change its state, either of rest, or of moving uniformly forward in a right line.

This force consists in the action only, and remains no longer in the body when the action is over. For a body maintains every new state it acquires, by its *vis inertiae* only. But impressed forces are of different origins, as from percussion, from pressure, from centripetal force.

DEFINITION V

A centripetal force is that by which bodies are drawn or impelled, or any way tend, towards a point as to a centre.

Of this sort is gravity, by which bodies tend to the centre of the earth ; magnetism, by which iron tends to the loadstone ; and that force, whatever it is, by which the planets are continually drawn aside from the rectilinear motions, which otherwise they would pursue, and made to revolve in curvilinear orbits. A stone, whirled about in a sling, endeavours to recede from the hand that turns it ; and by the endeavour, distends the sling, and that with so much the greater force, as it is revolved with the greater velocity, and as soon as ever it is let go, flies away. That force which opposes itself to this endeavour, and by which the sling continually draws back the stone towards the hand, and retains it in its orbit, because it is directed to the hand as the centre of the orbit, I call the centripetal force. And the same thing is to be understood of all bodies, revolved in any orbits. They all endeavour to recede from the centres of their orbits ; and were it not for the opposition of a contrary force which restrains them to, and detains them in their orbits, which I therefore call centripetal, would fly off in right lines, with an uniform motion. A projectile, if it were not for the force of gravity, would not deviate towards the earth, but would go off from it in a right line, and that with an uniform motion, if the resistance of the air was taken away. 'Tis by its gravity that it is drawn aside continually from its rectilinear course, and made to deviate towards the earth, more or less, according to the force of its gravity, and the velocity of its motion. The less its gravity is, or the quantity of its matter, or the greater the velocity with which it is projected, the less will it deviate from a rectilinear course, and the farther it will go. If a leaden ball, projected from the top of a mountain by the force of gunpowder, with a given velocity, and in a direction parallel to the horizon, is carried in a curved line to the distance of two miles before it falls to the ground ; the same, if the resistance of the air were taken away, with a double or decuple velocity, would fly twice or ten times as far. And by increasing the velocity, we may at pleasure increase the distance to which it might be projected, and diminish the curvature of the line which it might describe, till at last it should fall at the distance of 10, 30, or 90 degrees, or even might go quite round the whole earth before it falls ; or lastly, so that it might never fall to the earth, but go forwards into the celestial spaces, and proceed in its motion *in infinitum*. And after the same manner that a projectile, by the force of gravity, may be made to revolve in an orbit, and go round the whole earth, the moon also, either by the force of gravity, if it is endued with gravity, or by any other force, that impels it towards the earth, may be continually drawn aside towards the earth, out of the rectilinear way which by its innate force it would pursue ; and may be made to revolve in the orbit which it now describes ; nor could the moon without some such force be retained in its orbit. If this force was too small, it would not sufficiently turn the moon out of a rectilinear course ; if it was too great, it would turn it too much, and draw down the moon from its orbit towards the earth. It is necessary that the force be of a just quantity, and it belongs to the mathematicians to find the force that may serve exactly to retain a body in a given orbit with a given velocity ; and *vice versa*, to determine the curvilinear way into which a body projected from a given place, with a given velocity, may be made to deviate from its natural rectilinear way, by means of a given force.

The quantity of any centripetal force may be considered as of three kinds : absolute, accelerative, and motive.

DEFINITION VI

The absolute quantity of a centripetal force is the measure of the same, proportional to the efficacy of the cause that propagates it from the centre, through the spaces round about.

Thus the magnetic force is greater in one loadstone and less in another, according to their sizes and strength of intensity.

DEFINITION VII

The accelerative quantity of a centripetal force is the measure of the same, proportional to the velocity which it generates in a given time.

Thus the force of the same loadstone is greater at a less distance, and less at a greater : also the force of gravity is greater in valleys, less on tops of exceeding high mountains ; and yet less (as shall hereafter be shown), at greater distances from the body of the earth ; but at equal distances it is the same everywhere ; because (taking away, or allowing for, the resistance of the air), it equally accelerates all falling bodies, whether heavy or light, great or small.

DEFINITION VIII

The motive quantity of a centripetal force is the measure of the same, proportional to the motion which it generates in a given time.

Thus the weight is greater in a greater body, less in a less body ; and, in the same body, it is greater near to the earth, and less at remoter distances.   This sort of quantity is the centripetency, or propension of the whole body towards the centre, or, as I may say, its weight ; and it is always known by the quantity of an equal and contrary force just sufficient to hinder the descent of the body.

These quantities of forces, we may, for the sake of brevity, call by the names of motive, accelerative, and absolute forces ; and, for the sake of distinction, consider them with respect to the bodies that tend to the centre, to the places of those bodies, and to the centre of force towards which they tend : that is to say, I refer the motive force to the body as an endeavour and propensity of the whole towards a centre, arising from the propensities of the several parts taken together ; the accelerative force to the place of the body, as a certain power diffused from the centre to all places around to move the bodies that are in them ; and the absolute force to the centre, as endued with some cause, without which those motive forces would not be propagated through the spaces round about ; whether that cause be some central body (such as is the loadstone in the centre of the magnetic force, or the earth in the centre of the gravitating force), or anything else that does not yet appear. For I here design only to give a mathematical notion of those forces, without considering their physical causes and seats.

Wherefore the accelerative force will stand in the same relation to the motive, as celerity does to motion. For the quantity of motion arises from the celerity multiplied by the quantity of matter ; and the motive force arises from the accelerative force multiplied by the same quantity of matter. For the sum of the actions of the accelerative force, upon the several particles of the body, is the motive force of the whole. Hence it is, that near the surface of the earth, where the accelerative gravity, or force productive of gravity, in all bodies is the same, the motive gravity or the weight is as the body ; but if we should ascend to higher regions, where the accelerative gravity is less, the weight would be equally diminished, and would always be as the product of the body, by the accelerative gravity. So in those regions, where the accelerative gravity is diminished into one half, the weight of a body two or three times less, will be four or six times less.

I likewise call attractions and impulses, in the same sense, accelerative, and motive ; and use the words attraction, impulse, or propensity of any sort towards a centre, promiscuously, and indifferently, one for another ; considering those forces not physically, but mathematically : wherefore the reader is not to imagine that by those words I anywhere take upon me to define the kind, or the manner of any action, the causes or the physical reason thereof, or that I attribute forces, in a true and physical sense, to certain centres (which are only mathematical points) ; when at any time I happen to speak of centres as attracting, or as endued with attractive powers.

SCHOLIUM TO DEFINITION VIII

Hitherto I have laid down the definitions of such words as are less known, and explained the sense in which I would have them to be understood in the following discourse. I do not define time, space, place, and motion, as being well known to all. Only I must observe, that the common people conceive those quantities under no other notions but from the relation they bear to sensible objects. And thence arise certain prejudices, for the removing of which it will be convenient to distinguish them into absolute and relative, true and apparent, mathematical and common.

I. Absolute, true, and mathematical time, of itself, and from its own nature, flows equably without relation to anything external, and by another name is called duration : relative, apparent, and common time, is some sensible and external (whether accurate or unequable) measure of duration by the means of motion, which is commonly used instead of true time ; such as an hour, a day, a month, a year.

II. Absolute space, in its own nature, without relation to anything external, remains always similar and immovable. Relative space is some movable dimension or measure of the absolute spaces ; which our senses determine by its position to bodies ; and which is vulgarly taken for immovable space ; such is the dimension of a subterraneous, an aerial, or celestial space, determined by its position in respect of the earth. Absolute and relative space are the same in figure and magnitude ; but they do not remain always numerically the same. For if the earth, for instance, moves, a space of our air, which relatively and in respect of the earth remains always the same, will at one time be part of the absolute space into which the air passes ; at another time it will be another part of the same, and so, absolutely understood, it will be continually changed.

III. Place is a part of space which a body takes up, and is according to the space, either absolute or relative. I say, a part of space ; not the situation, nor the external surface of the body ; but their surfaces, by reason of their dissimilar figures, are often unequal. Positions properly have no quantity, nor are they so much the places themselves, as the properties of places. The motion of the whole is the same with the sum of the motions of the parts ; that is, the translation of the whole, out of its place, is the same thing with the sum of the translations of the parts out of their places ; and therefore the place of the whole is the same as the sum of the places of the parts, and for that reason, it is internal, and in the whole body.

IV. Absolute motion is the translation of a body from one absolute place into another ; and relative motion, the translation from one relative place into another. Thus in a ship under sail, the relative place of the body is that part of the ship which the body possesses ; or that part of the cavity which the body fills, and which therefore moves together with the ship : and relative rest is the continuance of the body in the same part of the ship, or of its cavity. But real, absolute rest, is the continuance of the body in the same part of that immovable space, in which the ship itself, its cavity, and all that it contains, is moved. Wherefore, if the earth is really at rest, the body, which relatively rests in the ship, will really and absolutely move with the same velocity which the ship has on the earth. But if the earth also moves, the true and absolute motion of the body will arise, partly from the true motion of the earth, in immovable space, partly from the relative motion of the ship on the earth ; and if the body also moves relatively in the ship, its true motion will arise, partly from the true motion of the earth, in immovable space, and partly from the relative motions as well of the ship on the earth, as of the body in the ship ; and from these relative motions will arise the relative motion of the body on the earth. As if that part of the earth, where the ship is, was truly moved towards the east, with a velocity of 10010 parts ; while the ship itself, with a fresh gale, and full sails, is carried towards the west, with a velocity expressed by 10 of those parts ; but a sailor walks in the ship towards the east, with 1 part of the said velocity : then the sailor will be moved truly in immovable space towards the east, with a velocity of 10001 parts, and relatively on the earth towards the west, with a velocity of 9 of those parts.

Absolute time, in astronomy, is distinguished from relative, by the equation or correction of the vulgar time. For natural days are truly unequal, though they are commonly considered as equal and used for a measure of time : astronomers correct this inequality for their more accurate deducing of the celestial motions. It may be, that there is no such thing as an equable motion, whereby time may be accurately measured. All motions may be accelerated and retarded, but the flowing of absolute time is liable to no change. The duration or perseverance of the existence of things remains the same, whether the motions are swift or slow, or none at all : and therefore this duration ought to be distinguished from what are only sensible measures thereof ; and from which we deduce it, by means of the astronomical equation. The necessity of this equation, for determining the times of a phenomenon, is evinced as well from the experiments of the pendulum clock, as by eclipses of the satellites of Jupiter.

As the order of the parts of time is immutable, so also is the order of the parts of space. Suppose those parts to be moved out of their places, and they will be moved (if the expression may be allowed) out of themselves. For times and spaces are, as it were, the places as well of themselves as of all other things. All things are placed in time as to order of succession ; and in space as to order of situation. It is from their essence or nature that they are places ; and that the primary places of things should be movable, is absurd. These are therefore the absolute places ; and translations out of those places, are the only absolute motions.

But because the parts of space cannot be seen, or distinguished from one another by our senses, therefore in their stead we use sensible measures of them. For from the positions and distances of things from any body considered as immovable, we define all places ; and then with respect to such places, we estimate all motions, considering bodies as transferred from some of those places into others. And so, instead of absolute places and motions, we use relative ones ; and that without any inconvenience in common affairs : but in philosophical disquisitions we ought to abstract from our senses, and consider things themselves, distinct from what are only sensible measures of them. For it may be that there is no body really at rest, to which the places and motions of others may be referred.

But we may distinguish rest and motion, absolute and relative, one from the other by their properties, causes, and effects. It is a property of rest, that bodies really at rest do rest in respect of one another. And therefore as it is possible, that in the remote regions of the fixed stars, or perhaps far beyond them, there may be some body absolutely at rest ; but impossible to know, from the position of bodies to one another in our regions, whether any of these do keep the same position to that remote body ; it follows that absolute rest cannot be determined from the position of bodies in our regions.

It is a property of motion, that the parts, which retain given positions to their wholes, do partake of the motions of those wholes. For all the parts of revolving bodies endeavour to recede from the axis of motion ; and the impetus of bodies moving forwards arises from the joint impetus of all the parts. Therefore, if surrounding bodies are moved, those that are relatively at rest within them, will partake of their motion. Upon which account, the true and absolute motion of a body cannot be determined by the translation of it from those which only seem to rest ; for the external bodies ought not only to appear at rest, but to be really at rest. For otherwise, all included bodies, besides their translation from near surrounding ones, partake likewise of their true motions ; and though that translation were not made, they would not really be at rest, but only seem to be so. For the surrounding bodies stand in the like relation to the surrounded as the exterior part of a whole does to the interior, or as the shell does to the kernel ; but if the shell moves, the kernel will also move, as being part of the whole, without any removal from near the shell.

A property, near akin to the preceding, is this, that if a place is moved, whatever is placed therein moves along with it ; and therefore a body, which is moved from a place in motion, partakes also of the motion of its place. Upon which account, all motions from places in motion, are no other than parts of entire and absolute motions ; and every entire motion is composed of the motion of the body out of its first place, and the motion of this place out of its place ; and so on, until we come to some immovable place, as in the before-mentioned example of the sailor. Wherefore, entire and absolute motions can be no otherwise determined than by immovable places ; and for that reason I did before refer those absolute motions to immovable places, but relative ones to movable places. Now no other places are immovable but those that, from infinity to infinity, do all retain the same given position one to another ; and upon this account must ever remain unmoved ; and do thereby constitute what I call immovable space.

The causes by which true and relative motions are distinguished, one from the other, are the forces impressed upon bodies to generate motion. True motion is neither generated nor altered, but by some force impressed upon the body moved ; but relative motion may be generated or altered without any force impressed upon the body.

For it is sufficient only to impress some force on other bodies with which the former is compared, that by their giving way, that relation may be changed, in which the relative rest or motion of this other body did consist. Again, true motion suffers always some change from any force impressed upon the moving body ; but relative motion does not necessarily undergo any change by such forces. For if the same forces are likewise impressed on those bodies, with which comparison is made, that the relative position may be preserved, then that condition will be preserved in which the relative motion consists. And therefore any relative motion may be changed when the true motion remains unaltered, and the relative may be preserved when the true suffers some change. Upon which accounts, true motion by no means consists in such relations.

The effects which distinguish absolute from relative motion are, the forces of receding from the axis of circular motion. For there are no such forces in a circular motion purely relative, but in a true and absolute circular motion, they are greater or less, according to the quantity of the motion. If a vessel hung by a long cord, is so often turned about that the cord is strongly twisted, then filled with water, and held at rest together with the water ; thereupon, by the sudden action of another force, it is whirled about the contrary way, and while the cord is untwisting itself, the vessel continues for some time in this motion ; the surface of the water will at first be plain, as before the vessel began to move ; but after that, the vessel, by gradually communicating its motion to the water, will make it begin sensibly to revolve, and recede by little and little from the middle, and ascend to the sides of the vessel, forming itself into a concave figure (as I have experienced), and the swifter the motion becomes, the higher will the water rise, till at last, performing its revolutions in the same times with the vessel, it becomes relatively at rest in it. This ascent of the water show its endeavour to recede from the axis of its motion ; and the true and absolute circular motion of the water, which is here directly contrary to the relative, becomes known, and may be measured by this endeavour. At first, when the relative motion of the water in the vessel was greatest, it produced no endeavour to recede from the axis ; the water showed no tendency to the circumference, nor any ascent towards the sides of the vessel, but remained of a plain surface, and therefore its true circular motion had not yet begun. But afterwards, when the relative motion of the water had decreased, the ascent thereof towards the sides of the vessel proved its endeavour to recede from the axis ; and this endeavour showed the real circular motion of the water continually increasing, till it had acquired its greatest quantity, when the water rested relatively in the vessel. And therefore this endeavour does not depend upon any translation of the water in respect of the ambient bodies, nor can true circular motion be defined by such translation. There is only one real circular motion of any one revolving body, corresponding to only one power of endeavouring to recede from its axis of motion, as its proper and adequate effect ; but relative motions, in one and the same body, are innumerable, according to the various relations it bears to external bodies, and, like other relations, are altogether destitute of any real effect, any otherwise than they may perhaps partake of that one only true motion. And there-fore in their system who suppose that our heavens, revolving below the sphere of the fixed stars, carry the planets along with them ; the several parts of those heavens, and the planets, which are indeed relatively at rest in their heavens, do yet really move. For they change their position one to another (which never happens to bodies truly at rest), and being carried together with their heavens, partake of their motions, and as parts of revolving wholes, endeavour to recede from the axis of their motions.

Wherefore relative quantities are not the quantities themselves, whose names they bear, but those sensible measures of them (either accurate or inaccurate), which are commonly used instead of the measured quantities themselves. And if the meaning of words is to be determined by their use, then by the names time, space, place, and motion, their sensible measures are properly to be understood ; and the expression will be unusual, and purely mathematical, if the measured quantities themselves are meant. On this account, they do strain the sacred writings who there interpret those words for the measured quantities.[1] Nor do those less defile the purity of mathematical and philosophical truths, who confound real quantities with their relations and sensible measures.

It is indeed a matter of great difficulty to discover, and effectually to distinguish, the true motions of particular bodies from the apparent ; because the parts of that immovable space, in which those motions are performed, do by no means come under the observation of our senses. Yet the thing is not altogether desperate ; for we have some arguments to guide us, partly from the apparent motions, which are the differences of the true motions ; partly from the forces, which are the causes and effects of the true motions. For instance, if two globes, kept at a given distance one from the other by means of a cord that connects them, were revolved about their common centre of gravity, we might, from the tension of the cord, discover the endeavour of the globes to recede from the axis of their motion, and from thence we might compute the quantity of their circular motions. And then if any equal forces should be impressed at once on the alternate faces of the globes to augment or diminish their circular motions, from the increase or decrease of the tension of the cord, we might infer the increment or decrement of their motions ; and thence would be found on what faces those forces

---

[1] Some seventeenth-century writers argued that the earth must be at rest because it said so in the Bible. Among the texts they quoted were *Ps.* 96. 10, ' The world also is stablished that it cannot be moved ', and *Joshua* 10. 12, ' And he said in the sight of Israel, Sun, stand thou still upon Gibeon, and thou Moon in the valley of Aijalon '.

ought to be impressed, that the motions of the globes might be most augmented ; that is, we might discover their hindmost faces, or those which, in the circular motion, do follow. But the faces which follow being known, and consequently the opposite ones that precede, we should likewise know the determination of their motions. And thus we might find both the quantity and the determination of this circular motion, even in an immense vacuum, where there was nothing external or sensible with which the globes could be compared. But now, if in that space some remote bodies were placed that kept always a given position one to another, as the fixed stars do in our regions, we could not indeed determine from the relative translation of the globes amongst those bodies, whether the motion did belong to the globes or to the bodies. But if we observed the cord, and found that its tension was that very tension which the motions of the globes required, we might conclude the motions to be in the globes, and the bodies to be at rest ; and then, lastly, from the translation of the globes among the bodies, we should find the determination of their motions. But how we are to obtain the true motions from their causes, effects, and apparent differences, and *vice versa*, how from their motions either true or apparent, we may come to the knowledge of their causes and effects, shall be explained more at large in the following treatise. For to this end it was that I composed it.

AXIOMS, OR LAWS OF MOTION

LAW I

Every body continues in its state of rest, or of uniform motion in a right line, unless it is compelled to change that state by forces impressed thereon.

Projectiles continue in their motions, so far as they are not retarded by the resistance of the air, or impelled downwards by the force of gravity. A top, whose parts by their cohesion are continually drawn aside from rectilinear motions, does not cease its rotation, otherwise than as it is retarded by the air. The greater bodies of the planets and comets, meeting with less resistance in freer spaces, preserve their motions both progressive and circular for a much longer time.

LAW II

The change of motion is ever proportional to the motive force impressed ; and is made in the direction of the right line in which that force is impressed.

If any force generates a motion, a double force will generate double the motion, a triple force triple the motion, whether that force be impressed altogether and at once, or gradually and successively. And this motion (being always directed the same way with the generating force), if the body moved before, is added to or subtracted from the former motion, according as they directly conspire with or are directly contrary to each other ; or obliquely joined, when they are oblique, so as to produce a new motion compounded from the determination of both.

LAW III

To every action there is always opposed an equal reaction : or, the mutual actions of two bodies upon each other are always equal, and directed to contrary parts.

Whatever draws or presses another is as much drawn or pressed by that other. If you press a stone with your finger, the finger is also pressed by the stone. If a horse draws a stone tied to a rope, the horse (if I may so say) will be equally drawn back towards the stone ; for the distended rope, by the same endeavour to relax or unbend itself, will draw the horse as much towards the stone as it does the stone towards the horse, and will obstruct the progress of the one as much as it advances that of the other. If a body impinge upon another, and by its force change the motion of the other, that body also (because of the equality of the mutual pressure) will undergo an equal change, in its own motion, towards the contrary part. The changes made by these actions are equal, not in the velocities but in the motions of bodies ; that is to say, if the bodies are not hindered by any other impediments.

For, because the motions are equally changed, the changes of the velocities made towards contrary parts are inversely proportional to the bodies. This law takes place also in attractions, as will be proved in the next Scholium.

RULES OF REASONING IN PHILOSOPHY

RULE I

We are to admit no more causes of natural things than such as are both true and sufficient to explain their appearances.

To this purpose the philosophers say that nature does nothing in vain, and more is in vain when less will serve ; for nature is pleased with simplicity, and affects not the pomp of superfluous causes.

RULE II

Therefore to the same natural effects we must, as far as possible, assign the same causes.

As to respiration in a man and in a beast ; the descent of stones in Europe and in America ; the light of our culinary fire and of the sun ; the reflection of light in the earth, and in the planets.

RULE III

The qualities of bodies, which admit neither intensification nor remission of degrees, and which are found to belong to all bodies within the reach of our experiments, are to be esteemed the universal qualities of all bodies whatsoever.

For since the qualities of bodies are only known to us by experiments, we are to hold for universal all such as

162

universally agree with experiments ; and such as are not liable to diminution, can never be quite taken away. We are certainly not to relinquish the evidence of experiments for the sake of dreams and vain fictions of our own devising ; nor are we to recede from the analogy of nature, which is wont to be simple, and always consonant to itself. We no other way know the extension of bodies than by our senses, nor do these reach it in all bodies ; but because we perceive extension in all that are sensible, therefore we ascribe it universally to all others also. That abundance of bodies are hard, we learn by experience ; and because the hardness of the whole arises from the hardness of the parts, we therefore justly infer the hardness of the undivided particles, not only of the bodies we feel but of all others. That all bodies are impenetrable, we gather not from reason, but from sensation. The bodies which we handle we find impenetrable, and thence conclude impenetrability to be an universal property of all bodies whatsoever. That all bodies are movable, and endowed with certain powers (which we call the *vires inertiae*) of persevering in their motion, or in their rest, we only infer from the like properties observed in the bodies which we have seen. The extensions, hardness, impenetrability, mobility, and *vis inertiae* of the whole, result from the extension, hardness, impenetrability, mobility, and *vires inertiae* of the parts ; and hence we conclude the least particles of all bodies to be also all extended, and hard and impenetrable, and movable, and endowed with their proper *vires inertiae*. And this is the foundation of all philosophy. Moreover, that the divided but contiguous particles of bodies may be separated from one another, is matter of observation ; and, in the particles that remain undivided, our minds are able to distinguish yet lesser parts, as is mathematically demonstrated. But whether the parts so distinguished, and not yet divided, may, by the powers of nature, be actually divided and separated from one another, we cannot certainly determine. Yet, had we the proof of but one experiment that any undivided particle, in breaking a hard and solid body, suffered a division, we might by virtue of this rule conclude that the undivided as well as the divided particles may be divided and actually separated to infinity.

Lastly, if it universally appears, by experiments and astronomical observations, that all bodies about the earth gravitate towards the earth, and that in proportion to the quantity of matter which they severally contain ; that the moon likewise, according to the quantity of its matter, gravitates towards the earth ; that, on the other hand, our sea gravitates towards the moon ; and all the planets one towards another ; and the comets in like manner towards the sun ; we must, in consequence of this rule, universally allow that all bodies whatsoever are endowed with a principle of mutual gravitation. For the argument from the appearances concludes with more force for the universal gravitation of all bodies than for their impenetrability ; of which among those in the celestial regions, we have no experiments, nor any manner of observation. Not that I affirm gravity to be essential to bodies : by their *vis insita* I mean nothing but their *vis inertiae*. This is immutable. Their gravity is diminished as they recede from the earth.

RULE IV

In experimental philosophy we are to look upon propositions collected by general induction from phenomena as accurately or very nearly true, notwithstanding any contrary hypotheses that may be imagined, till such time as other phenomena occur, by which they may either be made more accurate, or liable to exceptions.

This rule we must follow, that the argument of induction may not be evaded by hypotheses.

GENERAL SCHOLIUM [1]

The hypothesis of vortices is pressed with many diffi-

[1] The General Scholium was added in the 2nd edition 1713.

culties. That every planet by a radius drawn to the sun may describe areas proportional to the times of description, the periodic times of the several parts of the vortices should observe the square of their distances from the sun ; but that the periodic times of the planets may obtain the 3/2th power of their distances from the sun, the periodic times of the parts of the vortex ought to be as the 3/2th power of their distances. That the smaller vortices may maintain their lesser revolutions about Saturn, Jupiter, and other planets, and swim quietly and undisturbed in the greater vortex of the sun, the periodic times of the parts of the sun's vortex should be equal ; but the rotation of the sun and planets about their axes, which ought to correspond with the motions of their vortices, recede far from all these proportions. The motions of the comets are exceedingly regular, are governed by the same laws with the motions of the planets, and can by no means be accounted for by the hypothesis of vortices ; for comets are carried with very eccentric motions through all parts of the heavens indifferently, with a freedom that is incompatible with the notion of a vortex.

Bodies projected in our air suffer no resistance but from the air. Withdraw the air, as is done in Mr. Boyle's vacuum, and the resistance ceases ; for in this void a bit of fine down and a piece of solid gold descend with equal velocity. And the same argument must apply to the celestial spaces above the earth's atmosphere ; in which spaces, where there is no air to resist their motions, all bodies will move with the greatest freedom ; and the planets and comets will constantly pursue their revolutions in orbits given in kind and position, according to the laws above explained. But though these bodies may, indeed, persevere in their orbits by the mere laws of gravity, yet they could by no means have at first derived the regular position of the orbits themselves from those laws.

The six primary planets are revolved about the sun in circles concentric with the sun, and with motions directed towards the same parts, and almost in the same plane. Ten moons are revolved about the earth, Jupiter and Saturn, in circles concentric with them, with the same direction of motion, and nearly in the planes of the orbits of those planets. But it is not to be conceived that mere mechanical causes could give birth to so many regular motions, since the comets range over all parts of the heavens in very eccentric orbits ; for by that kind of motion they pass easily through the orbs of the planets, and with great rapidity ; and in their aphelions, where they move the slowest, and are detained the longest, they recede to the greatest distances from each other, and hence suffer the least disturbance from their mutual attractions. This most beautiful system of the sun, planets, and comets, could only proceed from the counsel and dominion of an intelligent and powerful Being. And if the fixed stars are the centres of other like systems, these, being formed by the like wise counsel, must be all subject to the dominion of One ; especially since the light of the fixed stars is of the same nature with the light of the sun, and from every system light passes into all the other systems : [1]and lest the systems of the fixed stars should, by their gravity, fall on each other, he hath placed those systems at immense distances from one another[1].

This Being governs all things, not as the soul of the world, but as Lord over all ; and on account of his dominion he is wont to be called Lord God παντοκράτωρ, or Universal Ruler. For God is a relative word, and has a respect to servants ; and Deity is the dominion of God not over his own body, as those imagine who fancy God to be the soul of the world, but over servants. The supreme God is a Being eternal, infinite, absolutely perfect ; but a being, however perfect, without dominion, cannot be said to be Lord God ; for we say, my God, your God, the God of Israel, [2]the God of Gods, and Lord of Lords[2] :

[1-1] Added in 3rd edition 1726.
[2-2] Added in 3rd edition.

but we do not say, my Eternal, your Eternal, the Eternal of Israel, [1-]the Eternal of Gods; we do not say, my Infinite, or my Perfect[-1] : these are titles which have no respect to servants. The word God[a] usually signifies Lord; but every Lord is not a God. It is the dominion of a spiritual being which constitutes a God : a true, supreme, or imaginary dominion makes a true, supreme, or imaginary God. And from his true dominion it follows that the true God is a living, intelligent, and powerful Being; and, from his other perfections, that he is supreme, or most perfect. He is eternal and infinite, omnipotent and omniscient; that is, his duration reaches from eternity to eternity; his presence from infinity to infinity; he governs all things, and knows all things that are or can be done. He is not eternity and infinity,[2] but eternal and infinite; he is not duration or space, but he endures and is present. He endures forever, and is everywhere present; and, by existing always and everywhere, he constitutes duration and space. Since every particle of space is always, and every indivisible moment of duration is everywhere, certainly the Maker and Lord of all things cannot be never and nowhere. [3-]Every soul that has perception is, though in different times and in different organs of sense and motion, still the same indivisible person. There are given successive parts in duration, coexistent parts in space, but neither the one nor the other in the person of a man, or

[a] Dr. Pocock derives the Latin word *Deus* from the Arabic *du* (in the oblique case *di*), which signifies *Lord*. And in this sense princes are called gods, *Psal*. lxxxii. ver. 6; and *John* x. ver. 35. And Moses is called a god to his brother Aaron, and a god to Pharaoh (*Exod*. iv. ver. 16; and vii. ver. 1). And in the same sense the souls of dead princes were formerly, by the heathens, called gods, but falsely, because of their want of dominion.

[1-1] In 2nd edition ' we do not say, my Infinite, your Infinite, the Infinite of Israel; we do not say my Perfect, your Perfect, the Perfect of Israel.'

[2] In 2nd edition, ' He is not eternity or infinity.'

[3-3] Added in 3rd edition.

his thinking principle ; and much less can they be found in the thinking substance of God. Every man, so far as he is a thing that has perception, is one and the same man during his whole life, in all and each of his organs of sense. God is the same God, always and everywhere.⁻³ He is omnipresent not virtually only, but also substantially ; for virtue cannot subsist without substance. In him ᵃ are all things contained and moved ; yet neither affects the other : God suffers nothing from the motion of bodies ; bodies find no resistance from the omnipresence of God. It is allowed by all that the supreme God exists necessarily ; and by the same necessity he exists always and everywhere. Whence also he is all similar, all eye, all ear, all brain, all arm, all power to perceive, to understand, and to act ; but in a manner not at all human, in a manner not at all corporeal, in a manner utterly unknown to us. As a blind man has no idea of colours, so have we no idea of the manner by which the all-wise God perceives and understands all things. He is utterly void of all body and bodily figure, and can therefore neither be seen, nor heard, nor touched ; nor ought to be worshipped under the representation of any corporeal thing. We have ideas of his attributes, but what the real substance of anything is we know not. In bodies, we see only their figures and colours, we hear only the sounds, we touch only their outward surfaces, we smell only the smells, and taste the savours ; but their inward substances are not to be known either by our senses, or by any reflex act of our minds ;

ᵃ This was the opinion of the ancients. So Pythagoras in Cicero, *de Nat. Deor.* lib. 1. Thales, Anaxagoras, Virgil, *Georg.* lib. iv, ver. 220 ; and *Aeneid*, lib. vi, ver. 721. Philo *Allegor.* at the beginning of lib. 1. *Aratus* in his *Phaenom.* at the beginning. So also the sacred writers ; as St. Paul, *Acts* xvii, 27, 28. *St. John's Gosp.* xiv, 2. Moses in *Deut.* iv, 39 and x, 14. David *Psal.* cxxxix, 7–9. Solomon I, *Kings* viii, 27. Job xxii, 12–14. Jeremiah xxiii, 23–24. The idolaters supposed the sun, moon, and stars, the souls of men, and other parts of the world, to be parts of the Supreme God, and therefore to be worshipped ; but erroneously.

much less, then, have we any idea of the substance of God. We know him only by his most wise and excellent contrivances of things, and final causes ; we admire him for his perfections ; but reverence and adore him on account of his dominion : [1] for we adore him as his servants ; and a god without dominion, providence, and final causes, is nothing else but Fate and Nature. Blind metaphysical necessity, which is certainly the same always and everywhere, could produce no variety of things. All the diversity of natural things which we find suited to different times and places could arise from nothing but the ideas and will of a Being necessarily existing. But, by way of allegory, God is said to see, to speak, to laugh, to love, to hate, to desire, to give, to receive, to rejoice, to be angry, to fight, to frame, to work, to build. For all our notions of God are taken from the ways of mankind by a certain similitude, which, though not perfect, has some likeness, however.[1] [2] And thus much concerning God ; to discourse of whom from the appearances of things, does certainly belong to Natural Philosophy.[2]

Hitherto we have explained the phenomena of the heavens and of our sea by the power of gravity, but have not yet assigned the cause of this power. This is certain, that it must proceed from a cause that penetrates to the very centres of the sun and planets, without suffering the least diminution of its force ; that operates not according to the quantity of the surfaces of the particles upon which it acts (as mechanical causes use to do), but according to the quantity of the solid matter they contain, and propagates its virtue on all sides to immense distances, decreasing always as the inverse square of the distances. Gravitation towards the sun is made up out of the gravitations towards the several particles of which the body of the sun is composed ; and in receding from the sun,

[1] Added in 3rd edition.
[2] This sentence was not in the original draft of the Scholium but was added by Newton as the second edition was going through the press.

decreases accurately as the inverse square of the distances as far as the orbit of Saturn, as evidently appears from the quiescence of the aphelions of the planets ; nay, and even to the remotest aphelions of the comets, if those aphelions are also quiescent. But hitherto I have not been able to discover the cause of those properties of gravity from phenomena, and I frame no hypotheses.[1] For whatever is not deduced from the phenomena is to be called an hypothesis ; and hypotheses, whether metaphysical or physical, whether of occult qualities or mechanical, have no place in experimental philosophy. In this philosophy particular propositions are inferred from the phenomena, and afterwards rendered general by induction. Thus it was that the impenetrability, the mobility, and the impulsive force of bodies, and the laws of motion and of gravitation, were discovered. And to us it is enough that gravity does really exist, and acts according to the laws which we have explained, and abundantly serves to account for all the motions of the celestial bodies, and of our sea.

And now we might add something concerning a certain most subtle spirit which pervades and lies hid in all gross bodies ; by the force and action of which spirit the particles of bodies attract one another at near distances, and cohere, if contiguous ; and electric bodies operate to greater distances, as well repelling as attracting the neighbouring corpuscles ; and light is emitted, reflected, refracted, inflected, and heats bodies ; and all sensation is excited, and the members of animal bodies move at the command of the will, namely, by the vibrations of this spirit, mutually propagated along the solid filaments of the nerves, from the outward organs of sense to the brain, and from the brain into the muscles. But these are things that cannot

---

[1] *Hypotheses non fingo.* It should be noticed that this famous remark only refers to the problem of the cause of gravity and only to that as discussed in the *Principia*. In the *Opticks* Newton does put forward a hypothesis about its cause, but there as always he distinguishes between this hypothesis and the results, such as the inverse square law of gravitational attraction, established by the ' analytical' method.

be explained in a few words, nor are we furnished with that sufficiency of experiments which is required to an accurate determination and demonstration of the laws by which this electric and elastic spirit operates.

FROM THE *OPTICKS*

QUERY 15 (1704)

Are not the species of objects seen with both eyes united where the optic nerves meet before they come into the brain, the fibres on the right side of both nerves uniting there, and after union going thence into the brain in the nerve which is on the right side of the head, and the fibres on the left side of both nerves uniting in the same place, and after union going into the brain in the nerve which is on the left side of the head, and these two nerves meeting in the brain in such a manner that their fibres make but one entire species or picture, half of which on the right side of the sensorium comes from the right side of both eyes through the right side of both optic nerves to the place where the nerves meet, and from thence on the right side of the head into the brain, and the other half on the left side of the sensorium comes in like manner from the left side of both eyes. For the optic nerves of such animals as look the same way with both eyes (as of men, dogs, sheep, oxen, etc.), meet before they come into the brain, but the optic nerves of such animals as do not look the same way with both eyes (as of fishes and of the chameleon) do not meet, if I am rightly informed.

BEGINNING OF QUERY 21 (1717)

Is not this medium [1] much rarer within the dense bodies of the sun, stars, planets and comets, than in the empty celestial spaces between them ? And in passing from them

[1] Queries 17–20 concern a hypothetical 'ethereal medium'.

to great distances, doth it not grow denser and denser perpetually, and thereby cause the gravity of those great bodies towards one another, and of their parts towards the bodies ; every body endeavouring to go from the denser parts of the medium towards the rarer ? For if this medium be rarer within the sun's body than at its surface, and rarer there than at the hundredth part of an inch from its body, and rarer there than at the fiftieth part of an inch from its body, and rarer there than at the orb of Saturn ; I see no reason why the increase of density should stop any where, and not rather be continued through all distances from the sun to Saturn, and beyond. And though this increase of density may at great distances be exceeding slow, yet if the elastic force of this medium be exceedingly great, it may suffice to impel bodies from the denser parts of the medium towards the rarer, with all that power which we call gravity. . . .

END OF QUERY 28 [1] (1706)

. . . And therefore to make way for the regular and lasting motions of the planets and comets, it's necessary to empty the heavens of all matter, except perhaps some very thin vapours, steams or effluvia, arising from the atmospheres of the earth, planets and comets, [2-] and from such an exceedingly rare ethereal medium as we described above.[-2] A dense fluid can be of no use for explaining the phenomena of nature, the motions of the planets and comets being better explain'd without it. It serves only to disturb and retard the motions of those great bodies, and make the frame of nature languish : and in the pores

---

[1] Newton is here arguing against the wave theory of light as held, in particular, by Huygens. He has claimed that the wave theory could not explain the peculiar refractive properties of Iceland spar and that it was also disproved by the fact that light does not bend round obstacles. He now puts forward the additional objection that an aether would slow down the motion of the planets and comets.

[2-2] Added in 1717.

of bodies, it serves only to stop the vibrating motions of their parts, wherein their heat and activity consists. And as it is of no use, and hinders the operations of nature, and makes her languish, so there is no evidence for its existence, and therefore it ought to be rejected. And if it be rejected, the hypotheses that light consists in pression or motion propagated through such a medium, are rejected with it.

And for rejecting such a medium, we have the authority of those the oldest and most celebrated philosophers of Greece and Phoenicia, who made a vacuum and atoms, and the gravity of atoms, the first principles of their philosophy ; tacitly attributing gravity to some other cause than dense matter. Later philosophers banish the consideration of such a cause out of natural philosophy, feigning hypotheses for explaining all things mechanically, and referring other causes to metaphysics : whereas the main business of natural philosophy is to argue from phenomena without feigning hypotheses, and to deduce causes from effects, till we come to the very first cause, which certainly is not mechanical ; and not only to unfold the mechanism of the world, but chiefly to resolve these and such like questions. What is there in places almost empty of matter, and whence is it that the sun and planets gravitate towards one another, without dense matter between them ? Whence is it that nature does nothing in vain ; and whence arises all that order and beauty which we see in the world ? To what end are comets, and whence is it that planets move all one and the same way in orbs concentric, while comets move all manner of ways in orbs very eccentric, and what hinders the fix'd stars from falling upon one another ? How came the bodies of animals to be contrived with so much art, and for what ends were their several parts ? Was the eye contrived without skill in optics, and the ear without knowledge of sounds ? How do the motions of the body follow from the will, and whence is the instinct in animals ? Is not the sensory of animals that place to which the sensitive substance is present, and into which the sensible species of things are carried through the nerves and brain, that there they may be perceived by their immediate presence to that substance ? And these things being rightly dispatch'd, does it not appear from phenomena that there is a Being incorporeal, living, intelligent, omnipresent, who in infinite space, as it were in his sensory, sees the things themselves intimately, and throughly perceives them, and comprehends them wholly by their immediate presence to himself : of which things the images only carried through the organs of sense into our little sensoriums, are there seen and beheld by that which in us perceives and thinks. And tho' every step made in this philosophy brings us not immediately to the knowledge of the first cause, yet it brings us nearer to it, and on that account is to be highly valued.

BEGINNING OF QUERY 31 (1706)

Have not the small particles of bodies certain powers, virtues or forces, by which they act at a distance, not only upon the rays of light for reflecting, refracting, and inflecting them, but also upon one another for producing a great part of the phenomena of nature ? For it's well known that bodies act one upon another by the attractions of gravity, magnetism, and electricity ; and these instances show the tenor and course of nature, and make it not improbable but that there may be more attractive powers than these. For nature is very consonant and conformable to herself. How these attractions may be peform'd, I do not here consider. What I call attraction may be perform'd by impulse, or by some other means unknown to me. I use that word here to signify only in general any force by which bodies tend towards one another, whatsoever be the cause. For we must learn from the phenomena of nature what bodies attract one another, and what are the laws and properties of the attraction, before we enquire the cause by which the attraction is perform'd. The attractions of gravity, magnetism, and electricity, reach to very sensible distances, and so have been observed by vulgar eyes, and there may be others which reach to so small distances as hitherto escape observation; [1]−and perhaps electrical attraction may reach to such small distances, even without being excited by friction.−[1]

For when salt of tartar runs *per deliquium*,[2] is not this done by an attraction between the particles of the salt of tartar, and the particles of the water which float in the air in the form of vapours? And why does not common salt, or saltpetre, or vitriol, run *per deliquium*, but for want of such an attraction? Or why does not salt of tartar draw more water out of the air than in a certain proportion to its quantity, but for want of an attractive force after it is satiated with water? And whence is it but from this attractive power that water which alone distils with a gentle lukewarm heat, will not distil from salt of tartar without a great heat? And is it not from the like attractive power between the particles of oil of vitriol and the particles of water, that oil of vitriol draws to it a good quantity of water out of the air, and after it is satiated draws no more, and in distillation lets go the water very difficultly? And when water and oil of vitriol poured successively into the same vessel grow very hot in the mixing, does not this heat argue a great motion in the parts of the liquors? And does not this motion argue that the parts of the two liquors in mixing coalesce with violence, and by consequence rush towards one another with an accelerated motion? [3] . . .

END OF QUERY 31 (1706)

. . . And thus nature will be very conformable to herself and very simple, performing all the great motions of the

---

[1]−[1] Added in 1717.   [2] ' run per deliquium ' = to deliquesce.
[3] There follow various other chemical hypotheses concerned with attractive and repulsive forces.

heavenly bodies by the attraction of gravity which intercedes those bodies, and almost all the small ones of their particles by some other attractive and repelling powers which intercede the particles. The *vis inertiae* is a passive principle by which bodies persist in their motion or rest, receive motion in proportion to the force impressing it, and resist as much as they are resisted. By this principle alone there never could have been any motion in the world. Some other principle was necessary for putting bodies into motion ; and now they are in motion, some other principle is necessary for conserving the motion. For from the various composition of two motions, 'tis very certain that there is not always the same quantity of motion in the world. For if two globes joined by a slender rod, revolve about their common centre of gravity with an uniform motion, while that centre moves on uniformly in a right line drawn in the plane of their circular motion ; the sum of the motions of the two globes, as often as the globes are in the right line described by their common centre of gravity, will be bigger than the sum of their motions, when they are in line perpendicular to that right line.[1] By this instance it appears that motion may be got or lost. But by reason of the tenacity of fluids, and attrition of their parts, and the weakness of elasticity in solids, motion is

---

[1] This is a strange example. Newton seems to be arguing thus : if the globes are of mass m, the rod of length $2r$, the linear velocity of the centre of gravity v, and the angular velocity ω, then when the rod is at right angles to the direction of motion, one globe will have a velocity of $v + \omega r$, the other of $v - \omega r$. When the rod is parallel to the direction of motion, each globe will have a velocity of $\sqrt{v^2 + \omega^2 r^2}$. Thus the quantity of motion in one case appears to be $m(v + \omega r) + m(v - \omega r) = 2mv$; in the other $2m\sqrt{v^2 + \omega^2 r^2}$. But this is to regard momentum as a scalar, not as a vector quantity, and elsewhere, e.g. when discussing collision of bodies, Newton recognizes that momentum is a vector quantity. Clearly if one takes in this example the momentum in the two directions, parallel and at right angles to the direction of motion, then the amount in each direction is constant, i.e. $2mv$ and 0 respectively.

much more apt to be lost than got, and is always upon the decay. For bodies which are either absolutely hard, or so soft as to be void of elasticity, will not rebound from one another. Impenetrability makes them only stop. If two equal bodies meet directly *in vacuo*, they will by the laws of motion stop where they meet, and lose all their motion, and remain in rest, unless they be elastic, and receive new motion from their spring. If they have so much elasticity as suffices to make them rebound with a quarter, or half, or three quarters of the force with which they come together, they will lose three quarters, or half, or a quarter of their motion. And this may be tried, by letting two equal pendulums fall against one another from equal heights. If the pendulums be of lead or soft clay, they will lose all or almost all their motions : if of elastic bodies they will lose all but what they recover from their elasticity. If it be said, that they can lose no motion but what they communicate to other bodies, the consequence is, that *in vacuo* they can lose no motion, but when they meet they must go on and penetrate one another's dimensions. If three equal round vessels be filled, the one with water, the other with oil, the third with molten pitch, and the liquors be stirred about alike to give them a vortical motion ; the pitch by its tenacity will lose its motion quickly, the oil being less tenacious will keep it longer, and the water being less tenacious will keep it longest, but yet will lose it in a short time. Whence it is easy to understand, that if many contiguous vortices of molten pitch were each of them as large as those which some suppose to revolve about the sun and fix'd stars,[1] yet these and all their parts would, by their tenacity and stiffness, communicate their motion to one another till they all rested among themselves. Vortices of oil or water, or some fluider matter, might continue longer in motion ; but unless the matter were void of all tenacity and attrition of parts, and communication of motion, (which is not to be supposed) the motion

[1] In 1706 edition ' as large as the Cartesian vortices '.

would constantly decay. Seeing therefore the variety of motion which we find in the world is always decreasing, there is a necessity of conserving and recruiting it by active principles, such as are the cause of gravity, by which planets and comets keep their motions in their orbs, and bodies acquire great motion in falling ; and the cause of fermentation, by which the heart and blood of animals are kept in perpetual motion and heat ; the inward parts of the earth are constantly warm'd, and in some places grow very hot ; bodies burn and shine, mountains take fire, the caverns of the earth are blown up, and the sun continues violently hot and lucid, and warms all things by his light. For we meet with very little motion in the world, besides what is owing to these active principles.[1] And if it were not for these principles the bodies of the earth, planets, comets, sun, and all things in them would grow cold and freeze, and become inactive masses ; and all putrefaction, generation, vegetation and life would cease, and the planets and comets would not remain in their orbs.

All these things being consider'd, it seems probable to me, that God in the beginning form'd matter in solid, massy, hard, impenetrable, moveable particles, of such sizes and figures, and with such other properties, and in such proportion to space, as most conduced to the end for which he form'd them ; and that these primitive particles being solids, are incomparably harder than any porous bodies, compounded of them ; even so very hard, as never to wear or break in pieces : no ordinary power being able to divide what God himself made one in the first creation. While the particles continue entire, they may compose bodies of one and the same nature and texture in all ages ; but should they wear away, or break in pieces, the nature of things depending on them would be changed. Water and earth composed of old worn particles and fragments of particles, would not be of the same nature and texture now,

[1] In 1706 ' owing either to these active principles or to the dictates of a will '. The next sentence ' And if . . . orbs ' was added in 1717.

with water and earth composed of entire particles, in the beginning. And therefore that nature may be lasting, the changes of corporeal things are to be placed only in the various separations and new associations and motions of these permanent particles ; compound bodies being apt to break, not in the midst of solid particles, but where those particles are laid together, and only touch in a few points.

It seems to me farther, that these particles have not only a *vis inertiae*, accompanied with such passive laws of motion as naturally result from that force, but also that they are moved by certain active principles, such as is that of gravity, and that which causes fermentation, and the cohesion of bodies. These principles I consider not as occult qualities, supposed to result from the specific forms of things, but as general laws of nature, by which the things themselves are form'd : [1-]their truth appearing to us by phenomena, though their causes be not yet discover'd. For these are manifest qualities, and their causes only are occult. And the Aristotelians gave the name of occult qualities not to manifest qualities, but to such qualities only as they supposed to lie hid in bodies, and to be the unknown causes of manifest effects : such as would be the causes of gravity, and of magnetic and electric attractions, and of fermentations, if we should suppose that these forces or actions arose from qualities unknown to us, and uncapable of being discovered and made manifest. Such occult qualities put a stop to the improvement of natural philosophy, and therefore of late years have been rejected.[-1] To tell us that every species of things is endow'd with an occult specific quality by which it acts and produces manifest effects, is to tell us nothing : but to derive two

---

[1-1] In 1706, this read, ' Nam Principia quidam talia revera existere, ostendunt phaenomenae naturae : licet ipsorum causae quae sint, nondum fuent explicatum,' i.e. ' For natural phenomena show that such principles really exist : although it has not yet been explained what are their causes.' These changes were almost certainly made with Leibniz's objections in mind.

or three general principles of motion from phenomena, and afterwards to tell us how the properties and actions of all corporeal things follow from those manifest principles, would be a very great step in philosophy, though the causes of those principles were not yet discover'd : and therefore I scruple not to propose the principles of motion above mention'd, they being of very general extent, [1-] and leave their causes to be found out.[-1]

Now by the help of these principles, all material things seem to have been composed of the hard and solid particles above mention'd, variously associated in the first creation by the counsel of an intelligent agent. For it became him who created them to set them in order. And if he did so, it's unphilosophical to seek for any other origin of the world, or to pretend that it might arise out of a chaos by the mere laws of nature ; though being once form'd, it may continue by those laws for many ages. For while comets move in very eccentric orbs in all manner of positions, blind fate could never make all the planets move one and the same way in orbs concentric, some inconsiderable irregularities excepted which may have arisen from the mutual actions of comets and planets upon one another, and which will be apt to increase, till this system wants a reformation. Such a wonderful uniformity in the planetary system must be allowed the effect of choice. And so must the uniformity in the bodies of animals, they having generally a right and a left side shaped alike, and on either side of their bodies two legs behind, and either two arms, or two legs, or two wings before upon their shoulders, and between their shoulders a neck running down into a back-bone, and a head upon it ; and in the head two ears, two eyes, a nose, a mouth, and a tongue, alike situated. Also the first contrivance of those very artificial parts of animals, the eyes, ears, brain, muscles, heart, lungs, midriff, glands, larynx, hands, wings, swimming bladders, natural spectacles, and other organs of sense and motion ; and the

[1-1] Added in 1717.

instinct of brutes and insects, can be the effect of nothing else than the wisdom and skill of a powerful ever-living agent, who being in all places, is more able by his will to move the bodies within his boundless uniform sensorium, and thereby to form and reform the parts of the universe, than we [1] are by our will to move the parts of our own bodies. [2]-And yet we are not to consider the world as the body of God, or the several parts thereof, as the parts of God. He is an uniform Being, void of organs, members or parts, and they are his creatures subordinate to him, and subservient to his will ; and he is no more the soul of them, than the soul of man is the soul of the species of things carried through the organs of sense into the place of its sensation, where it perceives them by means of its immediate presence, without the intervention of any third thing. The organs of sense are not for enabling the soul to perceive the species of things in its sensorium, but only for conveying them thither ; and God has no need of such organs, he being every where present to the things themselves.-[2] And since space is divisible in infinitum, and matter is not necessarily in all places, it may be also allow'd that God is able to create particles of matter of several sizes and figures, and in several proportions to space, and perhaps of different densities and forces, and thereby to vary the laws of nature, and make worlds of several sorts in several parts of the universe. At least, I see nothing of contradiction in all this.

As in mathematics, so in natural philosophy, the investigation of difficult things by the method of analysis, ought ever to precede the method of composition. This analysis consists in making experiments and observations, [3]-and in drawing general conclusions from them by induction, and admitting of no objections against the conclusions, but such as are taken from experiments, or other certain truths. For

[1] In 1706 instead of ' we ', ' our spirit which is in us the image of God '.

[2-2] Added in 1717.　　　　[3-3] Added in 1717.

hypotheses are not to be regarded in experimental philosophy. And although the arguing from experiments and observations by induction be no demonstration of general conclusions ; yet it is the best way of arguing which the nature of things admits of, and may be looked upon as so much the stronger, by how much the induction is more general. And if no exception occur from phenomena, the conclusion may be pronounced generally. But if at any time afterwards any exception shall occur from experiments, it may then begin to be pronounced with such exceptions as occur.[-3] By this way of analysis we may proceed from compounds to ingredients, and from motions to the forces producing them ; and in general, from effects to their causes, and from particular causes to more general ones, till the argument end in the most general. This is the method of analysis : and the synthesis consists in assuming the causes discover'd, and establish'd as principles, and by them explaining the phenomena proceeding from them, and proving the explanations.

In the first two books of these optics, I proceeded by this analysis to discover and prove the original differences of the rays of light in respect of refrangibility, reflexibility, and colour, and their alternate fits of easy reflexion and easy transmission, and the properties of bodies, both opaque and pellucid, on which their reflexions and colours depend. And these discoveries being proved, may be assumed in the method of composition for explaining the phenomena arising from them : an instance of which method I gave in the end of the first book. In this third book I have only begun the analysis of what remains to be discover'd about light and its effects upon the frame of nature, hinting several things about it and leaving the hints to be examin'd and improv'd by the farther experiments and observations of such as are inquisitive. And if natural philosophy in all its parts, by pursuing this method, shall at length be perfected, the bounds of moral philosophy will be also enlarged. For so far as we can know by natural philosophy what is the first cause, what power He has over us, and what benefits we receive from Him, so far our duty towards Him, as well as that towards one another, will appear to us by the light of nature. And no doubt, if the worship of false Gods had not blinded the heathen, their moral philosophy would have gone farther than to the four cardinal virtues ; and instead of teaching the transmigration of souls, and to worship the sun and moon, and dead heroes, they would have taught us to worship our true Author and Benefactor.

APPENDIX B

EXTRACTS FROM LETTERS RELATING TO THE CORRESPONDENCE

1. Leibniz and Newton to Conti.
2. Leibniz to Wolff and Bernoulli.
3. Leibniz's Correspondence with Caroline.

I.—LEIBNIZ AND NEWTON TO CONTI

The following extracts contain the passages of philosophical interest in the letters which Leibniz and Newton wrote to Conti about each other at the same time as the Leibniz-Clarke exchange was taking place. See Introduction, p. x.

Leibniz to Conti. Nov. or Dec. 1715. [Raphson, *History of Fluxions*, London 1715 (actually 1717), and Des Maiseaux, *Receuil*, Vol. II.]

His [i.e. Newton's] philosophy appears to me rather strange and I cannot believe it can be justified. If every body is heavy it follows necessarily (whatever his supporters may say and however passionately they deny it) that gravity will be a scholastic occult quality or else the effect of a miracle. I did at one time convince M. Bayle that whatever cannot be explained by the nature of created things is miraculous. It is not sufficient to say : God has made such a law of Nature, therefore the thing is natural. It is necessary that the law should be capable of being fulfilled by the nature of created things. If, for example, God were to give to a free body the law of revolving around a certain centre, he would either have to join to it other bodies which by their impulsion made it always stay in its circular orbit, or to put an angel at its heels ; or else he would have to concur extraordinarily in its motion. For naturally it would go off along the tangent. God acts

continually on his creatures in the conservation of their
natures, and this conservation is a continual production of
that which is in itself perfection.   He is *intelligentia supramundana* because he is not the soul of the world and has no
need of a sensorium.

I do not find the existence of a vacuum proved by the
argument of M. Newton or his followers, any more than
the universal gravity which they suppose, or the existence
of atoms.   One can only accept the existence of a vacuum
or of atoms, if one has very limited views.   M. Clarke
contests the opinion of the Cartesians who believe that God
cannot destroy one part of matter to make a vacuum, but
I am astonished that he does not see that if space is a
substance different from God, the same difficulty occurs.
Now to say that God is space, is to give him parts.   Space
is the order of co-existents and time is the order of successive
existents.   They are things true but ideal, like numbers.

Matter itself is not a substance but only *substantiatum*, a
well-founded phenomenon,[1] and which does not mislead one
at all if one proceeds by reasoning according to the ideal
laws of arithmetic, geometry, dynamics, & etc.   Everything I put forward in that seems to me proved.   As to
dynamics or the doctrine of forces, I am astonished that
M. Newton and his followers believe that God has made his
machine so badly that unless he affects it by some extraordinary means, the watch will very soon cease to go.
This is to have very narrow ideas of the wisdom and power
of God.   I call extraordinary every operation of God
demanding something other than the conservation of the
natures of created things.   I believe the metaphysics of these
gentlemen *a narrow one*[2] and their mathematics *arrivable*[2]
enough ;   this does not prevent me from estimating very

---

[1] 'un phénomène bien fondé'.

[2] In English in the original.—In some proof sheets of the Des
Maiseaux *Receuil* in Cambridge University Library, the word *arrivable* is
followed by the words *c'est-à-dire commune ou superficielle* which are deleted
in ink.

highly the physico-mathematical meditations of M. Newton ; and you would, Sir, do a great service to the public, if you would persuade this able man to give us his recent conjectures in physics. I strongly approve of his method of drawing from phenomena what can be drawn without making any suppositions, even if sometimes this is only drawing conjectural consequences. However, when the *data* are not sufficient, it is permissible (as one does sometimes in deciphering) to imagine hypotheses, and if they are good ones to hold them provisionally, waiting for new experiments to bring us *nova data* and for what Bacon calls *experimenta crucis*, in order to choose between hypotheses. As I have learned that certain Englishmen have misrepresented my philosophy in their *Transactions*, I have no doubt that, with what I send you here, I can be justified. I am strongly in favour of the experimental philosophy but M. Newton is departing very far from it when he claims that all matter is heavy (or that every part of matter attracts every other part) which is certainly not proved by experiments, as M. Huygens has already asserted ; gravitating matter could not itself have that weight of which it is the cause and M. Newton adduces no experiment or sufficient reason for the existence of a vacuum or of atoms or for the general mutual attraction. And because we do not yet know perfectly and in detail how gravity is produced or elastic force or magnetic force, this does not give us any right to make of them scholastic occult qualities or miracles ; but it gives us still less right to put bounds to the wisdom and power of God and to attribute to him a sensorium and such things. Furthermore I am astonished that the followers of M. Newton have produced nothing to show that their master has taught them a good method ; I have been more fortunate in my disciples.

Newton to Conti. 26th Feb. 1716. [Raphson and Des Maiseaux.]

Hitherto Mr. Leibnitz avoided returning an answer to

the *Commercium Epistolicum* [1] by pretending that he had not seen it. And now he avoids it by telling you that the English shall not have the pleasure to see him return an answer to their slender reasonings (as he calls them) and by endeavouring to engage me in disputes about philosophy and about solving of problems ; [2] both of which are nothing to the question.

As for philosophy, he colludes in the signification of words, calling those things miracles which create no wonder ; and those things occult qualities, whose causes are occult, though the qualities themselves be manifest ; and those things the souls of men, which do not animate their bodies. His *harmonia praestabilita* is miraculous and contradicts the daily experience of all mankind ; every man finding in himself a power of seeing with his eyes, and moving his body by his will. He prefers hypotheses to arguments of induction drawn from experiments, accuses me of opinions which are not mine ; and instead of proposing questions to be examined by experiments before they are admitted into philosophy, he proposes hypotheses to be admitted and believed before they are examined. But all this is nothing to the *Commercium Epistolicum.*

Leibniz to Conti. 9th April 1716. [Des Maiseaux.]

I do not wish here to go into detail about what M. Newton says rather bitterly against my philosophy and in favour of his own. This is not the place. I call a *miracle* any event which can only occur through the power of the Creator, its reason not lying in the nature of created things ; and when nevertheless one would attribute it to the qualities or powers of created things, then I call this quality a

[1] The *Commercium Epistolicum* was a collection of letters and manuscripts relating to the Newton-Leibniz calculus controversy, selected and published together with a report by a special committee of the Royal Society.

[2] Leibniz had ended his letter to Conti by propounding a problem whose solution involved the calculus ' in order to feel the pulse of the English analysts '.

scholastic occult quality ; that is one that it is impossible to render clear, such as a primitive heaviness ; for the occult qualities which are not chimerical are those whose cause we do not know but do not exclude. And I call the soul of man that simple substance which perceives what happens in the human body and whose desires or acts of will are followed by the exertions of the body. I do not prefer hypotheses to arguments drawn by induction from experiments ; but things are sometimes passed off as general inductions when they only consist in particular observations, and sometimes passed off as a hypothesis when they are capable of demonstration. The idea which M. Newton gives here of my pre-established harmony is not that which many able men outside England have, and I cannot believe that you yourself have had a similar idea or have it now unless you have just changed your views.

II.—Leibniz to Wolff and Bernoulli

Leibniz to Wolff. 23rd Dec. 1715. [Dutens ii, p. 105.]

Her Royal Highness the Princess of Wales, who read my *Theodicy* very attentively and was delighted with it, recently, as she herself told me, argued about it with a certain English clergyman who has access to court. She attacked Newton and his followers for holding that God needs to correct and reanimate his machine. She thinks that my opinion according to which everything proceeds well from what is pre-established, and there is no need of divine correction but only divine sustentation, is more conformable with the perfections of God. He gave her Royal Highness a paper written in English in which he tries to defend Newton's view and attack mine. He would impute to me the denial of divine governance, if everything proceeds well by itself. But he does not realize that the divine governance of natural things consists in sustentation, and must not be taken in an anthropological sense. I replied immediately and sent my reply to the Princess.

Leibniz to Bernoulli. June 1716.

[*Leibnitii et Bernoullii Commercium.* Lausanne & Geneva 1745, vol. ii, p. 381.]

You perhaps already know that I am at present engaged in a philosophical quarrel with Newton or, what amounts to the same thing, with his defender Clarke, a royal pensioner.[1] You know that Keill and the writer of the preface [2] to the new edition of Newton's *Principia* wished to attack my philosophy. I therefore wrote to Her Royal Highness the Princess of Wales, who as befits her excellent ability is interested in these matters, saying that philosophy or rather natural theology is declining considerably among the English—— [Leibniz then summarizes his first letter in the Correspondence.] The Princess of Wales communicated excerpts of this letter to Clarke. He gave her a paper in reply written in English which she sent to me, I replied, he answered, I wrote a second paper ; he a third, I, just now, a fourth, that is I answered his third paper.

III.—LEIBNIZ'S CORRESPONDENCE WITH CAROLINE

Letters exchanged by Princess Caroline and Leibniz from the year 1706 until his death are printed in O. Klopp, Die Werke von Leibniz, *Vol. XI, Hanover 1884. The first paper in the Leibniz-Clarke Correspondence is an extract from one of Leibniz's letters to her, and the papers that followed were transmitted by Caroline in the course of their general correspondence. (Klopp prints French versions of the Leibniz-Clarke papers as part of this correspondence.) The following extracts from the letters of Leibniz and Caroline contain all except the most insignificant references to the exchanges with Clarke. The rest of their correspondence concerns personal, political, and religious questions.*

Some of the letters are also printed in J. M. Kemble : State Papers, Correspondence illustrative of the Social and Political State of Europe . . ., *where the editor has preserved Caroline's original spelling (Dr. Glerck, Sr Eizack Newton, Monsieur L'Ebeniz, etc.).*

[1] ' Regis Eleemosynario '.   [2] See p. x above.

Caroline to Leibniz. 14th November 1715. [Klopp XI, 50.]

I have talked to-day to the Bishop of Lincoln about the translation of your *Theodicy* ; he assures me that there is no-one capable of doing it except Dr. Clarke, whose books I sent you by Oeynhausen. He is a close friend of Chevalier Newton.

Caroline to Leibniz. 26th November 1715. [Klopp XI, 52. *Presumably enclosed with Clarke's first paper.*]

I hope you received the books I sent you. Send me, please, your opinion on Dr. Clarke's works which I think have considerable merit although not comparable with the *Theodicy.* . . . We are thinking very seriously of getting your *Theodicy* translated ; but we are still looking for a good translator. Dr. Clarke is too opposed to your opinions to do it ; he would certainly be the most suitable person of all ; but he is too much of Sir Isaac Newton's opinion and I am myself engaged in a dispute with him. I implore your help ; he gilds the pill and is not willing to admit that Mr. Newton has the opinions which you ascribe to him, but you will see from the enclosed paper that it comes to the same thing. I can only ever believe what would conform to the perfection of God. I have found this much more perfect in your system than in that of Mr. Newton, where, in effect, God has to be always present to readjust his machine because he was not able to do it at the beginning. Neither Dr. Clarke nor Mr. Newton wishes to be thought a follower of Mr. Locke, but I cannot and would not wish to be one of theirs.

Leibniz to Caroline (no date, but mentions New Year). [Klopp XI, 58. *Enclosed with Leibniz's second paper.*]

. . . The writing which Your Royal Highness sent me is as good as it could be considering the weak position it has to defend. Dr. Clarke, who seems to be its author, does, however, at times appear somewhat embarrassed and I don't know if my reply enclosed here, will not increase his embarrassment. We shall soon see whether he continues ingenuously or whether he is capable of ridding himself of his prejudices. He shows a great desire to convict me of holding wrong opinions, but in vain. I have not wished to remark on this in order not to make our controversy bitter. I hope Your Royal Highness will have copies kept of what is given to her and of what I send, the better to be able to judge it.

I have gone through the two books of Dr. Clarke, or at least the greater part of them, but I shall have to re-read them more attentively. He often says very good things, but fails for want of following or envisaging my principles. He is right to maintain against Mr. Dodwell and against an anonymous writer that the soul is immortal because of its indivisibility and that whatever is composed of parts can have nothing in it except what is in its parts. That being so, I don't at all see how he can maintain that the soul is extended ; for wherever there is extension there are parts unless one takes the word in an unusual sense.

The truth, as Your Royal Highness has very properly argued, is that God has made the soul immortal, that is, that it is naturally immortal and could only be annihilated by a miracle, as God could annihilate the whole created universe. But to do that would be inconvenient. These gentlemen who strongly debase the idea of God do the same with the idea of the soul. It almost seems that according to them, the soul can perish naturally, that is by the ordinary operation of God who, according to them looks very much like being the soul of the world. One of their sect could easily persuade himself into believing that idea of some of the ancient writers which I have spoken about in my Discourse on the Conformity of Faith and Reason according to which souls are born when the machine is organized to receive it, as organ-pipes are adjusted to receive the general wind, and that they perish on the destruction of the bodily organs, the general wind no longer producing consciousness. Thus at bottom, there would only be one lasting soul, that is the soul of the world. I should not like to impute that view to them, but as long as they don't put forward principles contrary to that doctrine, their doctrine may lead to it.

My view is entirely different. Each soul is an image or living representation of the created universe according to its point of view ; it could no more perish than the universe of created things ; and there are souls everywhere But the rational soul is something more ; it is the image of the Deity. This is what the Holy Scriptures say so marvellously, as Your Royal Highness has so excellently insisted ; it is most creditable that she should single-handed maintain the truth against such able people. All souls keep their substance and are imperishable, even those of beasts ; but only rational souls still keep their personality, that is, the reflective knowledge of what they themselves are, or consciousness. This is what makes them capable of reward or punishment. I wish these gentlemen would explain their views about animals, whether they give them souls or not. And if they have souls (I mean immaterial ones) one must ask whether they perish or not, and, (if they hold that they are extinguished) on what they base the privilege of the human soul in being imperishable, whether on nature or only on grace, that is on an extra-ordinary operation of God, as is in effect the view of Dodwell and some modern, but bad, philosophers.

Thus it is important to know what one must say on Mr. Newton's principles. As for myself, I believe that I have explained distinctly in what consists the difference between the consecutions of animals which resemble reason and reasonings of men. It seems that my antagonists destroy the true difference between the miraculous and the natural ; and that according to them God's nature is always to act by miracles in actions which should be the most natural.

Caroline to Leibniz. 10th Jan. 1716. [Klopp XI, 71.
Enclosed with Clarke's second paper.]

I enclose a reply to your paper ; I considered very carefully the replies made on both sides. I do not know whether the bias I have for your merit makes me partial but I find all his replies are rather words than what could be called replies. You are right about the author of the reply ; they are not written without the advice of Chev. Newton, whom I should like to be reconciled with you. I do not know if you will consent, but the Abbé Conti and myself have made ourselves mediators ; it would be a great pity if two such great men as you and he were to be estranged by misunderstandings. . . .

I could not help myself saying to Dr. Clarke that your opinion seems the more conformable to the perfection of God and that any philosophy which would lead me away from it appears to me imperfect since in my opinion philosophy was made, or ought to be sought, in order to make us more tranquil in spirit and to strengthen us against ourselves and against everything outside us which may assail us, and I cannot believe it could have this effect if it showed us the imperfection of God. He talked to me a very long time in an effort to convert me to his opinion and wasted his breath. I beg you to reply.

Leibniz to Caroline. 25th February 1716. [Klopp XI, 78. *Enclosed with Leibniz's third paper.*]

Your Royal Highness shows her kindness towards me and her goodwill to others in wishing to reconcile me with Mr. Newton. I indeed believe that this reconciliation can take place since he has not yet been willing to appear publicly against me himself.

Caroline to Leibniz. 24th April 1716. [Klopp XI, 90.]

The Abbé Conti has succeeded in losing some of the papers which you wished me to entrust to him. He promises to find them again. This is what has prevented me from sending by this post Clarke's last reply. Last Saturday I had the Abbé Conti and Mr. Clarke with me from 6 till 10 o'clock. I should have liked you here to support me. Mr. Clarke's knowledge and his clear way of reasoning have almost converted me to believing in the vacuum.

I have seen the letter which Chev. Newton sent you through Conti. He claims that everything he has said in it is matters of fact. I eagerly await your reply. I am in despair that persons of such great learning as you and Newton are not reconciled. The public would profit immensely if this could be brought about, but great men are like women, who never give up their lovers except with the utmost chagrin and mortal anger. And that, gentlemen, is where your opinions have got you.

Caroline to Leibniz. 15th May 1716. [Klopp XI, 93. *Enclosed with Clarke's third paper.*]

I send you herewith Dr. Clarke's reply which fortunately has been found. . . .

. . . Tomorrow we are going to see the experiments on colours, and one which I have seen on the vacuum has almost converted me. It is for you to lead me back into the right way, and I await the answer which you make to Mr. Clarke.

Leibniz to Caroline. 12th May 1716. [Klopp XI, 100.]

The passage printed by Clarke in his edition of the Correspondence (p. 43 above) as a postscript to Leibniz's fourth paper is in fact a postscript to this letter, and is a reply to Caroline's mention of the vacuum in her letter of 15th May 1716.

Caroline to Leibniz. 26th May 1716. [Klopp XI, 112.]

I have been watching experiments and I am more and more charmed by colours. I cannot prevent myself from being a little biassed towards the vacuum ; but I think there is a misunderstanding, since what these gentlemen call a vacuum is meant to signify nothing but something which is not matter.

Leibniz to Caroline. 2nd June 1716. [G. VII, 378–9. *Gerhardt says that the draft from which he published this letter, was written by Leibniz on the same folio as contained his fourth paper.*]

I thank Your Royal Highness for her kindness in wishing to see my lost papers again ; I will get them recopied. I enclose herewith a reply to the last paper of M. Clarke ; he, and his like, do not properly understand that great principle that nothing happens without a sufficient reason for it and, what follows, that even God cannot choose without having a reason for this choice. This is the error of vague indifference or the absolutely absolute decree, which I have refuted in the *Theodicy*. This error is also the source of the vacuum and atoms.

It seems to me that there is nothing in my reply to the Abbé Conti which marks a troubled mind ; there is also nothing which slanders M. Newton. But since he attacks me I defend myself and do so in polite terms. What use is it to exhort me to peace when sending me challenges ?

I am afraid that we shall dispute about the vacuum as uselessly as about other things. I have not sufficient time to spare to waste it in amusements. There are more important things to do. I do not believe that there is any space without matter. The experiments which are said to produce a vacuum only exclude a gross matter, which is drawn from the glass cavity by the weight of mercury with Torricelli or by the pump with M. Guerike. For the rays of light which are not devoid of some subtle matter pass through the glass. I would not have touched on this question of the vacuum if I had not found that the theory of the vacuum detracts from the perfections of God, as do almost all the other philosophical principles which are contrary to mine. For mine are almost all bound up with the great principle of sufficient reason and the perfection of God. Thus I have no fear that Your Royal Highness will lightly abandon those of my opinions which she has had the leisure to penetrate fully ; the acuteness of her mind and her zeal for the glory of God are my surety.

In asking Your Royal Highness to communicate to the Abbé Conti my discussions with M. Clarke, my intention was that they should thus be communicated to other friends ; but since the Abbé has lost part of them, I shall get them all copied again and I think it would be best to communicate them to others so that the papers will not be lost again so easily.

Caroline to Leibniz. 26th June 1716. [Klopp XI, 114. *Enclosed with Clarke's fourth paper.*]

I have not been able to reply sooner to your letter of the 2nd. Dr. Clarke, who was away in the country, has just brought me the reply.

Leibniz to Caroline. 18th August 1716. [Klopp XI, 131. *Enclosed with Leibniz's fifth paper.*]

I enclose here part of my reply to Mr. Clarke's fourth paper ; the other half will follow by the next post. This reply is very full since I have wanted to explain everything completely and to see whether there is any hope of making Mr. Clarke see reason. For if he falls back on repeating himself, there will be nothing to be done with him and one will have to try politely to come to a close.

Caroline to Leibniz. 31st August 1716. [Klopp XI, 181.]

I read with pleasure the replies which you have made to Mr. Clarke. I do not know if he will be able to reply to them.   Clarke is a man of the greatest vivacity and of an eloquence which is, in my opinion, unequalled.

Leibniz to Caroline.   11th September 1716.   [Klopp XI, 182.]

I cannot judge of elegance in English, but I think I can at least judge of the clarity of the expressions.   Mr. Clarke is certainly not without it, but we shall soon see whether it is accompanied by sincerity, and whether he is the man to hold out his hands to the truth : that would undoubtedly do him more honour than the detours which he might take to avoid it.   If he continues to dispute my great principle *that nothing happens without there being a sufficient reason why it happens, and why it happens thus rather than otherwise,* and if he still claims that something can happen by a *mere will of God* without any motive, an opinion perfectly refuted in my *Theodicy* and again in my last paper, he will have to be left to his opinion or rather to his obstinacy.   It is difficult for him not to be touched by it at the bottom of his soul, but I believe that the public will not let him off.

Caroline to Leibniz.   19th September 1716.   [Klopp XI, 185.]

Although I have already replied to your last letter, I write on behalf of Mr. Clarke to whom I have spoken and with whom I have read your papers.   It appears that you want to have them printed.   He earnestly begged me to persuade you that if you would have them printed, you should have the papers printed in the language in which they are written, and he promises on his side to do the same.

Caroline to Leibniz.   26th September 1716.   [Klopp XI, 197.]

I have given Dr. Clarke your papers and he is making a collection of them all for me.

Caroline to Leibniz. 29th October 1716. [Klopp XI, 198. *Enclosed with Clarke's fifth paper.*]

I write these few lines to accompany Dr. Clarke's reply. I hope you will at least find it agreeable even if not satisfactory.

INDEX OF NAMES